COMPREHENSIVE WORK RE
CUSTOMER SERVICE TRAINING PROGRAM

Includes: lecture content, in-class exercises with answers, personalized participant worksheets, competency statements and tracking forms, section review key concepts, scenarios that can be used for skill building or certification/final tests, and more

Jay Goldberg, MBA

Contains all the content from the four books in DTR Inc.'s Training Series: Workplace Basics, Workplace Skills, People Skills, and Customer Service plus tools for instructors

Classroom books (lecture content and certification scenarios only) are available. Visit www.DTRConsulting.BIZ for more information.

www.DTRConsulting.BIZ

The opinions expressed in this manuscript are solely the opinions of the author and do not represent the opinions or thoughts of the publisher.

This book was written to help individuals understand and improve their workplace skills. The information detailed in the book is based on the experience, knowledge and observations of Jay Goldberg. Since hiring, firing, and promoting employees varies by company and the person performing the task, there is no guarantee by the author or publisher, expressed or implied that following everything in this book will result in employees who implement what they learn and become exceptional employees.

COMPREHENSIVE WORK READINESS and CUSTOMER SERVICE TRAINING PROGRAM
For Classroom and On the Job Training, Courses and Certification Programs

Includes all the materials from DTR Inc.'s Work Readiness Certification Series

Workplace Basics
Workplace Skills
People Skills
Customer Service

A classroom copy of this book (without the answers) is available. Visit www.DTRConsulting.BIZ for more information.

Printer/Publisher: CreateSpace.
Thanks to Stuart Kroll for his help in editing this book.

Contact the author, via email, at Book@DTRConsulting.BIZ. Please type "your work readiness book" in the subject line of the email to ensure that your email is not deleted as junk mail.

PowerPoint presentations are available. Visit www.DTRConsulting.BIZ for more information or to order more books.

ISBN - 978-1492804956

TABLE OF CONTENTS

ORIENTATION

Participant/Employee Orientation

This program is run like a structured workplace, not like a typical classroom. Therefore, your success in this program is tied to demonstrated competencies, some of which are assessment tests, but many of which are based on individual behaviors.

Listed below are some rules for this program that need to be followed <u>all</u> <u>the</u> <u>time</u> during this program. To ensure that you have read and understood each rule you need to write your initials after reading each rule. In fact, writing your initials after each rule (if you do not understand a rule, please ask the instructor before initialing), is the first of many competency statements you will need to pass in this course. In order to obtain full certification or honors in this program you need to pass all competencies. In terms of the workplace, think of these rules as an employee handbook.

Participant/employee program handbook rules

Rule   Initials

Penalties for not adhering to company (program) policies

There are consequences for not following the company (program) policies in this document. The consequences are failing a competency, and since most of these competencies are behavior based and proven over the entire length of the program, they CANNOT be made up by taking an individual module over again at a later date. Therefore, if a participant fails even one of these competencies, that participant will not be able to obtain full credit or honors for the program   _____

Interacting with supervisors (instructors)

In this program, your instructor needs to be considered your supervisor. So at all times you will be required to:

- ✓ Be respectful to your supervisor (instructor)
- ✓ Act professionally when interacting with your supervisor (instructor)
- ✓ Use appropriate language when talking to your supervisor (instructor)

_____

Interacting with coworkers (other participants)

At all times you will be required to:

- ✓ Be respectful to your coworkers (other participants)
- ✓ Act professionally when interacting with your coworkers (other participants)
- ✓ Use appropriate language when talking to your coworkers (other participants)

To clarify the above, this means that if a participant answers a question incorrectly in class, there will be no laughing, whispering behind someone's back, etc. Also all contributions to team exercises need to be taken seriously and no one's serious contribution should be made fun of.

There will be times when your supervisor (instructor) informs the class that they can have fun with an exercise and act informally. When this occurs, do so for that exercise only, and then return to the more "structured" classroom environment.

Teamwork

A number of exercises throughout this program are done in teams. When you are a member of a team you must contribute to the work the team is performing. In some cases, it is possible that specific roles for team members will be assigned by the supervisor (instructor) or an assigned team leader (a classmate). In those cases you are responsible for your assigned role, but can receive help from other team members. In other cases, the team itself will determine roles in a manner decided by the team. In all cases you cannot fight with your team, get a bad attitude and desert your team, etc. You must be a good team player and not "check out" or sit silently and let your team members do the work.

Speaking in public

As a good employee you will need to be able to speak in front of your coworkers (classmates) and supervisors (instructors). Shyness may be endearing in social situations, but not speaking up in the workplace makes your supervisors assume that you are either not interested or that you have nothing of value to say. Either way that is not good. During this program you will be required to participate in group presentations. This is not optional. No exceptions can be made.

Ethical approach to exercises and worksheets

You may not formally do the exercises and worksheets contained in this book until they are assigned by your supervisor (teacher). This means you cannot bring written notes to class regarding the answers to these exercises and worksheets (in the book or using separate paper) or ask prior participants about these exercises and worksheets. You are also prohibited from asking prior participants about the questions on the certification tests.

Ethical approach to the program

Since this program is run like a training program at work and not an educational course; you will be observed not just on your work output but on your approach to your work. Among other things, this means:

- ✓ You must always be attentive, and show that you are attentive in class
- ✓ You cannot talk over the supervisor (instructor) or your co-workers (classmates) when they are participating in classroom discussions; you need to be listening to what is being said and talking over someone not only impacts your ability to learn, but your co-workers (classmates) as well
- ✓ There are a number of individual worksheets that are required to be filled out during this program; you must answer all the worksheets honestly and completely (note – there will be random checks to ensure that this is being done)

Clear communication

When you are called on in the training session to answer questions, you must answer them in a clear and concise way; there should be no ambiguity in your answers.

Ready for work (class)

You must show up to class every session with all of the required materials; which includes this book. No exceptions will be made for not being prepared to work.

Dress and grooming code

There is a dress code in effect for this company (class). The dress code can be for the entire program or for specific days in the program. Please ask the instructor what the dress code is. The dress code MUST also be followed per the instructions of your instructor (if there are exceptions – for example school rules or events - the exceptions need to be agreed to before showing up in violation of the instructors dress code).

Please write the dress code for your program here; including the days (all or just specific days of the week) that the dress code needs to be followed.

The grooming code follows. It is possible, depending upon the venue for the program; that additions will be made to the items below. Please ask the instructor if there are any additions to the items below.

Have no body odor (including bad breath)
Have neat, clean hair

Please write any additional grooming items required in your program in the box below.

Attendance policy

There are no (none, cero, нул, ゼロ, null, zéro, etc.) unexcused absences permitted in this program. If a participant (employee) has even one unexcused absence, they fail a competency and cannot obtain full credit for this program (think of it as being fired during your probation period).

Just like a real job, all child care, transportation, etc. issues are expected to be solved before starting the job (starting this program program), not after starting the job, and all employees (participants) are expected to have backups in place in case problems arise.

Punctuality (tardiness) policy

There is no unexcused tardiness permitted in this program. If an employee (participant) is late even one, they fail a competency and cannot obtain full credit for this program (think of it as being fired during your probation period).

Punctuality and tardiness refers to the following:

- ✓ Be at your desk ready to work on time. This means not even 10 seconds late!
- ✓ Be back from all breaks and at your desk ready to work on time. Again, not even 10 seconds late!
- ✓ Stay for the entire session, cannot leave early

WORKPLACE BASICS

The Profit Motive of Business

In the National Football League (NFL), the amount of money set aside for employee salaries (players) is a set percentage of revenue earned by the owners. The more money earned by the League, from ticket sales, television contracts, etc., the more money the players make. The contract negotiated between the owners and players clearly shows the relationship between the business and its employees. If the league negotiates more money from the television networks, player salaries rise. If NFL games suddenly do poorly in the ratings, and the league gets less money in its television contracts, player salaries decline. If the league suddenly could not get any television contracts, employees could lose their jobs (player rosters could be cut).

While most businesses do not have a negotiated rate of revenue which they use on employee wages, the concept is the same. The more money a business makes, the more money it has to spend on employee salaries and benefits, and the less likely it is to have layoffs (employees lose their jobs).

Therefore, you are similar to an NFL player. Your team is the business that hires you. Your game is your day to day job. Your opposition is businesses that sell similar products and services, and/or businesses that are after the same pot of money and customers that your business serves but sells different product or services.

For example, if you work for the consumer electronics company Best Buy and listen closely you can hear the game announcer saying: "Starting for the Best Buy Giants at Senior Sales Representative, is Jay Goldberg. Goldberg is on a twenty day streak of generating sales revenue of over $20,000 a day. Goldberg's run has moved Best Buy into first place, just ahead of the BrandsMart Cowboys. It has also kicked in his sales bonus making Goldberg one of the highest paid salesmen in his field. Perhaps best of all, unbeknownst to Goldberg, his recent sales streak has allowed Best Buy management to keep John Doe on full time. Without the extra revenue earned by Goldberg, Doe's hours would have been cut and he would have had trouble earning enough money to pay his rent, which would have created a difficult situation for him, his wife, and two children."

The paragraph above was written to show a fun example. I have no knowledge about the compensation structure, or sales goals of Best Buy or any other consumer electronics company. I have also bought and been a satisfied customer of both Best Buy and BrandsMart and having Best Buy win the above competition in no way indicates that I prefer Best Buy to BrandsMart.

Another old "wise" tale I heard from an old wise man at a meeting; in my days generating a work readiness program and curriculum for a South Florida client, follows.

The owner of a small manufacturing firm in Florida called his entire staff together for a meeting. Everyone knew the meeting was about the status of a pending contract. The manufacturing company had worked on previous contracts for the company for whom it was awaiting word on a new contract. In the past, contracts with this company resulted in a lot of highly stressful work, which included long hours and tight timeframes for product delivery. The owner then announced that the company did <u>not</u> get the contract. There were cheers all around the room because workers were relieved that they would not have to go through the long days and stressful times again. The next day many started being fired from their jobs. Without that client, the manufacturing company did not have the funds to keep everyone employed.

Your job is available because the company that employs you is conducting enough business, and making enough money, for that job to be needed. Therefore, your job and associated pay scale are tied directly to the success of the business you work for. In addition, one of the best ways for your pay to increase is to stay with the same company for at least two or three years to show that employer or potential future employers that you have both the ability to commit to a company, and have gained the experience and knowledge to take on a job with more responsibilities at higher pay. Therefore, it is very important to you that the business you work for is profitable so you can keep your job, improve your resume, and grow your earnings, instead of continually jumping sideways.

As a final exercise, let's assume you are the owner of a small business. Five years ago you took a $75,000 loan to start up the business and used the equity in your home as collateral. Over the past five years you have struggled to grow the business, putting most of the money you earned back into the business. In doing so, your credit card debt has grown to $25,000. Now, in year five, your sales have exploded. You are able to finally take a good salary, start significantly paying down your debt and can hire a three person sales force and a full time customer service representative. What has to happen for you to keep those four people employed? <insert 30 seconds of game show music here>

The answer is that the money brought in by the three salespeople has to at least cover the money you are paying the four of them (including benefits, taxes, and their overhead).

Let's say in year one, the three salespeople bring in enough to cover all their expenses plus 10%. You decide to split the 10% profit with your employees by using half of those profits to increase their base pay. Now, in year two the three salespeople come up 20% short of all the money it costs you to employ them. That 20% shortfall comes out of your pocket. That was money you were using to help pay down your credit card and home loans. However, your employees still expect a raise. If you give them a raise and they have the same year next year that they did in year two, the money you earn will go down even more.

Now you're thinking that you took the risk to start the business; you are the person in debt because of the business; so why should you be the one whose earnings go down while everyone else's salary goes up?

You would not be wrong, but business owners also realize that if the business does well, they stand to profit more than their employees (deservingly so since the owners take the risks).

Therefore, you decide that you'll take a hit and reward your best employees, but you won't take the full hit. You decide to give raises to your two top salespeople and your customer service representative. You also fire your worst salesperson and split his/her work amongst the other two salespeople, feeling no guilt since they are getting raises, while, you the owner, are taking less compensation. You also have a plan in place to cut back the hours for the customer service representative if the two salespeople do not show improvement over last year's sales volume within four months.

See - if you were an owner, the amount of money you pay your employees, and how many employees you hire would depend upon the profits your business was making. After all you took the risk, you deserve a salary, and you have bills to pay.

In this example, the owner could have easily decided to fire the salesperson with the least time in the business, or the salesperson that the owner did not get along with, if the sales results were fairly even, or if the owner believed that the remaining sales people could improve. Workers livelihoods are directly tied to the success of the business with whom they are employed.

The above example works for large businesses and chains as well as small businesses. Owners still base jobs and worker's pay on the profitability of the business. For company-owned chain stores, store managers' compensation (and job security) is often tied to the profitability of the store he/she is managing.

EXERCISE WB1

You are running a 27 week, 10 team, 50 years old plus outdoor basketball league. All teams play each other three times. Each team supplies its own coach and there are two refs per game. There are no playoffs. If teams tie for first, the winner of the head-to-head series between the teams is crowned the winner of the league. All 12 members of the winning team get a trophy. The league supplies uniforms for all team members.

Q1. How many people will you need to hire?
Q2. List all the expenses that might be involved, including staff expenses.
Q3. How much do you think you can charge each team?
Q4. Total up all your expenses.
Q5. Calculate your revenue (# of players times what you are charging each player).
Q6. Since the main goal for every business is to make profits; is the league profitable?
Q7. What other factors could impact profits plus or minus?

Time Is Money

Pink Floyd's classic album, *Dark Side of the Moon* contains songs titled "Time" and "Money." Many consider this album one of the best rock albums ever. Certainly, I do. So did Pink Floyd subconsciously incorporate these two keys as songs on their album to assure its success? Perhaps. Or maybe the cosmos rewarded them for discovering this successful workplace connection. Hmmm. Or maybe they're just very talented and I'm pointing out random facts to help introduce this topic. Actually, that sounds about right.

Absenteeism

When an employee takes off from work unexpectedly, the amount of work that has to be completed on the job doesn't change. That means the co-workers of the employee that misses work, now have more work to do. So workers that make a habit of missing days due to illness or personal problems that need to be taken care of during work hours are <u>not</u> popular with their co-workers. It doesn't matter why. Whether for car problems, day care problems, a hang nail, etc., co-workers will be annoyed with people who do not show up to work when scheduled for work. If a worker doesn't show up because his/her day care provider cancelled, co-workers aren't going to say, "No problem, you do what you have to. I don't mind not being able to go on even a bathroom break today because your day care provider didn't show up." It's more likely that your co-workers (who are more like friendly neighbors than tried and true friends) will say, "Great, I have to suffer because that a*****e doesn't have a backup plan in place in case of emergencies. Here I am living with no air conditioning for two days so I can wait until a day off to have a repair person come over and fix it so I won't miss work, and now I have to have a tough day because my co-worker didn't show up."

But that's not the worst of it. That worker's supervisor will now have to help out to get the work completed. After all, that supervisor is being paid to assure all work is completed successfully; work he or she normally does, and work done by his or her staff. In fact, the supervisor may have to stay late to finish the additional work. And most supervisors are on salary, not a per hour rate so they do not get overtime pay.

Now keep in mind that this supervisor is the person who determines employee raises; keeps that worker and others employed, and recommends employees for promotions. Therefore inconveniencing the supervisor who will now have to do his or her normal work plus help out performing additional work to make up for the absent employee, is not the ideal career move.

So how happy do you think supervisors are with employees who do not show up to work on their scheduled days? If you were a supervisor, how pleased would you be? So absenteeism has a negative impact on your co-workers and supervisor.

In addition, all companies have policies on absenteeism. Therefore, not staying within those work rules comes with consequences. Excessive absenteeism is grounds for being fired. And being fired leaves a big hole in one's resume when he or she looks for their next job.

Use of sick days

Please be aware that in trying to be fair to employees many companies allow a generous amount of sick days. Often the longer you work for a company, the more sick days you earn.

Sick days are not vacation days or even personal days. They are an insurance policy the company provides to its employees. They are to be used only when an employee is sick. Since sick days are an unplanned absence, when used there is a negative impact on the workplace. If all employees used all their sick days a company would have no choice but to reduce sick days for everyone. Think how high your car insurance would be if every driver except you had two accidents a year. Insurance companies cannot pay out money it does not have. They cannot survive if they pay out more money than they take in. No business could. In this case everyone's car insurance rates would go up (including yours) to an amount where the insurance company was taking in more money than it was paying out.

Therefore, employees who abuse their sick days are hurting their co-workers. That makes that employee someone that the workplace would be better off without.

Let's say that Jane Doe has worked for the business for ten years and has used only 10 sick days during that time. Furthermore, during that time Jane has accrued (built up a backlog of) 50 sick days. Then she gets very sick and will have to be hospitalized for three weeks and stay in bed at home for an additional three weeks. This means she will miss 30 days. This is exactly what the sick days were provided to Jane Doe for. She will be paid for missing the 6 weeks of work because of the company's sick days (insurance) policy. This situation is also more controllable for the business. Knowing the amount of time that Jane Doe will be out, the company can hire a temp to help out, or build in a little time delay in delivering products/services when talking to customers. If these 30 days were used at random during that 10 year span, the company would not have been able to bring in a temp, and would not have known to build in time delays when talking to customers.

Now, let's look at a company where employees were misusing sick days. In order to curb the misuse, the company decides to cut the number of sick days allowed in half. Therefore, Jane Doe has earned 30 total sick days instead of 60 (50 backlog plus 10 she used). Since she used 10 sick days, Jane Doe only has 20 sick days left to cover her six week absence (30 days). Jane Doe's illness, therefore, would have resulted in her being out of work for 10 days (2 weeks) without pay. The result could be that she gets behind in her rent, never gets caught up, and either has to move or gets evicted.

Workers who abuse sick days are certainly hurting the company, hurting their co-workers, and hurting their supervisor.

Here is a final car insurance, sick day analogy. You pay for car insurance and if you do not get into an accident you do not get your money back from the insurance company. You pay for insurance in case you need it. In fact, insurance is the ultimate good neighbor product because you not getting into accidents meant that some of the money you paid for the insurance went to help other people who got into accidents (the money has to come from somewhere). Sick days are exactly the same. If you do not get sick you do not earn any money for days that go unused. However, it means that the company can have a good sick day policy to help employees who need to use them. And one day that just may be you.

Finally, if you use your full allotment of sick days because you have a lot of one day illnesses, your job could be in jeopardy. In the National Football League (NFL), a player that gets injured often may find it difficult to stick with a team. If a team cannot count on that player being available on game day, his roster spot could go to a lesser player who that team can rely on. It is no different in business. If a company is relying on five people to man the phones for calls from customers, and often comes up short because "a player" is on the "injured list" (one specific employee is often out sick), the supervisor could fire that employee (cut the player) who is the cause of the company losing customers and money because the company is constantly operating "one man down" (only four people on the phones).

Tardiness

By now you should have a good idea of what I am going to say about showing up late for work, extending lunches, and extending breaks. If you are tardy you are not only a "bad workplace neighbor", but quite frankly, a bad employee.

A lot of thought and analysis goes into creating work schedules. Often department A cannot start its work until department B completes its work. Other times, in order to meet customer expectations, to satisfy and keep those customers, work must be completed within specific timeframes.

Tardiness is the villain of both of these situations. If you show up 30 minutes late and do a phenomenal job, but that meant that the company had people sitting around doing little for a half hour until you showed up and completed your work; the company just wasted money. If the company now has to pay those workers overtime to finish their work, who is management going to blame? You will be subject of management's scorn.

Another possibility is that management will expect the workers who were delayed by you to finish their work within the normal work day. There go those bathroom breaks again. Who do you think those workers will be angry at? Sure they will be angry a bit at management. But it is you being late that caused the tough work day, so it is you, their "bad workplace neighbor" who they will be annoyed with the most. You will be creating problems in the workplace, and if tardiness (even 5 minutes) is a repeat problem, you stand an excellent chance of being fired. Your supervisor will have no choice. If you come late, others will expect management to deal with you or they will start coming late to work as well. That would throw off work schedules even more, increase costs through overtime, and mean missing customers' deadlines, which could result in losing those customers which mean lower profits. And by now you know that lower profits means fewer jobs and less money for employees. What a mess your five, ten or thirty-minute tardiness created.

Businesses can't risk it. Therefore, being tardy is a sure way to get fired.

Straight forward: reporting times for work are part of the company's policies making not reporting on time a serious offense with a consequence which is, almost assuredly, being fired.

Phone center example

To show you how quickly a phone center can get out of control, let's say a co-worker of yours comes in 15 minutes late (I know you wouldn't come in late). During those 15 minutes callers are on hold longer than usual because the phone center is down one staff member, so 10 callers hang up because they have to leave to go to work. These 10 <u>dissatisfied</u> customers are now going to call back later in the day adding unexpected call volume to those time frames. Let's say that all ten call during their lunch break. Now the phone center is understaffed during lunch because it was staffed for ten less calls than it gets. So during lunch time callers will be on hold longer than expected and some of them will hang up because they have to eat. This creates more dissatisfied customers and adds more unexpected call volume to other time periods in that day or the next day. That in turn will create even more dissatisfied customers and create future time periods where there will be more calls, longer hold times than desired and additional customer hang-ups.

As you now see, this fifteen minute tardiness could result in a problem that lasts for days and causes many customers who are dissatisfied. And dissatisfied customers could take their business elsewhere reducing the profitability of the business. This, as we know, can have a negative impact on employee jobs, compensation, and benefits.

Now if you added in the fact some workers come back late from lunch, or take a bathroom break at a bad time, or call in with an unexcused absence, etc. you see the importance of being punctual and not taking off days unnecessarily

Attendance and tardiness worksheet

1. What problems can arise from employees who are absent a lot and constantly tardy?

_____
_____
_____
_____
_____

2. How does an employee benefit from good attendance and being punctual (on time)?

_____
_____
_____
_____
_____

3. What will you do to ensure you will get to work on time every day?

_____
_____
_____
_____
_____

4. What are some of your personal lifestyle habits and obstacles that could hinder your efforts to get to work on time and be punctual while on the job?

_____
_____
_____
_____
_____

5. List some contingency plans and strategies to help overcome the items you listed in #4 above.

_____
_____
_____
_____
_____
_____

EXERCISE WB2

Below is a list of reasons workers use for staying home from work. Please indicate if the excuse is good, bad, or depends upon the circumstance. Then explain why you believe the choice you made is the correct choice.

Q1. Your car will not start.

Q2. Your child is sick.

Q3. You stayed out late, are very tired, and wake up with a major headache.

Q4. You have a fever of 102.

Q5. You have an appointment with the local cable company scheduled that day.

Q6. There is a death in your family.

Q7. Your best friend needs to you watch his or her kids because they have a doctor's appointment.

Q8. You had a fight with your spouse and are too upset to work.

Q9. You have a second, part-time job and they told you, "We need you today three people are out with the flu; if you can't come in today and help out we will need to fire you and hire someone who can fill in when we have emergencies."

Q10. Your child's teacher called and needs to talk to you about something very important.

Safety in the Workplace

For some reason the word safety always makes me think of an underrated song and album from the late seventies, "Safety in Numbers" by Crack the Sky. If you don't know it; check it out on You Tube. A little known fact is that their debut album, *Crack the Sky*, released in 1975, was declared the debut album of the year by *Rolling Stone* magazine and included memorable songs such as, "A Sea Epic" and "Robots for Ronnie." Oh, well, now on to the topic.

All workplaces have safety rules. Some rules are generated by the company, but most are required by OSHA (Occupational Safety and Health Administration). If companies do not follow these rules they can get fines or even shut down until proper safety precautions are implemented.

From the OSHA web site: "Under the OSH Act, employers are responsible for providing a safe and healthful workplace. OSHA's mission is to assure safe and healthful workplaces by setting and enforcing standards, and by providing training, outreach, education and assistance. Employers must comply with all applicable OSHA standards. Employers must also comply with the General Duty Clause of the OSH Act, which requires employers to keep their workplace free of serious recognized hazards."

OSHA enforcement information follows (from the OSHA web site):

OSHA Jurisdiction:

- Covers private sector employers
- Excludes self-employed, family farm workers, and government workers (except in state plan states)
- Approves and monitors 27 State Plan states which cover private and public sector employees.
- Assists Federal Agency Programs

OSHA Inspections:

- Conducted without advance notice
- On-site inspections, or Phone/Fax investigations

- Highly-trained compliance officers

Inspection Priorities:

- Imminent danger
- Catastrophes
- Worker complaints and referrals
- Targeted inspections - high injury/illness rates, severe violators
- Follow-up inspections

Therefore, you must follow the safety rules in your workplace and wear the proper and required safety clothing and equipment. Also, ensure that your co-workers do the same. Do not look the other way. The only way for you to be safe, is for everyone to act safely. The person who starts an electrical fire is not necessarily the only one who will get hurt.

Some items you need to be aware of include:

✓ Know workplace warning signs (physical signs or tags):
  - white/black = housekeeping hazards
  - green = first aid and safety equipment
  - blue = caution against using unsafe equipment
  - orange = physical hazards
  - red = danger, stop, and fire protection equipment
  - yellow = general caution

✓ Working with electricity
  - do not fix electrical problems yourself
  - do not use machines with red or yellow tags
  - report machines not working properly or with frayed cords
  - always plug in machines with the power button off

✓ Fire extinguishers
  - locate all fire extinguishers so you know where they are before you need them
  - read the labels to know what type of fires each fire extinguisher is to be used for; using the fire extinguisher on the wrong type of fire can make the problem worse
  - class A fire extinguishers are for wood, paper, cloth, trash plastics
  - class B fire extinguishers are for flammable liquids (gasoline, oil, grease, acetone)
  - class C fire extinguishers are for electrical
  - class D are for metals
  - water (H_2O) extinguishers are for class A fires only
  - carbon dioxide (CO_2) extinguishers are for class B and C
  - dry chemical (DC) can be for A,B,C or just B,C

✓ Emergency evacuation
- know where the exits are
- know the evacuation procedure

✓ Injuries
- know and wear all required safety equipment to avoid injuries
- know where the medical emergency kit is located
- always use latex gloves where dealing with blood spills
- for serious problems seek medical help

Below are some statistics from the U. S. Department of Labor's web site for 2006:

Number of deaths   5,703

Transportation related	2,423
Assaults/violent acts	754
Equipment/object related	983
Falls	809
Harmful substance/work environment	525
Fires/explosions	201

Percent of workers:

| Who get hurt/sick on the job | 4.4% |
| Who missed time from injuries/illness | 1.3% |

While the percentages may look low, this means that almost a half a million workers got hurt or sick on the job in 2006.

Another way to look at the numbers is that on average over 13,000 people got injured or sick on the job, and over 15 people died on the job, every day in 2006.

Consequences of accidents on businesses

The equation to determine the success of a business is simple:
Revenues – Expenses = Profits

Businesses need to be profitable to stay in business, keeping its workers employed.

Revenues are the monies that the business makes selling its products or services.

Expenses are monies that it costs the business to operate.

Expenses include employee costs, and insurance such as workman's comp.

Expenses can be fixed (such as mortgage on a building) or variable (such as the number of workers hired to complete a specific job or contract).

If a business isn't making profits, and can not raise its prices or increase its sales, it cuts expenses.

Fixed costs cannot be cut; variable costs can be cut.

Accidents are an expense to a business.

Accidents can carry fines, result in shut downs, and increase the amount of money the business must pay for workers (workman) compensation insurance. This increases expenses. Another result of accidents in the workplace could be bad press leading to negative word of mouth for the company. That can lead to a reduction in customers, which obviously, has a negative impact on revenues.

Increases in expenses and/or reductions in revenues means that the business will need to cut expenses (and, yes, employees and employee salaries and benefits are on the table for cuts).

Therefore, co-workers who are not safety conscious (i.e. who do not play by the company's "safety rules"), or who fake injuries to collect workers compensation, may just cost you your job, or cause you to get a lower pay increase, or even see your compensation or benefits cut. Everything is connected. The extra business expenses from workplace accidents, higher insurance premiums, and loss of revenue from bad press have to be taken from somewhere.

This is why minimizing accidents on the job is a joint venture between the workers and the business. In addition to caring about its employees health and safety, and meeting OSHA standards; it is just good business for a company to provide a safe work environment while it makes sense for all workers to follow all safety rules, procedures and policies to remain safe, healthy and employed at a good wage.

So be sure you and your co-workers work safely and that no one takes advantage of worker compensation insurance.

Now the following points should make sense and be important to you:

(1) When an employee uses worker's comp fraudulently it is not just between that worker and the company; that worker is placing you and your co-workers' jobs, benefits, and wages in jeopardy. Remember, if one worker gets away with it, more will try.

(2) There are some situations where using your personal medical insurance instead of workman's comp to pay for your medical expenses may be the best choice as you work in partnership with your employer to ensure your health and the health of that business.

Safety consequences worksheet

If It Wasn't True It Would Be Funny, Inc. averages three employee accidents a week, in part because of some employees not following safety procedures, and in part because the company does not have sufficient safety policies in place.

List three consequences that could happen to the business.

1. _____

2. _____

3. _____

Assuming you worked for this company, list two consequences that could happen to you because of the situation at If It Wasn't True It Would Be Funny, Inc.

1. _____

2. _____

Steps to Take to Limit Accidents at Work

Be alert for possible dangers. Knowing the type of emergencies that may occur in your workplace means that you will be better prepared to avoid those dangers.

Keep your mind on your work. By concentrating on the work at hand there is a lower probability of an accident occurring.

Get training (formal or informal) on the proper and safe use of all equipment that you will be using in the workplace. The better you are trained, the less likely you will have an accident due to the lack of understanding of how to the use that equipment; and the more aware you will be regarding the potential dangers of using that equipment incorrectly.

Check your workplace for the location of safety equipment. If you know where equipment such as fire extinguishers, first aid kits, etc., are, you can respond to an accident more quickly and minimize the damage.

Know what to do if an accident occurs. By being prepared for common workplace accidents you can respond properly to emergency situations and avoid making the situation worse.

EXERCISE WB3

You are a full time employee for Electric Electricians located at 111 Main Street, Ridgway, PA. You are a tradesperson whose occupation is an electrician.

While on the job you sprain your wrist when you brace your fall off a ladder while doing electrical work in the ceiling while working at 222 First Street, DuBois, PA. It is not serious but will need to be wrapped for three weeks. First aid was administered at the work site and that was the only treatment needed. When you leave the area it is safe. The incident happened on January 25th, 2006 at 11:15 AM. The agency of the injury was powered equipment. You decide not to notify the Department of Industrial Relations.

The name of the W.H.S.O. is Bill Jones. His phone number is 555-111-2222.

The form that follows is used for all accidents at If It Wasn't True It Would Be Funny, Inc. Once completed, your supervisor will sign the form. There are no other attachments needed for this incident.

Make a copy of the form on the next page and fill it out using this information.

Sample accident report

INCIDENT NOTIFICATION FORM

READ NOTES / DIRECTIONS PRIOR TO COMPLETION OF THIS FORM – PLEASE PRINT

Type of incident
☐ work injury ☐ serious bodily injury ☐ work caused illness ☐ dangerous event ☐ dangerous electrical event
Notify Department of Industrial Relations ☐ Yes ☐ No ☐ serious electrical incident
Was injury/illness fatal? ☐ Yes ☐ No   If an electrical incident, has the area been made safe? ☐ Yes ☐ No

Details of injured person

Given names		Surname	
Residential Address		D.O.B.	
	Postcode	☐ Male ☐ Female	

Basis of employment

Full time	☐	Part time	☐
Casual	☐	Volunteer	☐
Member of public	☐	Other	☐
Self-employed	☐		

Type of employment

Occupation [   ]

Administration	☐	Tradesperson	☐	Apprentice/trainee	☐
Technical	☐	Professional	☐	Student	☐
Other	☐				

Nature of work injury or work caused illness, eg. fracture, sprain & strain, electrical shock, burns, etc. [   ]

Bodily location of injury or work caused illness [   ]

Medical treatment ☐ nil ☐ first aid ☐ doctor only ☐ hospital admitted to: [   ]
(if overnight)

Mechanism of injury/disease

Falls, trips and slips	☐	Sound and pressure	☐	Biological factors	☐
Hitting objects with part of body	☐	Body stressing	☐	Mental stress	☐
Heat radiation and electricity	☐	Chemicals and other substance	☐	Other and unspecified mechanisms of injury	☐

Agency of injury/disease

Machinery and (mainly) fixed plants	☐	Mobile plant and transport	☐	Animal, human and biological agencies	☐
Powered equipment, tools and appliances	☐	Non-powered handtools, appliances and equipment	☐	Environmental agencies	☐
Chemicals and chemical products	☐	Materials and substances	☐	Other and unspecified agencies	☐

Details of how incident occurred

Day   Month   Year   Time of incident: ☐☐ ☐☐ am/pm
Description of incident (Attach report)

[   ]

Name of employer/self-employed person/principal contractor [   ]

Address of employer/ self-employed person/ principal contractor		Location address of workplace where incident occurred	
Name of W.H.S.O. and phone no. (if any)		Phone ( )	

Employer/Self-Employed Person/Principal Contractor Signature

	Day	Month	Year

OFFICE USE ONLY	
District Reference No. ☐☐☐☐☐☐☐☐	Action
Plant No. ☐☐☐☐☐☐☐	
Date: Day Month Year	
Workplace/Construction Workplace No. ☐☐☐☐☐☐	
Licence No.	

(Refer Reverse Page)

PRIVACY STATEMENT The Department of Industrial Relations respects your privacy and is committed to protecting personal information. The information provided on this form is for

EXERCISE WB4

The machines Fred works on give off sparks. Everyone is required to wear safety goggles. Fred's wife Wilma comes to the plant to give Fred his lunch box that he left at home. She is dressed in her work clothes for her job and walks directly up to Fred at his work station and hands him his lunch box, says a couple of words and then leaves.

Q1. If you were Wilma would you have done the same thing?

Q2. Why or why not?

Be a Positive Force in the Workplace

The old children's show host, Mr. Rogers was right. "Be a good neighbor." Living next to someone who blasts loud music all the time, lets his/her lawn grow wildly, is the king (or queen) of the pop over, is constantly arguing very loudly, throws trash on the common grounds, doesn't pick up after his/her dog, allows his/her kids to play loudly outside at 7:00 AM Saturday morning, etc., is annoying. This neighbor is someone who doesn't know how (or chooses not) to be a good neighbor.

In life, you may have limited options to escape that self-centered neighbor. Work is different. Part of everyone's job is to be a good neighbor to other workers. If you are superb in your work, but are a "bad workplace neighbor", you may not get the pay raises you expect. You certainly are unlikely to get a promotion where you will be in charge of those neighbor workers. You could even get fired.

Think about it. Your employer needs more than one good worker. So, even if you are the best worker but your "bad workplace neighbor" actions result in other workers being unhappy at work, who can the company afford to lose; you or three or four others? Furthermore, if other workers were to leave because of a bad work environment due to a "bad workplace neighbor" it is usually good workers who leave because they will be the most coveted by other employers.

Therefore, it is very difficult for a business to keep a good worker who is a "bad workplace neighbor." Worst case, the supervisor gives that employee a mixed performance appraisal (usually this comes with only a below-average to average pay raise). The supervisor's hope is that that employee will improve as a workplace neighbor to get a larger raise during his/her next performance review.

So while many workers believe their pay is only about doing their job well, that is not true. Their supervisor cannot overlook bad behavior in the workplace. High employee turnover (workers constantly leaving) is very expensive, cutting into business profits (and we now know that can negatively impact jobs and wages). New employees have to be trained; meaning that a person in the company is training a new employee rather than being productive elsewhere. Also, new employees need time before they are at full productivity (takes time before the new employee can produce work at expected levels) so it costs the company more money to produce the same amount of work until the new employee is up to speed.

Even if workers' "bad workplace neighbor" behaviors do not cause their fellow employees to quit, it will still have a negative impact on overall productivity. Workers who are unhappy in the workplace often make more mistakes, look for any excuse to be absent from work, and think about their job as short term, not long term, so come up with fewer suggestions to solve customer and work related problems.

Luckily for the employer, if these problems can be solved by firing one employee, even if he/she is a top employee in terms of productivity and quality of work, it can, and often will, do so.

Entering the workplace is like moving to a foreign country. Some of the behaviors needed to be a good neighbor in the country will be common sense, while others have to be explained and, possibly, learned.

What follows are some common behaviors workers will need to follow to become "good workplace neighbors." I'm sure many of you will find the majority of these as common sense; behaviors you would do in the workplace even if you hadn't read this book. That's fine. But the one or two that you may not have known will help you, and now you know that the items that follow below are expected in the workplace, not optional if you want to keep your job and maximize your pay.

Be dependable and responsible

Dependable refers to the person, while responsible refers to a person's action. It is a fact that you must show up to work when scheduled and never be late. I'm confident that you will, as the famous Starship Captain Picard says, "Make it so." By performing this one feat you attain a workplace behavior highly-valued by employers; being dependable. Your supervisor will know he/she can count on you being at work when he/she needs you at work. This will help you keep your job. But is it enough? No, it is not. If your employer can depend on you, but cannot rely on you to get your job done, then your dependability will go somewhat unnoticed.

However, if you are responsible by completing all your work assignments satisfactorily, and combine that with being dependable, you become a highly-valued employee, and will be on your way to a long successful working career.

Grooming

Everyone knew that guy or gal in college who partied all night, came home very late and kept hitting the snooze button on his/her alarm clock until he/she finally got up five minutes before class was starting. Still reeking badly from the odors of his/her night on the town, but with no time to shower, he/she runs off to class au natural (makes me think of the old theme song from the television show *The Monkees*, "Here we come, walking down the street, get the funniest looks from everyone we meet"). Or worse, he/she takes a "deodorant shower" (or the just as bad "laying on the perfume/after shave shower" mixing bad smells with over-powering factory-created smells). It didn't work then and doesn't work now. While in college that may have been overlooked because of the "hey I might need to do that some day" factor; in the workplace it will not. Co-workers will avoid working next to that person at all costs and may complain to supervisors. Depending upon the supervisor's personality, he/she will either confront the "smelly worker," will give the co-worker assignments where he/she is working alone, or will do nothing. It is the second and third options that will doom the "smelly worker." In the case of separating that worker from the other workers in the "pack," that worker's future with the company is dead in the water. In the case where the situation is ignored, the smelly worker's days with the company could be numbered.

So do not party all night, roll out of bed and come to work. If you do you are just shooting yourself in the foot by being a "bad workplace neighbor."

The second topic in this section is a bit more delicate. Most of you reading this will think, "Duh, why even mention it?" However, you may have known someone in your life who did not follow what is written next. Some may be individuals who came to the United States from overseas where daily practices are different. Below are standard hygiene practices used in the United States and will need to be followed to be considered a "good workplace neighbor."

✓ Shower every day using soap
✓ Use deodorant every day before coming to work
✓ Brush your teeth every day before coming to work
✓ Use mouthwash every morning
✓ Make sure your hair is neat and clean every day
✓ Wear clean and odor free clothes to work every day
✓ Wear clothes that are appropriate for your workplace
✓ Do not use too much perfume/cologne/after shave, (many people are sensitive to smell)

Mannerisms and habits

Since there are a lot of people with diverse behaviors that comprise a workplace; rules are established to avoid workplace conflicts. Many of these rules get in the way of individuals habits. However, think of this like a clubhouse, gym, pool, tennis court, etc. in your community. There are all sorts of rules governing these shared places. For example, no running by the pool (slip and fall in a wet area, have an accident, the accident costs the community pool money, insurance rates increase, and suddenly it costs every member of the community more money to use the pool – just like a safety issue in business).

Therefore, to be a "good workplace neighbor" and a valuable employee, play by the rules of the workplace as it relates to personal behavior. If smoking is not allowed in the workplace, don't smoke. If there is a designated smoking area and you are a smoker, use it. If you are not allowed to eat at your desk, don't sneak food at your desk.

Also, be very conscious of your own bad habits and mannerisms. Your mom will look the other way and still love you if you use profanity (but probably be hiding a dirty look), but your co-workers and supervisor will not. For many people, using profanity is something that they do without thinking. It is not, however, something you should do at work. Even if you are not called on it, using profanity in your everyday speech or when angry at work will be viewed as unprofessional and limit your growth in the company. In fact, the supervisor that tells you to stop is doing you a favor because he/she is giving you an opportunity to correct that bad habit at work. The supervisor that says nothing has probably already limited your growth to your current job position in his/her mind. It is almost never that the supervisor thinks it is okay that you use profanity because even if he/she is not offended, he/she knows someone in the workplace will be, and will have options available to him/her to get the profanities to stop which will make the supervisor look bad.

There are other mannerisms and habits that people have that they can use with the people that know them well, but are inappropriate in the workplace. Examples include touching people on the shoulder when talking to them, giggling, chewing gum, telling ethnic-related jokes, etc. I cannot list them all. If you do not know yours, ask someone that knows you and do not be offended when you hear what that person tells you.

Grooming and bad habit worksheet

Look at the previous pages with the list of grooming items and bad mannerisms and habits.

Which grooming items do you need to add to you routine to comply with what is expected at work?

_____   _____   _____

What bad mannerisms and habits do you need to correct in order to compy with what is expected at work?

1. _____

2. _____

What habits do you currently have that you know you will have to curtail to assure that you are a "good workplace neighbor?"

1. _____

2. _____

3. _____

Positive attitude

Everyone likes to be around people with positive attitudes. It's infectious. At work, it is more than that. Workers who look at things in a negative light and communicate that negativity to other workers (either verbally or with negative nonverbal personal signals) are considered problems in the workplace by management.

If every time a supervisor informs his/her team of new work procedures, you say nothing but sit there with your arms crossed and a frown, you will be labeled a malcontent without even opening up your mouth!

Therefore, I have two pieces of advice depending upon your personality.

If you are someone who looks at the glass as half empty, someone who always initially reacts poorly to change, do not discuss your feelings with your co-workers. You will come across as negative and that will be a very big problem for you. Also, when you are being informed of changes make an effort win an academy award. That doesn't mean over act, but be conscious of your body language and avoid negative personal signals. The gloom and doom co-worker is a horrible "workplace neighbor."

On the other hand, if you are someone who looks at the glass as half full, someone who initially reacts positively to change, and tends to become a cheerleader for the cause, let your positive attitude shine through. Your co-workers will appreciate it since they will have to adapt to the changes and seeing that someone feels positive about the changes will make them feel good. Even better, your supervisor will appreciate your attitude and consider you a real team player.

Positive self-image

The previous topics were to help you be a "good workplace neighbor" in your interactions with others. This topic is to help put you in the right frame of mind to undertake that challenge.

Always remember that you are working in your job because the management of the company believed in you enough to hire you. The company's profits are based on the quality of work received from its employees, including you, so that was a big decision.

The company believes in you, the management of the company believes in you, so you should believe in yourself. Have a positive self-image!

Know that you were chosen for your job. That despite any negative vibes you may feel are going on around you, and despite some occasional negative comments being communicated to you, that you are still employed so management still believes in you. If your supervisor did not believe in you, you would have been fired. That doesn't mean your supervisor believes you are working at your peak performance levels. He/she may believe that there is room for improvement. However, in the end he/she believes you are contributing to the profitability of the business, that you are not just a drain on the company's expenses. Again, if you were, you would be fired.

So feel good about your role in the company and be a "good workplace neighbor." Also know that your supervisor is on your side. As in sports, some coaches (supervisors) are players-coaches (think Tony Dungy), while some coaches can be tough SOB's on their players (think Bill Parcells). In both cases, however, the coach (supervisor) wants, in fact, needs his players to play well. Their jobs are on the line. Even when genius coaches don't win enough, they get fired. So despite how tough your supervisor is on you, know that he/she wants, in fact, needs you to succeed.

Next, a positive self-image does not mean you must be perfect all the time. Even the great ones make mistakes. In a game in 2007, Hall of Fame coach, Joe Gibbs used back-to-back timeouts to freeze a field goal kicker. That was against the rules, something he should have known. He made a mistake. The result was a penalty on his team, making the kick a much easier one and his team lost because of that made field goal. You will make mistakes as well. The key is to learn from those mistakes and to not repeat the same ones. Also, to ask questions if you are unsure of something. Just take notes so you do not have to keep asking the same question over and over again.

Lifestyle compromises

If you were playing in a championship game tomorrow, you wouldn't spend the night before the game partying and drinking into the wee hours of the morning. At least you wouldn't if you wanted to be at your best for the game. Now if you win the game, celebrating could be in order the night after the game.

At work, everyday is like a championship game. If you don't do your job to the best of your ability, your business could lose customers. If your productivity is down you are not producing sufficient product, meeting customer time schedules, etc., etc., etc. In the end that means less profits for the business which means less job security and less money available for employee salaries. It also means that your job performance is below standard, your supervisor will notice that, and that could result in lower pay raises and less opportunities for advancement. It could also result in you being fired.

Therefore, if you like to go out and "party", do so on a night where you do not have work the next day. This will ensure that you can report to work on time, and that there will be no lasting effects from the prior night negatively impacting your work.

Another compromise you may have to make because of your "marriage-like" relationship with your employer is your bed time. To be at your best you need a good night's sleep. Be sure you get it. Today, with DVR, DVD recorders, TiVo, shows available on the Internet, etc., you can easily watch any late night show you like another time.

You also need to be aware that how you behave outside of work reflects on your employer. How many times have you met an obnoxious person, found out where he/she works and thought that's one place I'll never go to. So do not do anything that could drive customers away from your place of business (that includes making negative comments about the company you work for). The impact on you can only be negative, even if the behaviors and/or comments never get traced back to you. If your place of work suffers, it just leads to layoffs and less money available for you and your co-workers.

This also means be careful what you post on YouTube and Facebook. You are a representative of your company. Be sure you behave accordingly online as well as in your everyday life.

Lifestyle choices

There are things you can do in your everyday life to help you be the best you can be in your partnership with your employer. Many these will also help you outside of the workplace as well.

- ✓ Eat healthy
- ✓ Exercise
- ✓ Don't overindulge in alcohol
- ✓ Don't use illegal drugs
- ✓ Don't smoke

Take control of your life

One of the best ways to take control of your life is to hang out with friends who understand that you are serious about earning good money in the workplace, support you in your quest, and are positive influences in your quest. These are not people who get down on you because you no longer go out partying with them on Wednesday nights. These are people who understand your priorities and start getting together with you Friday nights (assuming you have off Saturdays and Sundays) instead.

Know that you are in control of what you do, and what you do not do. Take control of your life and do not just follow others. Know that things happen for a reason and develop a plan so that good things happen for you. Decide on a plan of action in life, and at work, and follow that plan. Do not allow others to talk you out of what you know you have to do to succeed. This is especially true when things are not going the way you want. Stay the course. Know that "true friends" will not use this occasion to tear down your plan. True friends will be supportive. They may even help you come up with ways to adjust your plan so that you have a better chance to succeed. They will not substitute their selfish goals for you (e.g. as a buddy to party with when you're in a weak moment), for what is truly important to you (helping you stay the course so you can succeed at work).

Two examples of taking control through planning

One of your goals in life is to be a good employee so you can stay employed and earn good money. How do I know this? You wouldn't be reading this book or taking a work readiness course if it weren't true!

Therefore, both of these examples will deal with planning to get to work on time.

(1) To get to work on time, you need reliable transportation. Therefore you need to:
- ✓ Keep your car in good working order (repairs and maintenance).
- ✓ Know all public transportation options that can be used in case of emergencies (method and time schedules).
- ✓ Exchange telephone numbers with at least one co-worker who lives in your area so you can contact each other in case either of you need a ride to work (also know how early you need to call your co-worker to ensure that both of you do not arrive late to work).
- ✓ Ask your neighbors where they work. Some may work close to you and you both can give each other rides to work in emergencies.
- ✓ Know that, worst case, you can always call a cab to get to work; then let your supervisor know that you took a cab and ask if he/she knows anyone outside of your department that lives in your area and can help you out for the next day or two while your car is being repaired.

(2) If you have children, to be able to get to work on time (or at all), you need reliable daycare. Therefore you need to:
- ✓ Have both a reliable primary and backup daycare plan in place for your children (whether a facility or a worker in your home).
- ✓ Know the schedules of family members and friends you trust to take care of your children so they can be used in emergencies.
- ✓ Develop a network of neighborhood parents who have daycare needs and use each other's daycare workers in emergencies.
- ✓ Know your child's school schedule in advance so you will know when exceptions to your normal daycare plan will occur. This will protect against last minute hunting for daycare services; you will be able to plan in advance.
- ✓ Know all after school programs that can be of use to you. Also, know in advance days that the after school program may not be available even though the school is open so you can plan for those days.
- ✓ Investigate all daycare businesses or individuals that you plan to use. Be sure that they are dependable and that they offer safe environments for your children. Ask for references. If possible, show up at the facility before you plan to use them and ask the parents dropping off their kids questions. One good question to ask is how long they have been using the facility. If all are relatively new to the facility (and the facility has been around for years), that could mean that others have left because of previous problems. For businesses you can also contact the Better Business Bureau to see if there have been complaints about that business.

In both of these cases, if you do not get to work on time (or at all), your supervisor will not accept either car trouble or child care issues as acceptable reasons for missing work. Potential car trouble and child care issues are problems that people know may occur. You will be expected to have backup plans in place.

What it all means

"Married to the job" is a phrase usually reserved for workaholics. However, it is really true for everyone. Like a marriage there are benefits, responsibilities, and compromises required of both the employer and the employees.

The benefits are money, heath insurance, etc. for the employee, and quality work being completed for the employer.

The responsibilities are many for the employee, as outlined in this book. The responsibilities for the employer are to provide a safe, harassment-free, discrimination-free work environment and more to its employees.

Now it's the compromises that are interesting and are often ignored by employees. Employers compromise by giving up a greater share of profits than they would like to pay for their employees' salaries and benefits. The compromises required by employees involve their lifestyles away from the job.

When in a committed personal relationship, both parties have to make changes in their lifestyles. For example, going to single bars may no longer be acceptable. Well, since your relationship with your employer is like a marriage there are compromises you have to make in your lifestyle so you can be at your best for you employer.

Life plan for succeeding at work worksheet

Review the subchapters starting with lifestyle compromises through what it all means. List two things you will need to change, modify or have under control to ensure that you are successful at work.

1. _____
   _____

2. _____
   _____

Now list the steps you will take to ensure that the change is successful.

1. _____
   _____

2. _____
   _____

3. _____
   _____

EXERCISE WB5

Q1. How can dependable employee be unreliable?

Q2. How can a reliable employee be undependable?

Q3. Which is more important, being dependable or being reliable?

Q4. You work as a fact checker and need to be alert on the job so that errors do not occur. You stay up late every night because you have a second job and often come to work very tired. You need the extra money. If your work suffers, will management understand and look the other way? What could be the consequence of working that second job?

Q5. You show up late for work because you had to bail your best friend out of jail. You call to ask your new supervisor for permission and you get permission. Is that the end of it? Could anything negative come out of this situation for you?

Avoiding Workplace Problems

Who knew that the band The Offspring sung songs about the workplace! I have heard that when the band first formed they welcomed Kevin "Noodles" Wasserman, the school janitor into the band, allegedly because he was old enough to purchase alcohol for Dexter Holland and Greg Kriesel, both of whom were under the legal drinking age. So while their song, "She's Got Issues", contains the line, "And check your baggage at the door", the band didn't follow its own advice, bringing alcohol to their workplace. Wasserman acted unethically helping underage kids get alcohol (consequences - if one of them got into a car accident while drunk, killed someone, and it was found out that he supplied the alcohol, he could have been charged along with the driver). Oh, to be young, reckless, and in a successful rock band.

Their message, however, is on the money for the workplace. Check your baggage (behaviors that others will find objectionable) at the door of your workplace. This is not a suggestion. It is required. If you do not, you will likely be fired.

Value of Diversity in the Workplace

Since the workplace is based on teamwork, the more diversified the team members, the stronger the team.

If a team has team members who can look at a challenge from a variety of backgrounds and viewpoints, the team stands a better chance of coming up with solutions that address all aspects of that challenge.

This includes a mix of workers of different gender, age, ethnicity, race, religion, etc. The company wants to do business with all customers. If a team is assembled to fix a problem, it is best if the people working on the solution can fairly represent the company's customers.

For that reason, companies that employ a large staff, often have a goal of assembling a diversified workforce. Many ill-advised workers may feel the diversification is due to pressure from forces outside the company. That is a foolish viewpoint. Workplace diversification is strength for a business.

Objectionable behaviors

What follows are behaviors that will get you fired on the spot. Be aware that is not you who decide if your behavior qualifies as one of these objectionable behaviors. It is a combination of the company and the person who finds the behavior objectionable. That is very important. I'll "say" it again, with emphasis this time. It is **not you** who determines if your behavior qualifies as one of these objectionable behaviors. It is a combination of the company and **the person who finds the behavior objectionable**.

Harassment

When most people think of harassment in the workplace, sexual harassment is the topic that comes to mind. However, harassment can also be racial, creed (religion), age, ethnicity, lifestyle, and handicap motivated.

Remember, it is not what you think is objectionable that defines your actions as harassment; it is company policies and what the object of the harassment thinks. A joke you tell innocently every day to your friends, with no malice intended, could be taken as harassment in the workplace.

Harassment can be in the form of words or actions. To help avoid harassment you need to avoid:

✓ Telling/distributing jokes making fun of specific groups of people
✓ Touching other people
✓ Commenting on a person's physical appearance (good or bad)
✓ Using words to describe groups of people that the group finds objectionable (slurs, slang, etc.)
✓ Making broad comments about groups of people (good or bad)
✓ Displaying photos, images, cartoons, etc. that contains materials, symbols, words, etc. that others find objectionable in your work area
✓ Cursing

Discrimination

The workplace, like our country, is a melting pot. You will interact with people of different races, creeds, ethnicities, lifestyles, and ages. You must treat everyone in your workplace with courtesy and respect. Who you hang out with, who you deal with in your personal life is up to you. Who you deal with, who you interact with in the workplace is up to your management. If you are organizing a company event, everyone must be allowed to attend. You cannot discriminate against the people in your workplace. If you do, the company will have to fire you.

Drug/alcohol abuse

You may drink or use recreational drugs in your personal life. However, if you come to work drunk, hung over, or high, you are seriously risking your job.

Using recreation drugs is illegal, hence unethical. With unethical behavior come potential consequences. In this case, the consequences will be you losing your job. Many places of employment have drug testing and make their employees sign a drug-free workplace pledge as a condition of employment. Using drugs is a serious workplace offense. It has brought down more than one professional athlete.

The same is true for alcohol. When you sign a drug-free workplace pledge, it includes alcohol. You cannot drink on the job, no matter how well you believe you can hold your liquor, and cannot show up drunk or hung over.

Violence

Violence in the workplace is not tolerated, even if no one is seriously hurt. If you have a temper, you must keep it in check. Just threatening violence could get you fired. If a co-worker gets you angry, just walk away.

A plan of action

There are attitudes you can adapt in the workplace to help you avoid missteps. They include:

1. Remember the Otis Redding written, Aretha Franklin made famous song, "Respect." Treat everyone with respect, the same respect with which you want to be treated.
2. Know that you are not in control; your management is in control. Be a good soldier.
3. Be color, gender, lifestyle, etc. blind.
4. When talking to others in the workplace, talk as is if everyone you know and care about is listening in (parents, kids, friends, neighbors, etc.).
5. When talking to others in the workplace, talk as if your supervisor is always watching, and your next pay raise is on the line.
6. Do not say anything about another person that you wouldn't want said about you.
7. In a heated argument, talk as though you are in a public library (talk softly, do not raise your voice) and that the local police and "ambulance-chasing" attorneys are present.
8. When interacting with others in friendly conversations keep your hands at your side (no touching).
9. Act as though your personal work space will be shown on the *Disney Channel* (everything rated "G").

Don't count on others in the workplace to follow this advice; if they do be pleasantly surprised. If they do not, walk away.

Workplace comportment worksheet

Indicate if each of the items in the above checklist comes naturally for you (yes if it does, no if it does not).

1. Yes   No   2. Yes   No   3. Yes   No   4. Yes   No   5. Yes   No
6. Yes   No   7. Yes   No   8. Yes   No   9. Yes   No

EXERCISE WB6

Foad works for Tony at a bank. Tony is very big on team building and starts a monthly group get together after work on the last Friday night of the month at the local pub. Foad's religious beliefs prohibit drinking alcohol and eating certain foods.

If Tony did not know Foad's religious beliefs, what might his reaction be if:
    Q1. Foad refused to join the group
    Q2. Foad joined the group but refused to drink
    Q3. Foad joined the group but refused to chip in for appetizers ordered by the group

Q4. If any of the above situations occurred, what problems could this have caused Foad at work?

Q5. If Tony knew about Foad's religious beliefs, how might he have reacted to ensure Foad's behavior was not a problem for him with his co-workers?

Q6. If Tony knew Foad's religious beliefs and still wanted to get his group together, what could he do differently?

Social Life at Work

Have you ever heard the phrase, "don't mix business with pleasure?" Well, your business is your job, and your job takes place at work. Therefore, the social connections you make at work must be treated with even more care than those you make outside of the workplace. If you have a fight with a friend you do not work with, you do not have to see, or deal with that person unless you want to. That is not true for friendships you develop at work. Let's say a friend from your workplace violates your trust in a situation that has nothing to do with work, and that violation of trust happens away from the workplace. In other words, this violation of trust is of no interest and no consequence to the management of your company. However, you will still have to see and interact with that person. In fact, you may have to rely on this person at work. How well you do your job may be dependent on him/her, meaning that this person may have an impact on your next pay raise. Now you are in a bind. If you bring your personal conflict with this person to the workplace (not leaving your baggage at the door), then it does become of interest to management, and not in a good way. Management may feel that it has to let one of you go. Or, management may have to change someone's job functions (50% chance it's you). And it won't be a step up. If this personal issue moves to the workplace, it will be held against you, even if your supervisor says it won't (he/she may even believe that, but more senior management will not look at you as supervisor material if you cannot control your personal issues at work).

The answer is not to avoid making friends at work. I have many friends who I met at work throughout my career. My best friends at work, however, were not the people I sat next to, or whose work I needed to rely on. Those people I treated as "friendly- neighbors." These were people who I knew I might have to sit next to, or rely on at work, for a long time. These were people I could not afford to get into non-work related arguments with. So going to lunch with them yes; hanging out on Sunday watching football games, no. At times, after one of my "friendly-neighbor" co-workers moved on to another job, or when I moved on to another job, my friendship with some of my "friendly-neighbor" co-workers grew.

And if workplace friendships are this complicated, how complicated do you think office romances get?

Dating in the workplace

Employers expect their employees to "leave their issues at the door." When those issues involve an argument between co-workers who are dating, that is often difficult to do. In fact, co-workers dating can be so disruptive, that some businesses have a no dating a co-worker policy. Since not following company policies is unethical, if you decide to date a co-worker anyway, you can face severe consequences. One or both of you could be fired for violating company rules.

But what guidelines should you use if there is no company policy against dating in your workplace to avoid setbacks in your career and pay?

(1) <u>Do not date someone who you work next to or whose work you rely on.</u> Since dating comes with both good times and arguments, it will be almost impossible to avoid bringing your arguments to work if your dating partner is "in your face" all day at work. Besides, dating either leads to a permanent partnership or a breakup, with many more ending in a breakup than permanent partnership. More often than not, breakups are ugly, and people move on with their lives with the person he/she was previously dating no longer in his/her life. Obviously, that will not be the case if you dated a person you work with. Therefore, dating someone in this situation usually leads to one or both leaving a job that he/she was growing in, and starting over again in a new company. This can damage your resume, stunt your career growth, and put a dent in your earnings. Even if you stay with the company, the friction in the workplace can lead to your supervisor thinking you used poor judgment, and poor judgment is not a characteristic valued by employers. And employees who are believed to have poor judgment are not employees who are viewed as management material.

Now, you may feel this is unfair. That if you do your job well, you personal life (dating) is not fair to be used against you by the company. Normally that is true. However, it was you that opened the door for your personal life (dating) to be an issue on the job by dating a co-worker you deal with on a regular basis and, therefore, making it impossible for you to "leave your issues at the door." When you cannot "leave your issues at the door" it becomes a workplace issue. In this case, even if you have the ability to separate work from personal life, the person you are/were dating may not be able to do that. He/she has the ability to bring *your* personal business into the workplace and you can do absolutely nothing about it.

(2) <u>If you decide to date someone in your workplace who does not work in your area, and whose work you do not rely on, make sure it is someone you truly believe has the potential to be a lifetime partner.</u> There are a lot of successful marriages that started with the people meeting in the workplace. Many, however, took time to develop. The individuals involved got to know each other very well at work, sometimes as friends, before they started dating. In fact, by the time they started dating, there was already a strong connection.

(3) <u>Workplace "Romeos" may be popular with his/her co-workers, but he/she is not looked at favorably by management.</u> In fact he/she is looked at as a potential source of workplace turmoil. As individuals feel used, or "get dumped" they begin to feel uncomfortable at work, and that has a negative impact on productivity and quality. So do not look at your workplace as your pool for casual dating. If you use your co-workers for "one-night stands" (even if your co-worker is a willing participant), don't be surprised if your employer treats you the same way and you're cut loose in a hurry.

(4) <u>Be very aware of the line between asking a co-worker on a date and sexual harassment.</u> If you ask someone on a date whose pay and/or performance appraisal you control, just the act of asking that person out is sexual harassment. That is true, even if the person says yes. That is because the root of sexual harassment is control and power, not sexual deviance. No worker should be concerned, even a little, that not accepting a date with someone at work could lead to a lower pay raise or an unwarranted bad performance evaluation. A person that controls a worker's pay raises and/or job evaluations has that power. Therefore he/she should <u>never</u> place another person in this position, even if he/she is doing so with good intentions, and would never use a decline to give that co-worker a low pay raise or bad performance appraisal.

This should be common sense, because it is not only the person being asked out that is being put in a bad position, but so is the person doing the asking. What if the person being asked out, turns down the date and then turns out to be a below average worker and deserves a below-average pay raise and performance appraisal. What will the person (manager) who asked that worker out do? If he/she gives the worker the below average raise and performance appraisal, that worker may complain that he/she was only given that because he/she turned down a request for a date. If he/she gives the worker a better raise and performance evaluation than is deserved, it could take money out of the pocket of a more deserving employee. And what if that person's supervisor knows that the worker is below average and questions the raise and evaluation? People are not stupid. Your supervisor, like Frida (of ABBA), will know that there is something going on (sorry, I just like the song, "I Know There Is Something Going On" by Frida). Therefore, asking out a co-worker whose pay raise and/or job performance you control, is not only sexual harassment, but will put you in a very difficult position at work and could easily lead to management questioning your judgment.

Now, let's go back to something else I wrote. The act of asking someone whose pay and/or job performance you control is sexual harassment even if the person says yes (and means it). Let's say you two are dating and everything is going well. As much as you may try to hide that fact at work, it will become known. When it comes time for that person's performance review you give him/her a great review because he/she truly earned it. In fact he/she is doing so well that he/she gets a promotion to a new job that comes with higher pay and better benefits. Your supervisor knows how well that person is performing, and is the one who pushed for him/her to get the promotion. You feel good. You have clean hands. However, your dating partner's co-workers will not know how well the person you are dating is doing on the job. It is not their role to monitor his/her work. They have no idea how your dating partner's work stacks up against their own. All they know is that someone was "dating the boss" and now that someone has a promotion. They won't know that is was your supervisor's decision. This has many consequences. First, it makes you look bad, that getting ahead is a social decision, not a business decision. Second, your partner will be looked at as someone who "slept his/her way to the top." In this case it was clear that that didn't happen. However, that matters little.

Worst of all is that your relationship with the co-worker becomes sexual harassment to your dating partner's co-workers. They feel that to get ahead in their workplace they have to "date" their supervisor. Remember, sexual harassment is about power and control. They observed a situation where someone who in their eyes is "sleeping with the boss", a person in a position of power over their raises and performance appraisals, promoted a person he/she was "sleeping with."

(5) <u>If you are the person being asked out by someone who controls your pay and/or your job performance, know that you are being sexually harassed and you have the option of bringing it up with personnel (Human Resources), or more senior management.</u> You can also just deal with that person one-on-one to let him/her know what he/she has done. Of course my selfish preference is that you buy him/her a copy of this book, with paperclips on the pages dealing with this issue, and the appropriate text highlighted, and hand it to him/her. How you react depends upon what makes <u>you</u> feel most comfortable.

Social life at work worksheet

Have you ever dated and then broke up with someone who you worked with, or who lived in the same building, or was a next door neighbor?

1.   Yes   No

If yes; using the instance where the break up was the worst, how comfortable was it for you immediately after the break up while at work or at home?

2A. _____

If yes; using the instance where the break up was the worst, how comfortable do you believe it was for the other person immediately after the break up while at work or at home?

2B. _____

If no; if it was a bad break-up, how comfortable do you believe it would have been for you immediately after the break up while at work or at home if that person lived next door to you or worked next to you?

3A. _____

If no; if it was a bad break-up, how comfortable do you believe it would have been for the other person immediately after the break up while at work or at home if that person lived next door to you or worked next to you?

3B. _____

EXERCISE WB7

Marie works for Phil. They find out they have a lot in common and start dating. They try to keep their relationship hidden because there are rules against a supervisor dating one of his or her employees. One day, Gene catches them making out in the parking lot and soon Joyce does as well. Soon after, Marie gets a promotion.

Q1. What problem could this cause for Marie with her coworkers?

Q2. Statement – If a supervisor makes sexual advances to a willing employee; that could still be considered sexual harassment because others in the company might construe that as something the supervisor favors when it comes to giving raises and promotions. Do you agree or disagree with this statement. Please support your answer.

Q3. If Marie was hired on merit, then Phil and Marie break up, and later the job proves to be too much for her, and for the betterment of the company Phil needs to replace her; why might Phil be reluctant to do so?

Your Employment Relationship

All teams have team rules. Some may make sense to you, some may not, but you have to follow them all. For example, Tom Coughlin who has coached the Jacksonville Jaguars and New York Giants, had a rule that players had to be five minutes early to team meetings or they would be considered late and fined. Early in his coaching stint with the Giants, one of the team's best players and team leaders, Michael Strahan, got angry because he was on time for the official start of a team meeting, but was not there five minutes early and was fined.

While many of the Giant players did not understand the rule, I did. Coughlin was trying to instill a workplace behavior in the players. That behavior is that in order to ensure that you are not late for an event; you need to plan to get there early. You do not plan to get there at the exact moment the event is starting. Let's say that in Coughlin's case he was starting off his meeting by talking about his defensive game plan for the next game, and Strahan, a key player on defense, was late. He would be faced with a decision to delay the meeting (throwing off the timing for the whole day), start the meeting and then re-start again when Strahan showed up, or catch Strahan up when the meeting was over. None of these options is ideal and all cause work delays.

This brings up another point. Just because you may feel that a rule does not make sense, there is almost always a legitimate reason for the rule. Often management will not explain the reason for the rule because they believe it will be too time consuming to explain their reasoning to everyone, or they do not do want to get into a debate about a rule they feel strongly about.

Your new team (your employer) therefore has team rules. So get a copy of the team rules, called the Employee Handbook, read it and ask your Supervisor or Human Resources Manager questions if you do not understand something in the Employee Handbook. Some small businesses do not have a formal book. They may have memos stating workplace rules, or the rules may be informal and passed on verbally.

In some instances the rules will not be told directly to new employees. The new employee will be expected to use common sense and observe the workplace to understand and follow the rules for their employer. If you find yourself in this situation, do not assume; ask questions. The best person to ask is your supervisor. You can ask your co-workers, but if they are confused about a rule or do not know a rule, you cannot use that as an excuse if you do something wrong by following your co-worker's wrong information. There are situations where your Supervisor will pair you up with a co-worker and tell you to learn from him/her.

That is a different situation. Ask that co-worker questions. However, if that co-worker tells you something that does not make sense (even if you like the information such as Fridays you can leave two hours early if you finish your work), check with your Supervisor to be sure the information is correct.

There are no cases where businesses have no work rules! So you must know, understand, and follow the rules to be considered a valuable member of the team (your employer).

Some common topics found in Employee Handbooks are listed below. If you do not know the "rules" in your place of business regarding these topics, ask questions to find out what the rules are.

Employee Benefits

Topics may include medical insurance, vacation time, holidays, sick days, personal days, pension plans, life insurance, tuition reimbursement, workers compensation insurance, disability, etc.

Company Policies

Topics may include sexual harassment, discrimination, dating in the workplace, substance abuse, drug testing, smoking, leave of absence, severe weather, maternity leave, death in family leave, equal opportunity employer, reporting workplace accidents, use of company property for personal use, employee discounts, gifts from customers, confidential information, visitors, employees selling their own products in the workplace, employees holding a second job, grievances with co-workers/supervisors, employee discipline (suspension, termination), etc.

Compensation

Topics may include wage and salary schedules, performance appraisals, raises, promotions, overtime, pay periods, payroll deductions, tips, etc.

Employee Workplace Rules

Topics may include reporting times, attendance, punctuality, workplace safety, dress code, handling customer records, computer use, copier use, telephone etiquette, customer service, email etiquette, personal decorum in the workplace (no joking around, no arguing, etc.), problem resolution process, lunch, breaks, eating at your work station, etc.

Improve your skills to become more valuable to your employer

As an asset in the workplace, you are just like a stock on the Stock Exchange. If a company comes out with a great new product idea, one that will take the market by storm, you might be tempted to purchase that stock based on the potential of the new product. However, for that stock price to increase the company would have to make the product, introduce it to the marketplace; and then the product would have to perform as advertised. If not the stock price may not only fail to increase, but could decline.

The same concept is true in the workplace. You are hired based on the company's expectations. You need to meet those expectations to keep your job. To meet expectations, you will be expected to not only utilize the skills and knowledge indicated on your resume, but to learn how to apply them to the specific tasks you will be performing on your job. You will also be expected to be a positive influence in the workplace. To get a promotion, you may have to increase your skill and knowledge base (e.g. learning Excel and Access) and/or learn how to perform more complex functions at work (e.g. how to operate more complex machines so you can fill in when a co-worker is absent) and/or display abilities required of employees at higher job levels in the company (e.g. good leadership skills).

As you continue to add to your skill and knowledge base both on and off the job, your value to the company increases. So your "personal employee stock price" increases. As your "employee stock price" increases, your compensation (wages/salary plus benefits) increases as well.

Therefore, you <u>must</u> continue to learn on and off the job, if you want to grow your pay significantly. After all, as Simon and Garfunkel sang, "I am a Stock, I am an Island", or something like that.

Learning strategy

There are steps you can take to ensure that you continue to learn, which continues to make your "employee stock price" rise. They are:

- ✓ <u>Make learning a priority</u> – when given an opportunity to learn something new, take it, always. You never know when it will come in handy and it improves your value as an employee.
- ✓ <u>Seek out opportunities to learn</u> – be proactive, whether enrolling in courses, volunteering for new assignments at work, offering to become a co-worker's emergency backup, etc.; the more you learn, the more valuable you become.
- ✓ <u>Have a plan for learning</u> – set learning objectives (what you want to learn), research the best ways to obtain that skill/knowledge, and follow through and learn.
- ✓ <u>Remain enthused and motivated</u> – learning new skills and knowledge can be difficult, don't give up, stay focused and don't be afraid to ask for help during the learning process.
- ✓ <u>Know that learning is for you first, your employer second</u> – whenever you are given an opportunity (or even required) to learn, realize that you are helping yourself by increasing your "employee stock price" and if you leave that company, you take your higher "employee stock price" with you.
- ✓ <u>Approach everything new as an opportunity to learn and increase your value</u> – always be observant and ask questions. When someone at work is explaining how he/she performs a work task, don't "zone out"; listen carefully to what is being said, and learn how that task is done. If you do not understand something ask questions.

- ✓ <u>Do not limit what and where you learn</u> – you can learn on the job, you can learn away from work (e.g. ask a friend to show you how to use a computer program), you can learn at a community education program, you can learn at a school, you can even learn at social events. When someone in a higher position than you talks about his/her work and how he/she received a promotion, don't think of that person as boastful, or talking down to you, or self-centered (even if true); think of it as an opportunity to learn something that can increase your "employee stock price." Who cares why that person is saying what he/she is saying, just see if he/she is saying anything useful for your career.
- ✓ <u>Do not limit learning to work-related topics</u> – have you heard of the big sale that takes place on the golf course? This happens. Therefore, learn everything you can. For example, knowing current events could help you appear to be a more rounded person and that could be important if you were trying to get promoted to a job that included representing your company at social events.
- ✓ <u>Learn about yourself</u> – by looking objectively at who you are, you will be able to identify areas where you need to improve and find ways to learn to improve, so you can grow your "employee stock price."

A true story about raises

Let me share with you something that one of my new employees once said to me and how I responded.

He said, "I have been here a month and a half and I've been doing a really good job, so where is my raise?"

I responded, "You have been doing a really good job, thanks. But do you think I hired you to do a bad job? Or, maybe, that I hired you to do just an okay job? For the record, I hired you, and am paying you, to do a really good job. So since you are doing what I hired you to do, I'll let you keep your job."

I said the last sentence with a smile (positive personal signal) since at that point I was teasing him a bit. But I made my point to him, and hopefully to you. You are being paid to do a good job so do not expect extra rewards for doing what you are being paid to do. In my real life case, I then went on to explain to him the process and timetables for raises and informed him that if he kept up his performance, he could expect a nice raise at the appropriate time.

Raises

Raises usually come at specific times. Most often it is related to how long you have been working for the company. The most common timeframe is a year, hence the term "annual raise." Performance appraisals usually come before a raise. In fact, what is written on the performance appraisal often helps determine the amount of the raise. While this is the usual "rule of thumb," some companies do have different timeframes (for example: every 6 months, specific dates tied to the calendar, dates tied to personal accomplishments such as passing a test or obtaining a degree, etc.).

Raises usually have two components. The first is cost of living. This is a portion of the raise given to help offset increases in day-to-day living. This amount is often based on economic data, and not company data. The second part of the raise is performance based. This is the portion of your raise that is based on how well you are doing in your job (often as written in your performance appraisal). In some companies there are policies in place that employees with very bad performance appraisals are not even eligible for cost of living increases.

Keep in mind that some businesses, especially ones with unions, have predetermined raises. Unions often negotiate the timing and amount of raises and promotions. This is like a pass-fail evaluation rather than a test where you can get an A,B,C, etc. If you meet the job qualifications, personal qualifications, and job performance, you get a predetermined (union negotiated) pay increase. If you work for a union, find out the rules on raises and promotions so you can put yourself in a position to get raises and promotions.

Percent versus amount

Raises can be given as either dollar amounts or a percent increase over your existing pay. Dollar amount raises are straight forward, but often difficult to do because cost of living increases (to account for increases in every day life costs such as gas and food) varies by person. So if cost of living is said to have gone up by 2%, many businesses give a 2% cost of living increase as part of their employees' annual raises.

However, when employers account for cost of living and use percent raises, employees who exchange information on the amount of their raises (which you should not do because most people will lie about how much their raise was anyway), may come away confused. For example an employee with a very good performance appraisal may appear to have received a lower raise than an employee with an average performance appraisal. This is because of the cost of living factor and the nature of percents.

For example:

Alan has worked for the company for 25 years and is earning $60,000 and has an employee performance rating of fair.

Nancy has worked for the company for 3 years and is earning $40,000 and has an employee rating of excellent.

With a 3% cost of living increase and a 2% performance increase, Alan gets a 5% raise which equals $3,000.

With a 3% cost of living increase and a 4% performance increase (double the percentage Alan received), Nancy gets a 7% raise which equals $2,800.

If Alan and Nancy compared the amounts of their raises, Alan, the fair employee got $200 more than Nancy, the excellent employee.

This was only because Alan has been with the company much longer, so his salary was higher; making his lower percent raise result in more money than the higher percent raise that Nancy received.

As far as the company was concerned, Nancy received double the performance raise (4% vs. 2%) that Alan received.

So even if you compare raises and everyone is telling the truth, you have to know all factors before just looking at the dollar amount of the raise.

Promotions

Except when promotions are based on specific credentials, which is the exception not the rule, promotions can only occur when there is a job opening in the company.

A promotion occurs when an employee in a company is given a new job assignment that is considered a job function with more responsibility and a higher pay scale than that employee's current job.

If there are no open jobs at a higher level in the company than the job you are performing, there is no opportunity for a promotion for you.

In addition, many promotions are outside of your supervisor's work area. That means your supervisor can recommend you, but he/she is not the person making the decision on whether or not you get the job. It is the person you are interviewing with.

Employee stock price worksheet

List three things you can learn (or continue learning) that will help you become more valuable to your employer; hence improve your chances of increasing your pay.

1. _____

2. _____

3. _____

EXERCISE WB8

Q1. What is the difference between a raise and a promotion?

Q2. What are the reasons for raises?

Q3. What are the reasons for promotions?

Q4. What can you do to put yourself in position for a promotion?

Q5. Does getting a better raise than another worker always mean that that worker will receive more money than the other worker?

EXERCISE WB9

Q1. Using the information that follows; who would you promote to support person? Explain why you chose that person.

Let's say you are the supervisor of a work unit that has six phone representatives and one support person. The support person earns more money than the phone representatives because he/she has to know Microsoft Excel and Microsoft Access.

The support person generates management reports that you read and analyze. It is your insightful analysis that is going to help you go far and earn big bucks in the company. The "big boss" has been very impressed with your analysis of the data in the reports.

One of the reasons you are able to write insightful analyses is because your support person is a whiz at generating custom Excel and Access reports that helps organize the data that you analyze.

Then your support person leaves the company. Your supervisor says because the call volume is down, that you need to promote one of the phone representatives to the job of support person. The phone representative staff will now be down to five.

You look at your six phone representatives to determine who should get the promotion to support person (continues on next page).

- Person 1 has a performance rating of excellent, and has no computer experience.
- Person 2 has a performance rating of very good, and has no computer experience.
- Person 3 has a performance rating of good, and has some experience in Excel and Access.
- Person 4 has a performance rating of good, and has no computer experience.
- Person 5 has a performance rating of fair, and has no computer experience,
- Person 6 has a performance rating of poor, and knows Excel and Access very well.

Please note that as the supervisor, you were aware of all the facts presented here; as one of the phone representatives (worker, not a supervisor) you probably wouldn't be. Just understand that there are many factors that determine who gets promoted. While management wants to reward a deserving employee, the key is to place someone in the job that will perform it well.

WORKPLACE SKILLS

Required Workplace Skills

If someone says he or she is a singer, you expect that person to have a good voice. If someone says he or she is car mechanic you expect them to know how to change a tire and put oil in a car. If someone says he is a running back in the National Football league, you expect him to be a good athlete. I could go on and on, but I'll spare you.

Just like the examples mentioned above, if you say you are a good employee, there are certain skills that supervisors will expect you to possess. Some key ones follow.

Managing your time wisely

Self-management is the ability to understand how to best utilize your time, and the time of other people you interact with on the job, to maximize the work completed by all. Also, to do this without having your supervisor direct you every step of the way.

The areas that are under your control where you need to manage your time wisely include:

- ✓ Getting to work
- ✓ Lunch and breaks
- ✓ Completing work assignments
- ✓ Learning new work tasks
- ✓ Interactions with co-workers
- ✓ Interactions with supervisors
- ✓ Interactions with customers
- ✓ Using company phones for personal use
- ✓ Using the company's (or your personal) email
- ✓ Using the Internet
- ✓ Cell phone use

In all the areas listed, management will expect you manage your time and respect the time of others. If management has to tell you not to spend time talking on your cell phone, just having to tell you is a mark against you. You may think you get a pass because you hadn't been told yet, however, your supervisor will think that was something you should have known without having had to be told.

So do not have your cell phone constantly ringing during work, and do not spend work time making and taking personal calls. To accomplish this you may have to manage your friends and family. For example, let's say you decide to let all your calls go directly to voice mail and to listen to the messages and return any calls you need to during your scheduled break or lunch. That's an excellent personal policy. However, what if the call is for an emergency? You can instruct your family and closest friends to call you two times in a row if there is an emergency and he/she needs to talk to you immediately. Then when you get two calls in row from that family member or friend, take or return the second call immediately (or as soon as possible if you cannot get away at that exact moment). If you call back or take that call because of a real emergency, everyone should understand.

From the Workplace Basics section you know that companies are in business to make profits and the more profits a company makes, the more secure your job is, and the more money the company has available to pay for employee salaries and benefits. An efficient and productive workplace is a key for a business to be able to make profits. Therefore, you need to be a positive factor in the operation of the workplace, not someone who is the cause for work delays, wasted time, and conflict.

For example, you may be on a scheduled work break and decide to stop by and say hello to a friend who works in another area of the company. By doing so, you are preventing that person from completing his/her work. When you do this, no matter what happens, you lose in the eyes of your supervisor. Even if your friend completes all his/her work, your supervisor will believe it was despite your visit. So even if there is no negative impact on the amount of work that is produced; you will be viewed negatively because management will wonder how often you have done this before when there were work delays.

This doesn't mean if you pass a friend's desk and his/her nose isn't buried in work you can't say a quick hello and move on. However, if you want to enter into a discussion, see if you can schedule breaks or lunch together. If possible, your supervisors will comply. If it will cause work problems, your supervisors may not make a change in schedules. Just remember, your supervisors want happy, productive workers, so if it cannot be arranged it will be for a good reason. And you are not owed an explanation.

Another common area where many employees get into trouble is abusing the company's email account or the Internet. Save your personal use of the Internet for home.

Know two things. First, management may read any email in any company email account, even if the email was written to someone outside the company. And assume they will. So never write anything using your company email account that you wouldn't want management to read. That also means the company will know how often and to whom you email using the company email account. So if you make poor self-management decisions and abuse the time you spend writing non-work-related emails using your company email account, management will know it.

Second, every web site you go to on your computer at work, including personal email accounts sites, will be known by your management. Even if you delete the history and the cookies (which is often not allowed to be done by employees, or is allowed as a way to flag Internet abusers), your supervisors will know what web sites you have visited at work. So certainly, do not go to any site you would be embarrassed for your fellow co-workers and management to know you visited. Furthermore, ask what the policy is for using the Internet to go to web sites and to send personal emails when you are on a scheduled break or lunch. Then, of course, follow the company policies.

EXERCISE WS1

Which of the following items are good time management decisions, which are poor time management decisions? Write good or poor for each item below.

Q1. Stopping bye an attractive single person's desk get to know him or her every time you go to get coffee; even though you have to go out of your way to get to that person's desk.

Q2. Stopping bye an attractive single person's desk to get to know him or her every time you go to get coffee since that person's desk is right next to the coffee maker.

Q3. Going to lunch with your co-worker friends so that you can visit with them during lunch rather than visiting with them during work time.

Q4. Discussing a work-related topic with a co-worker as a line of customers backs up at your work station.

Q5. Learning new work tasks during your down time on the job.

Completing tasks accurately and efficiently

At home you may start projects and not complete them. You may have a bookcase with three legs that you started building in 2010, a masterpiece painting that you're waiting to frame, or a half-finished sweater that will no longer fit your best friend's kid anyway. And this may be just fine with you. You enjoyed the ride and the finished product was just a bonus. At work, however, this is not fine.

Completing job assignments in a timely manner is very important. If your supervisor assigns you work and you get it 95% complete, the reaction will not be, "Great job, you almost got the work done." In fact, you will get little credit, if any, for what you completed, even if you did great work.

At work, assignments are not to make you feel good, or to enjoy the ride. If the work is not completed entirely, it serves no purpose and management will look at it as wasted time.

This not only goes for regular work assignments, but for work you do above and beyond your regular assignments. Let's say you see a situation where an Excel spreadsheet will save a lot of time and be more accurate than a manual process that is currently being used on the job. It is not your regular work to create Excel spreadsheets, but you mention to your supervisor how an Excel spreadsheet will benefit the workplace. Your supervisor is thrilled, both because he/she likes the idea and because you are thinking about improvements in the workplace. So your supervisor gives you time to work on the spreadsheet. What just happened is that creating the spreadsheet has now become part of your regular work. There will be expectations that you will complete it. Some of you may be thinking, "I should not have opened my mouth." You would be wrong. Coming up with this idea is the type of workplace behavior that gets you noticed, brings you more in raises, and leads to more responsibility which can eventually lead to a promotion. However, after coming up with the idea, only volunteer, or take on the assignment if you can complete the work. If you do not complete the work, all of the good will (positive reactions) you received for the idea will turn negative. Your supervisor may feel you cannot back up what you say you can do, and may be reluctant to let you implement any more of your ideas.

So complete all work assignments, whether part of your regular work, or extra assignments. If you complete all your assignments in a timely manner, and provide quality work, you will become very valuable to your employer.

EXERCISE WS2

Your supervisor, Arnold D. Terminator, tells you that your job performance has not been up to his expectations. As a supervisor, he is known to fairly represent his name. He has terminated five employees in the last six months. Mr. Terminator informs you that he always has to check your work because you often do not complete tasks assigned to you. This is the same complaint that Mr. Terminator had with the previous five employees who were, gulp, terminated.

You look at your assigned work for the week and know you will have to complete tasks. This week you are assigned to work on and oversee the resolution to the problem dealing with the Freeze Machine, while keeping Mr. Terminator informed of the status through day-end status reports. The Freeze Machine is currently not working. When the Freeze Machine is down, production stops, and that costs the company money both in terms of paying employees who can't work because of the stoppage, and in terms of less product to sell reducing company profits. You know you can find out where in the process it breaks down, even the part of the machine that is not operating properly, and get a history of how often that machine has broken down in the past and been repaired. However, you do not repair machines, and do not have the authority to replace machines.

Q1. What is the specific task that needs to be completed?
Q2. Why is this task needed to be completed?
Q3. Assuming replacing or repairing the Freeze Machine can't happen until tomorrow, what is your last step to take today in your task? Please provide details for that task.
Q4. Since you do not repair machines, and do not have the authority to replace machines, is your task complete after performing the step you wrote in Q3? Explain your answer.

Since completing work assignments is not enough (the assignments must be completed correctly and the work product must be of high quality), companies often employ quality assurance practices in the workplace.

Therefore, expect your work to be reviewed, either in full, or in part; either all the time, or at random intervals. The main purpose for quality assurance is to verify that the work product is correct and of high quality. A side benefit of the process is that a supervisor can see where additional training is needed for specific employees. It also helps identify the good, the bad and the average, which is used for performance appraisals and determining merit raises.

So quality assurance functions and audits are a normal part of a workplace. They are not the product of an over-controlling boss and management not trusting its employees, or trying to make its employees' lives difficult.

Quality assurance worksheet

1. You work for a manufacturing company that makes car seats for infants. The company has an employee who checks some of your work. List some of the benefits to the company, the company's customers and to you of having this quality assurance person check some of your work.

A . _____
B . _____
C . _____
D . _____
E . _____

2. You are a teller for a bank. The company hires mystery shoppers to act as customers. They come into the bank and transact business with a teller and look around the bank. List some of the benefits to the bank, the bank's customers and to you of having this quality assurance person check some of your work.

A . _____
B . _____
C . _____
D . _____
E . _____

Following instructions and /directions

Instructions are steps you have to follow to complete something properly (such as the instructions for putting together a computer desk). Directions are the proper steps to follow to do something the desired way (such as evacuation procedures in case of an emergency to ensure everyone gets out of the building safely).

Most of us recognize the need to follow instructions. After all we bought the computer desk because we liked it, so we know we have to follow the instructions to ensure it is put together correctly.

On the other hand, many of us balk at following directions. We want to know why. After all there are other ways that the task at hand can be accomplished. Why do I have to go down the hall to the right and all the way across the building to exit during an evacuation when if I made a left there is an exit door right there? Hey, in an emergency I want to get out as fast as I can.

At work you have to think like you are in the army and follow all instructions and all directions exactly. If you believe you have a better way to build the computer desk (better instructions) or a better way to exit the building in an emergency (better directions), then inform your supervisor of your ideas and live by the decision of management.

In all cases, at the time when you are required to follow the instructions or directions, follow them exactly. The time to discuss your ideas for improvement is not at the time the instructions or directions are being followed, it is after the fact to suggest improvements.

Another good idea is to read all instructions in full before starting to follow them. Writing instructions is a skill and not all instructions are written by individuals with expertise in that skill. Most of us have been exposed to the exercise where we have to follow a set of 25 instructions and step #25 says ignore steps 2 thru 24, only do step #1. It is an annoying exercise but it makes it point. If you read the instructions in full you may find that in certain circumstances not all steps need to be followed. For example if you bought the computer desk, a step in middle might say if you didn't purchase the optional light you do not have to punch out the hole on the top shelf. Punching the hole out may have been step two or three and since you do not have the light you may have preferred it without the hole punched out. However, because you did not read all the instructions first you may have punched the hole out before seeing that it wasn't necessary in your case. Also, you may find something confusing at first because you cannot picture it in your head. However, after reading through the entire instructions it becomes clear and you avoid making errors. Finally, by reading through the entire instructions at work, you can jot down your questions and go to your supervisor one time for an explanation/clarification instead of having to keep running back and forth to ask questions which makes you look inefficient (because you were) and a drain on your supervisor's productivity because of the constant stop and starts (all in all, poor time management). In this case many workers see the negative personal signals coming from their supervisors and stop interrupting them. Instead they start guessing at what needs to be done. This can lead to errors in their work, which is an even worse offense than the constant interruption.

So read the instructions in full before starting, jot down all your questions, interrupt your supervisor once to get your questions answered, and get the work completed correctly. The employee who follows these directions (process) for following instructions will be highly-valued by his/her supervisor.

Using Procedure Manuals

Procedure manuals are books written to help employees perform tasks required of them in their jobs. Not all companies have manuals, and those that do may not have them for every job function.

If there is a procedure manual for your job function, it is a very helpful tool to use to ensure that you are doing your job correctly. However, your goal is to become familiar with the procedure manual as quickly as possible so that it becomes a tool to use to complete tasks that are not everyday tasks and not a book to use all the time. Relying too much on a procedure manual can slow you down. So employers expect new employees to rely on procedure manuals more than experienced employees.

When you are presented with a procedure manual read it completely to get an idea of what will be expected of you on the job and to understand how the procedure manual is laid out so you can easily find specific information in the manual. After you have worked on the task for a few days and are starting to get a good feel for how it is done, reread the procedure manual to start absorbing the job functions in full. By rereading the manual after performing the job function live, you may find that the procedures make more sense to you.

Ethics

In Stephen King's epic tale of good versus evil, *The Stand*, all of the survivors of a biological catastrophe are driven to split up into two camps; the good camp (Mother Abigail), and the evil camp (Randall Flagg). There was no middle ground.

It is the same with ethics. A behavior is either ethical (right) or unethical (wrong). There is absolutely no gray area. Being ethical means doing the right thing. What determines whether something is ethical or unethical is the behavior itself, not the circumstances surrounding the action taken, not the relationship between the people involved, not an individual's culture, not a person's value system, not life's experiences, etc., etc., etc.

If you were robbed by someone who needed the money to feed his/her kids, the act of robbery makes this an unethical behavior. In this case, surrounding circumstances such as that the robbery was out of desperation for the robber who needed to have money to feed his/her children is irrelevant when determining whether or not the act was ethical. Stealing is wrong, hence it is unethical. Besides, who's to say that the money he/she stole from you wasn't going to make it difficult for you to feed *your* kids?

That said, people are unethical all the time and being unethical does not make someone a bad person. For example, breaking the law is wrong, hence unethical. How many of you have driven a little over the speed limit? Well, that is against the law, making it an unethical act, but it does not make you a bad person.

The key to understanding ethics is to be able to define whether an act is ethical or unethical. Once you have identified the ethical behavior, then you decide what to do. In other words, to either do the ethical behavior or do the unethical behavior. This is where circumstances, relationships, culture, values, life's experiences, etc., etc., etc. come into play. You decide in each situation if you are going to act ethically or unethically.

There will be times in life that you feel strongly that choosing the unethical behavior is the right choice for you. However, you must be aware that if you choose to do the unethical behavior there can be **severe consequences**. Therefore, if you choose to act unethically, know what those consequences can be, and be prepared to accept those consequences for making the decision to act unethically. In the case of the person who committed the robbery above, let's say that the individual came in, explained his/her situation and you gave them $100 for food out of the store's cash register. You may feel strongly that helping that person's family was the right thing to do. However, you just stole money from your place of employment. A consequence of your action could be that you get fired when the amount in the register doesn't box to the day's activity.

More realistically, let's say that as soon as your boss comes back you tell him/her what you did and that you want him/her to take the $100 out of your next pay check. Now instead of stealing, you forced your employer to loan you $100. That is also wrong, hence unethical. You cannot force someone to loan you money. You could still get fired and be charged with stealing. Your boss could also say okay and take the money out of your next check. In either case what you did was unethical, only in one case there was a consequence (being fired) and in another there were no consequences. The key, however, is that you thought it through, knew the potential consequences, and decided that performing the unethical act was worth the risk to you. In this case it was an unethical act you thought was the right thing to do.

As a side note, this is a case where you acted unethically because of your value system. It's possible; however, that your boss' value system was different. He/she may have called someone they knew who worked for the local Workforce Development Board to arrange a meeting between that person and a Job Counselor to help that person get a job. That would have been teaching that person to fish (long term solution) rather than giving him/her money to buy fish (short term solution). This is a good example why the ethics of a situation comes down to the underlying behavior and ignores items such as personal values.

Next, let's look at the possible consequences for the unethical act of robbery from the parent's (robber's) point of view. The parent who stole from you may have felt he/she had no choice because he/she had to feed his/her kids. When making that choice, he/she should have been prepared for a possible arrest for committing the unethical, illegal act of robbery, and worse, for potentially losing his/her children if Social Services now deemed him/her an unfit parent. In the driving scenario, if you choose to drive over the speed limit, you have to be prepared to pay a speeding ticket, see your insurance rates increase, and know that you may have given the police officer cause to search your vehicle.

The case of Don Imus

Imus was the morning Dee Jay on "W*O*L*D", I mean WFAN (sorry, I just like that old Harry Chapin song). His show was simulcast on MSNBC. As a shock jock, saying outrageous things was part of his job. One morning on his show, during an impromptu comedy routine, Imus used derogatory terms (not serious, in jest) in his public forum to describe members of the predominately African-American women's basketball team at Rutgers University. In his professional life, Imus is very charitable, allowing his national radio show to be used for fund raising by charities for causes such as SIDS (Sudden Infant Death Syndrome). In his personal life, he is even more charitable having established the Imus Ranch for kids with cancer, a working cattle ranch surrounded by an old western town. Children with cancer come to the ranch and work the ranch alongside of Imus and his family. Therefore, not only does Imus spend money on kids with cancer, but he spends time with them as an active participant interacting during their visits. Children of all races and creeds attend his ranch.

Was Imus' remark ethical or unethical? When determining the ethics, first eliminate the surrounding circumstances. That means the fact that he is a shock jock and therefore expected to say some outrageous things, is irrelevant when determining the ethics. Don't agree? Well, is it okay for a hitman to kill someone because it's his/her job? Also, the fact that he is very charitable, and that he helps people of all races and creeds are also irrelevant. Using a public forum to denigrate (even in jest) college kids is wrong. Therefore, it is unethical. Does this make Imus a bad person? No, he does a lot of good in his life. It's possible the fact that he was doing his job and that he has a solid record of doing good made him feel that he could say what he did and it would be understood that he meant no harm. Irrelevant! Surely his loyal listeners would know that he said it in jest and he meant no harm. Irrelevant! The reality of the situation is that being on the public airways meant that people who were not his listeners would hear about it and react to it. Even that is irrelevant! It is the underlying behavior (using public airways to denigrate college kids) that determined his action to be unethical. And remember, doing something unethical means that there could be consequences. Were there consequences for Don Imus? Yes, he and his staff were fired, and his reputation took a hit from people who primarily knew of Imus through this event. While Imus made it back on the air on a different radio station, and is simulcast on a television station that does not currently go into as many homes as MSNBC, he still paid a price for his unethical act. It just wasn't a life sentence.

Let's say that there were no consequences to Don Imus; that the comment went through with no reaction. Would that have changed the ethics of the situation? Of course it would not have. The behavior is the same regardless of the consequences paid for the unethical act. Certainly the person who gets away with murder is not ethical, while the person who gets caught for committing murder is unethical. All unethical acts bring the possibility of consequences. Not all unethical acts have consequences attached to them. If you drove ten miles over the speed limit and there were no radar traps, cameras, or police officers around, you won't get a ticket. However, you still performed an illegal, hence an unethical act. By driving ten miles an hour over the speed limit, you were willing to risk getting a ticket and were prepared to pay a fine if you were caught. After all, if you weren't prepared for the possible consequences, you shouldn't have been speeding.

Music downloads

The Internet is amazing technology. It allows people all over the world to access other peoples' computers. That includes the ability to copy files from one computer to another computer. That is called downloading.

So networks were created for individuals to share music files. Someone would buy a music CD, copy the songs on the CD to their computer's hard drive, and allow other people to access their computer and download the songs. That one CD could now be owned by hundreds, if not thousands of people. How nice. How giving. How unethical.

The artists who wrote the songs and recorded the album certainly were not expecting to share the royalties (profits) of one CD amongst thousands of customers. Downloading music for free is directly stealing money from the record company and the band that recorded the

CD. Not to mention retailers who would have generated sales to some of the people who would have bought the CD if they could not get it for free and the workers who lost their jobs because the retailers were not making as much money. In addition, music is copyrighted material so downloading it for free is against the law which is another fact in making it unethical. Of course, the ethical way to download music is to pay for the songs you download at websites like iTunes, which is legal and results in royalties for the artists.

Since downloading music without paying is unethical, that means that there are potential consequences for downloading music for free. What are those potential consequences? The obvious is that if caught, you could pay significant fines. Don't believe me? The RIAA (Record Industry Association of America) website posted a write-up on December 6, 2007 indicating that 396 pre-litigation letters (sent out to settle before pursuing a lawsuit) have been sent to individuals (primarily students) at 22 universities.

The settlement figure is thought to be around $750 per song; so illegally downloading only 5 songs would cost someone $3,750 to settle. If these college kids do not settle and go to court, they are risking a lot more in money damages. Jamie Thomas, a single mother of two, was ordered to pay the RIAA (representing the record labels) $222,000 worth of damages for 24 pirated songs. Remember, only the behavior determines the ethics, the fact that Jamie Thomas is a single mother of two is irrelevant when determining the ethics in this situation.

Think the punishment doesn't fit the crime? **First**, when you act unethically it is not you who decides what the consequences will be for that unethical act. It is the damaged party or the court system. **Second**, "according to non-profit research group Institute for Policy Innovation, global theft of sound recordings cost the U.S. economy $12.5 billion in lost revenue and more than 71,000 jobs and $2 billion in wages to U.S. workers per year." This quote is from the RIAA website in a write-up *RIAA Pre- Lawsuit Letters Go To 22 Campuses In New Wave Of Deterrence Program* posted on December 6, 2007.

It seems to me that illegally downloading music is kind of like playing the lottery in reverse. With the lottery you pay $1 to buy a ticket to try to win a lot of money. And only a few random people win. With the illegal downloading of music, instead of paying $1 to buy a song, you download it for free and try to avoid paying a lot of money (if caught). And only a few random people lose.

Let's also look at this issue from the band's perspective. If a band puts out new albums on CDs and does not generate sufficient income from those albums, the band could break up and stop making new music. After all, they need to eat. Some bands are better studio bands than live bands and some musicians like making music but do not like to tour. These bands would quickly disappear if the band could not earn money from the sale of its albums.

On the same front: if you are using portions of this book from photocopies; that may also be a copyright infringement, making it illegal, and unethical. Writing this book is something I have done to not only help the readers, but to put food on my table.

Let's say you work for a bank as a teller. Stated in the qualifications for the job is that you must have a high school diploma or GED. One day a co-worker mentions to you that he/she is really excited because next month he/she is finally getting his/her GED. Your co-worker is a great worker, in fact last month he/she won employee of the month for the third month in a row. What are the ethics in this situation for both your co-worker and yourself?

_____
_____
_____
_____
_____
_____
_____
_____
_____
_____
_____
_____
_____
_____
_____

My take on ethics scenario #1

For your co-worker the ethics are straight forward. The fact that he/she was untruthful on the job application is in violation of company rules and, therefore, an unethical act. What are the consequences? If found out, that employee could (and most likely would) be fired even though he/she was a top employee.

What about the situation you are in? The ethical behavior would be to inform your supervisor. I know, I know, many of you are thinking that is not what you would do. I'm sure some of you feel that telling your supervisor is snitching and you are no snitch. Others of you feel that it is not your job; that is/was either the Human Resources Department job or your supervisor's job to find this out. So many of you would not inform your supervisor, you would just let the comment go.

What you are doing is applying your own set of values to the situation and deciding that acting unethically is the correct action to take. I am not going to preach about what you should do. Just remember that acting unethically (which does not make you a bad person) comes with potential consequences. Don't think there is any possibility of consequences here? Think again my friend.

Let's say that your supervisor finds out that your co-worker did not have his/her high school diploma or GED when he/she was hired. Maybe your co-worker celebrates when he/she finally gets the GED, or someone sends that person flowers as congratulations. When your co-worker is called onto the carpet by his/her supervisor, your co-worker comments that he/she didn't think it was a big deal and that he/she mentioned it to you and you did not think it was a big deal either. That statement by your co-worker just brought you into this mess.

As a result of the lie on the application your co-worker gets fired (this is usually a policy; companies cannot start looking into the degree of each lie on a job application). Nothing happens to you. You keep your job and, in fact, have no idea that your name was brought up in the meeting between your now fired ex-co-worker and your supervisor. However, your supervisor now feels that your priorities are wrong. You do not have the best interests of the company in mind. If you thought you would be admired for not "tattling" on a co-worker who was untruthful on his/her job application, you may be by some misguided co-workers, but you won't be by people of influence in the company.

A year later there is a promotion opportunity in the company. You believe you are perfect for the job. You don't get it. The same thing happens nine months later, then fifteen months after that. Unfair (you think)! However, it all goes back to your having deciding to act unethically. It is the fact that management in the company does not believe they can count on you to do the right thing for the company that is preventing you from advancing in the company. And you have totally forgotten that event, and never got a chance to explain your side of things, although I doubt that that would have made a difference anyway.

This happens all the time. Everyone is held accountable for how they act in the workplace. And more often than not, workers are unaware of how much management knows about what is going on. You are judged more by your supervisor's observations on what is going on and comments by third parties than you would believe.

Therefore, often consequences for choosing to do an unethical act are hidden consequences. Sometimes you hear people saying," I have had a run of bad luck." Perhaps that bad luck is really just hidden consequences from unethical behaviors (not karma, but direct results like not getting the promotion in this example). Or, maybe it is just bad luck.

Now here's the million (or at least thousand) dollar question. What would your author, Jay Goldberg do in this situation?

First, I would immediately recognize that my co-worker put me in an uncomfortable situation. This is a situation I did not ask to be in, and would not have volunteered to be in. Second, I would understand that people usually act for a reason. What my co-worker was doing was bringing in another person (me) to their situation. He/she may never have to use the "Jay Goldberg card" (e.g. telling the boss Jay knew and didn't think it was a big deal); but it was there if needed. Third, I would know that what my co-worker did was wrong and, therefore, unethical. Fourth, I would understand that my co-worker placed me in a position where I would have to act ethically or unethically. What I would not do, is ignore the situation like it never happened. I would make a decision based on full knowledge of what could happen if I were to choose to say nothing.

Okay, okay, I'll give you my decision based on the ethics and my personal set of values. I would approach my co-worker and tell him/her that he/she placed me in an uncomfortable situation. That he/she knows full well that you have to have your high school diploma or GED to be a bank teller. I would then tell him/her that he/she needs to speak to our supervisor and inform our supervisor of the situation. Furthermore, I would tell my co-worker that if he/she did not do this, that I would have no choice but to tell our supervisor myself. I would finish up by telling my co-worker that I am extremely angry with him/her for having put me in this position.

That is how I would handle the situation. Some of you will not agree with how I handled this. That's okay. I wouldn't risk my career because a co-worker was untruthful on a job application and decided to make me part of the lie.

Now, what if unbeknownst to my co-worker and myself was that the bank policy for mandatory high school diplomas or GEDs for all tellers came about when a major client of this fictional bank had numerous severe errors when conducting business with the bank's tellers seven years ago. The errors were all done by under-qualified tellers. To keep that client, the bank started a policy that all tellers would have at least a high school diploma or GED and promised that major client it would comply with that requirement 100%. Based on that promise the client stayed with the bank and became the #1 account for the bank in terms of profitability. Every year, the client reminds senior bank management of the bank's promise to only hire tellers with high school diplomas or GEDs.

Would this change your thinking, or at least provide you with a better understanding of why you would have shot yourself in the foot if you had acted unethically in this situation?

As an aside, "I'm not a tattler" is a playground stance, not a recognized position in the law. Ever hear of aiding and abetting? Or obstruction of justice? Or perjury? I don't think law officials or judges will say, "That's okay, you knew of a crime, or you know who committed a crime, but I respect you; you're no tattle tail." Consider the Personnel Department the law official and Management the judge for the workplace.

Worksheet: ethics work scenario #2

What if your supervisor asks you to do something that is illegal? For example, your supervisor asks you to not ring up a sale to avoid reporting the sale for sales tax purposes. What are your thoughts regarding this situation?

_____

_____

_____

_____

_____

_____

_____

_____

_____

_____

_____

_____

_____

_____

My take on ethics scenario #2

Obviously, not reporting all sales to stiff the government of the proper sales tax is illegal, and therefore, unethical, so you should not agree to do this. Even if you agree that taxes are too high (who doesn't); if sales taxes are underreported, the government will just find its money elsewhere. Maybe your real estate taxes will increase because your supervisor (and others like him/her) is not paying what is properly owed.

But your supervisor told you to do it.

What your supervisor tells you does not supersede the law. It is not an excuse to the court that you were only doing what your boss told you to do. Besides, if caught and faced with fines, want to bet how stand up your supervisor would be. I would bet your supervisor would know nothing about you not ringing up the sales, especially if he/she was not ringing up sales to avoid paying sales tax; but to steal money from the company. How quickly do you think it would take for your supervisor to blame you for the thefts? You'd be fired on the spot. And then, what if the owners decided to make you an example of you for his/her other employees, and had you prosecuted.

Even if the truth came out in court, your supervisor was arrested, and you were cleared of any wrongdoing; you would still have legal fees, lots of stress, and be out of a job. Telling the owner that you knew your supervisor was not ringing up all sales, but thought it was for cheating the government out of sales tax and not that he/she was stealing money from the company, would not result in you saving your job.

Unethical behaviors can have serious consequences. Do not act unethically just because your supervisor told you it is "okay" or even "expected." Remember, your personal values, etc. are not part of determining the ethics of any situation. So if you agree with your supervisor's position and perform the unethical act, just know you may have to pay the consequences for that unethical act alongside your supervisor. If you constantly are put in these kind of difficult situations, transfer to another department, talk to Human Resources, or find another employer.

Worksheet: ethics work scenario #3

You work in a donut shop. "Mmm, donuts!" Every morning on their way to work your buddies stop there to say hi and eat. Most days you are there with your supervisor. On rare occasions when your supervisor is not there with you, you give your friends free coffee. You know that this game of your friends guessing when they will get free coffee is the only reason that they come every day. It's the fun, not the money. If you stopped doing this your friends might drop by once a month instead of five times a week. Even when they get the free coffee, they spend a lot of money on breakfast sandwiches, donuts and more. What are your thoughts regarding this situation?

_____

_____

_____

_____

_____

_____

_____

_____

_____

_____

_____

_____

_____

_____

_____

_____

My take on ethics scenario #3

First, let's look at the ethics. Giving customers, even friends and relatives, free merchandise (food in this case) is stealing. What if you worked in a music store instead and you were giving away free CDs, not free coffee. Or if you worked in an electronics store and the merchandise you were giving away were free flat screen, high definition, televisions. The underlying behavior is the same in all of these cases. What the actual product being given away for free is does not matter. That is irrelevant.

In this situation you might know that if you were not giving the occasional free coffee away that it would cost the business money in the long run because your friends would stop coming every day. Furthermore, you might have worked previously for a restaurant that would occasionally buy their loyal repeat customers a drink because it was good for business. And in your observation it was not just good for business, but great for business. In fact, your past experience is the reason you decided to give the free coffee on occasion to your buddies. And it worked out great for the Donut Shop. They now come in every day.

All of that is irrelevant when deciding the ethics of the situation. If the business you work for has a different view about a policy that worked well in your prior business, it is not your place to independently implement your own rules, even if you truly believe it would be for the good of your employer.

Now, you may ask, "so Jay you told me that the profitability of my employer is very important to me, and now you tell me I should *not* do something that is bringing in more profits to the business?" Huh?

In this scenario what I would do is have a talk with my supervisor and explain the old policy at the restaurant where I used to work. I would then inform him/her what I would like to do for my friends because I believed it would result in them coming to the Donut Shop more often and, in the long run, be a more profitable situation for the business.

Then I would be prepared to follow whatever the supervisor stated was the policy of the Donut Shop.

Remember, you do not know the whole story. It's possible that this was tried before and got out of hand with employees giving away too much free stuff. It is also possible that the Donut Shop had complaints in the past from customers because they saw/heard that some other customers got free coffee while they never did. Maybe, when customers stop coming as often and do not get free coffee, they get angry and never come again. It could also be that you were giving away the product (coffee) that has the largest profit margin, and that the profits from the other food are minimal. In that case, maybe your supervisor tells you not to give free coffee, but is okay to give a free donut. What worked for one business may have been tried and did not work for another business. Also, you are not privy to the profit model for the company that has employed you.

Stealing from an employer is not only stealing money

While the scenario above is an obvious case of stealing a product from an employer, another less obvious theft is stealing your wages.

If you show up late, extend breaks and lunches, leave early, do personal business on your employer's time, etc., you are being paid by your employer for time that you are not working for your employer. Stealing time, therefore, is stealing money, which is unethical and comes with potential consequences.

Likewise, if you show up to work drunk, high, or hung over, you have put yourself in a position to be less productive on the job, which again is stealing money since you are being paid to be at your best. This is also unethical and, if caught, can come with severe consequences.

The Employee Handbook

Ethics in the workplace has an additional item that employees must pay attention to; the Employee Handbook. This can be a formal document, informal memos, or even word of mouth.

As long as the rules of this employer do not violate ethics (underlying behaviors, not your values), then if you do not follow the rules, your behavior is unethical. That means consequences could follow. You could be fired from your job.

So, know the rules of your workplace, and follow them.

EXERCISE WS5

During this work readiness and customer service training program you develop a quick friendship with someone who will be in the program with you. In fact, you make plans with that person to get together over the weekend. That person tells you that he/she has serious financial problems at home. During the first day of this program you learn that there are businesses that will hire graduates right away at a good wage to work part time if they pass all assessments and competencies. Your initial thought is that this is an excellent opportunity for your new friend.

When you get together over the weekend with your new friend he/she tells you that you wouldn't believe the great luck he/she had. When leaving the building he/she saw a Teacher Guide on a desk in an unattended room. He/she then goes on to say that the guide has all then answers to the exercises and quizzes, even some lame exercise about business ethics. He/she further states that since you two are friends, you are the only person with whom he/she will share the answers. He/she also states that this is a great opportunity for him/her to complete the program, and get a job that is critical to his/her family's eating well.

Q1.   Did the person who took the Teacher Guide do an ethical or unethical act?

Q2.   Explain your answer.

Q3.   What is the ethical thing for you to do?

Q4.   If you decided to say nothing, but did not use the answers, what would happen if your friend was caught and said, "It's no big deal. Even <you> knew about it and didn't think it was a big deal", and you were doing very well in the program?

Q5.   If your friend was not caught, what negative consequences could happen because of his/her cheating?

Reading in the Workplace

The goal of education is to teach knowledge and skills, not to get students "ready for work." Toward that end, when teaching reading, the education system unintentionally provides some information that goes against how that skill is best applied in the workplace. Reading in the workplace is different than reading outside the workplace. Reading a novel is different than reading a memo at work.

When you were taught reading in school you were encouraged to "read between the lines." It is not just what is written, but what the author's real meaning is behind the actual words on the page. Debates are held in classrooms all across America about the "real meaning" behind a cleverly written passage in a book. When reading a mystery novel, readers are encouraged to look for clues to help solve the mystery before it's revealed by the author. At times a book is vague because the author wants you to fill in the blanks yourself so you will be surprised when you read what actually happens (or feel good when you guessed the correct outcome).

This is not true when reading memos at work. There is no reading between the lines, there is no "solving mysteries" and if something is vague, you do not fill in the blanks yourself.

A work document is straightforward. It says what it means and there are no hidden meanings. If you are reading something into a document that is not stated directly, then your thinking is probably wrong. If you believe a work document is hinting at something that is not directly stated, ask your supervisor for clarification. Do not assume. This is also how workplace rumors start. Someone "reads between the lines" of a business memo; mentions his/her thoughts to a co-worker, and a rumor starts spreading. Eventually the starting place of the rumor is forgotten, and the topic of the rumor is thought to be have been said directly by someone in the company. So don't read between the lines, take workplace memos at face value, and ask questions for clarification if you are unsure of anything.

Another way that leisure reading and workplace reading differs is that when reading a novel, the author expects readers to bring preconceptions with them. That is not the case when reading memos at work. If I told you that Pat was a gold digger and then asked you to describe Pat, your first thought might be that Pat is someone who is looking to marry for money. However, what if in reality Pat works in a mine, digging for gold.

Again, your preconceptions can nudge you into reading more into a business memo than what is there. For example a memo may contain the following:

"We have become aware that not everyone is wearing a safety helmet when using machine ABC. It is a serious offense not to wear a safety helmet. If we catch anyone in the future without his or her helmet on, we will be forced to let them go."

Now from the Workplace Basics section, you know that this is written from two points of view: management's concern for its employees, and management's concern for violating OSHA rules and regulations.

However, if a co-worker reads this memo and brings to the table the preconceptions that management is snooping on its employees, or that management is too controlling; he/she might interpret the memo in a negative way. That co-worker may tell you:

"Did you read that memo; management is treating us like kids. If I want to risk not wearing a safety helmet who are they to tell me what to do. I bet they are looking for reasons to fire us."

This statement can start rumors. When spread throughout the company, it could end up being shortened to, "Management is looking to fire people." The original source, a misguided employee brining his/her preconceptions to a business memo and "reading between the lines", gets lost in translation.

Reading perceptions group discussion worksheet (write the answers on a board for all three, then go to page 90 to continue the discussion)

In the next story Jack is a professional basketball player. Without reading the story, what do you know about Jack?

_____

_____

_____

_____

In the next story Robin is a cheerleader. Without reading the story, what do you know about Robin?

_____

_____

_____

_____

3. On his first day on the job, Stu was nervous and shook hands with his boss using his left hand. Did Stu do anything wrong?

_____

_____

_____

_____

In all of these examples you will have an image of the person and situation just based on the brief description supplied to you. In fictional writing, the author often counts on that to help cement the character in your mind, or to make the character appear more real to you because you compare that character to someone you know.

That is not the case at work; do not bring preconceptions to business memos. Ask questions, do not assume.

Speed reading

A slow reader will read every word in a sentence, one at a time. If this describes the way that you read, notice how many times your eyes move as you proceed across a line of text. Reading every word and "fixing" your eyes on each word requires a considerable amount of time. Before you get to the end of a long sentence, chances are you have forgotten the beginning of that sentence, so you look back at the beginning - just to make sure that you got all of the information. The same process occurs with paragraphs, or with whole essays or textbook chapters.

If you train yourself to read quickly, rather than slowly, you will notice that several changes will occur in the way that you absorb and remember information from your reading.

- ✓ You will move your eyes fewer times, so you get through a reading passage more quickly.
- ✓ Since you get through a reading passage more quickly, you will be more likely to remember what you have read without having to look back to the beginning of a long sentence. This ability to remember more happens when you begin to process ideas, rather than single words.
- ✓ You will finish reading assignments more quickly and remember what you have read more accurately.

Reading for main topic

The main idea is, most often, stated in a topic sentence of a paragraph. In effective business documents, the topic sentence is usually the first sentence in the paragraph, but it may be the last sentence or any other sentence. The remaining sentences in the paragraph add supporting details to explain or tell more about the main idea. More than one paragraph may give supporting details about one main idea. In the paragraph that follows, the first sentence is the topic sentence. It states the main idea of the paragraph. The other sentences add information to explain the main idea.

> Every good music collection needs albums by Al Stewart. Most know Al Stewart from two songs, "Year of the Cat" and "Time Passages." However, he has many other excellent songs, and all of his albums are high quality from first song to last song. In addition, Al Stewart is unique in that he writes rock (or folk rock) songs about events in history. In fact one of his albums, *Between the Wars*, has songs that chronicle events from 1918 to 1939.

The main topic here is "Every good music collection needs albums by Al Stewart."

Reading for details

There are two ways to read for details. The first is when you are reading to absorb all the information contained in the piece you are reading. The second is when you are trying to find the answer to a specific question.

Reading for details: absorbing all information

When reading to absorb all information, you need to read the entire document, understand the main topic(s) and focus on the key characteristics for the topic(s). At work, this information will be vital to your job, so you need to take notes to help you remember the key points that you read. Taking notes also allows you to quickly review key points so that you do not have to go back to the original document and find that information again.

Your notes should be in the form of:

Topic   Specific item 1
                             Specific item 2
                             Specific item 3

Using the Al Stewart piece, the notes, containing the details of the write-up would be:

Best known songs   "Year of the Cat"
                             "Time Passages"

Album characteristics   Good songs throughout
                             Songs and entire albums about events in history

After taking notes, you should read and review your notes from time to time to help you remember what you read. Also remember that it has been proven that reading quickly helps with long term memory more than reading slowly.

Additional note taking methods

In addition to writing down notes you can use a yellow highlighter to highlight key points (assuming you own the source material). If you do not own the material make a work copy for yourself (if feasible) and use a highlighter on your work copy. If you do not want to mark up your original copy, use yellow stick'em notes and write the key points on those and stick them to the appropriate page.

When reading to find specific information, you do not need to read the full text. You can skim to find the specific information you require (do not read every word; look for a key word or words; can use finger to help guide you while skimming).

EXERCISE WS6

Skim the flash fiction story below to determine **the name of the famous educated rapper**. Please skim the story, do not read it. The purpose is the find the answer to the question as quickly as you can. If you want to read it in full after the exercise, I will be honored. I wrote this piece for a flash fiction contest at Associated Content. For the contest I had to write a flash fiction piece starting with the line, "He had not been expecting a letter." Associated Content has been absorbed by Yahoo.

You only have three minutes to complete this exercise. Wait until the instructor says start.

****

Life's Little Annoyances

He had not been expecting a letter. Especially since letters had gone the way of high-def televisions, digital cameras and video cell phones; so last century.

After giving the postmaster private a hundred dollar bill, and getting a dirty look for such a small tip; the man looked at the letter. For a long moment he stood there just staring at the darn thing until he remembered that he was actually going to have to read it himself. He thanked the Alien Who Is Our God that he took the reading elective in college.

The letter was dirty, crumpled and looked very old. In fact the letter was very old. There was an expiration date in red in the upper right corner. That date couldn't be true thought the man, the date was in the 1990's.

Confused and a little scared, the man's mind went racing. His first thought was that the letter was from the "Time of Viruses", one of the most evil periods in history. Would he get a virus if he opened the letter? He remembered the scary stories of his childhood where viruses arose seemingly from nowhere to wipe out memory. But those stories couldn't be true; they were just made up tales. Weren't they?

His next thought was, "if this is from the 1990's, it may be a collectable." Then he remembered that even if it was a collectible it was missing the highly valuable shrink wrap that all written materials came in back then, so it probably wouldn't be worth much anyway.

After much thought and procrastination, the man decided to throw caution to the windmill and open the letter. So he took the letter and placed it in his non-biological de-sheller. After thirty minutes the letter appeared on the product tray.

Looking over the letter the man concluded that it was from the famous educated rapper, Ed. MC Mahon, known for his hardcore rap about how not knowing about your credit is whack and knowing your credit score is wicked; and his heezy, fogelberg, spoken-word rap about the power of gold being able to be turned into cash.

He then wondered why this educated rapper would write him a letter asking him to buy magazines; and why Mahon felt that the chance to win $10,000,000; a relatively small sum, would incent him to do so.

So the man dictated a letter to his ambulatory she-bot computer. The letter simply said, "No thank you." It took him an hour to word it just right.

Using one of the stamps that came with the letter, the man used his Peabody and Sherman Way Back Machine to send the letter to Mahon.

Unfortunately for the man the letter was delivered to the wrong address, where the wrongful recipient wrote, "Return to sender" and placed it back in the mail.

The next day the man, who had not been expecting a letter, received the letter again. Commanding his ambulatory she-bot computer to shake its fist, the man said, "Darn you MC Mahon, you're a crafty son of a photon torpedo; I guess I'll just have to buy some of your magazines or I'll risk getting the Bill Murray disease and be turned into a ground hog."

****

> **EXERCISE WS7**
>
> Read the business memo that follows and then answer the questions in the next exercise box.

****

Memo To: All Staff

From: Randall F. Crowl, President

RE: Recent Problems in our Customer Service Dept

Date: November 15, 2012

===

As you are all aware, we have been getting a lot of complaints from our customers regarding our telephone service. To determine if these complaints were the exception or the rule, we sent out surveys to all customers that used our Phone Center in the last three months. The response from our customers was overwhelming. Our response rate from the surveys was 35%, well above industry averages of 20%.

While our response rate for the surveys was good, the results showed that we need a lot of improvement in how our Phone Center performs its customer service functions. The survey results clearly showed that the complaints we were getting from our customers were the rule, not the exception.

Some of the more alarming complaints from our customers were:

- Our phone representatives are sometimes rude to our customers.

- Our phone representatives often lack the knowledge to solve our customers' problems.

- Our customers often wait a long time before their calls are answered or get busy signals.

- When our customers do get through to a phone representative, they are often placed on hold for long intervals.

This is unacceptable! We are implementing a comprehensive plan to correct our poor service. However, to make the plan work we will need the commitment and understanding of our entire staff, especially our phone representatives.

The company will make a significant capital investment in both equipment and staff to correct the problems. But we will also expect more from our phone representatives.

To correct our capacity problem (long wait times before calls are answered and customers getting busy signals) we are purchasing a new phone system that will allow us to have more phone lines. We also plan to hire 10 additional phone representatives. We are making this investment to help both our customers and to ease the work burden on our staff. However, we are also asking for a commitment from our phone representatives. We are implementing a strict policy for time logged into our new phone system. Tardiness will no longer be accepted. If you are supposed to be at your work station and logged into the phone system at 8:00 AM, you must be there at precisely 8:00 AM. 8:01 AM or 8:02 AM will not do!

In addition, we will track every phone representative's talk time. Your goal should be an average talk time of two minutes. Remember, if you spend ten minutes with a customer you are giving that customer great service, but if three other customers have to wait ten minutes before they speak to a phone representative because of that call, we are providing poor service to those three customers. Great service for one and poor service for three is unacceptable. Therefore, manage your talk time.

To correct the other issues that are directly related to the performance of our phone representatives, we plan to implement a comprehensive training program. The training program will cover topics like correct hold procedures, how to remain courteous even when dealing with angry or rude customers, and problem resolution knowledge. The training will be held during your off hours, when you are not scheduled to be on the phone. However, we will pay you double time for attending the training sessions. Once again this is a situation where we are working together to solve our customers' problems. We are making a financial commitment both in terms of paying trainers and paying our phone representatives for additional work hours at twice your normal pay; but we need a commitment from our phone representatives to give up some of their free time and to take our training sessions seriously.

Finally, since we are a business, we need to be sure that our expenditures are worthwhile. Towards that end we will continue to survey our customers, and will start a test call and phone monitoring program.

Last but not least, we are implementing a Phone Representative of the Month award. Each month we will give a $500 check to the Phone Representative of the Month. The Phone Representative of the Month award will go to the phone representative with the highest score on our test call and phone monitoring programs who also has an average talk time of two minutes or less, and has not been late logging into the phone system all month.

Let's continue to work together to improve the service we provide to our customers so we can remain the best company in our industry.

Thank you.

****

EXERCISE WS7 (continued)

Q1.   What is the main idea of this business memo?

A. The company is going to start to track phone representatives more closely.
B. The company is implementing new programs to improve phone service.
C. The company is buying a new phone system.
D. $500 will be given to the top phone representative each month.

Q2.   If you were a phone representative, would you react positively or negatively to this memo?

Circle one (no wrong answer):   Positively   Negatively

Using specific details from the memo, give two reasons to support your positive or negative reaction.

_____
_____
_____
_____
_____

EXERCISE WS7 (continued)

Answer the following questions, True or False:

Q3. The response rate for the company's survey was industry standards.
     TRUE   FALSE

Q4. Phone representatives now had to log into the phone system in a timely manner. If
     they were scheduled to log in at 8:00 AM, they could log in at 8:01 AM or 8:02 AM
     but no later.
     TRUE   FALSE

Q5. The company is making a financial commitment to help solve the problem.
     TRUE   FALSE

Q6. The company is hiring 10 new employees who, in addition to helping with normal
     phone coverage, will be especially helpful covering for phone representatives that
     are attending training classes.
     TRUE   FALSE

Q7. The only goal for the test calls and phone monitoring is to help decide who wins
     the Phone Representative of the Month award.
     TRUE   FALSE

Q8. Every month a $500 check will be given to the employee who is selected as
     employee of the month.
     TRUE   FALSE

Reading perceptions in-class group discussion worksheet (from page 83)

1. In the next story Jack is a professional basketball player. Without reading the story what do you know about Jack?

Jack plays professional basketball in the Continental Basketball Association (CBA). He could not make the NBA because he was only 5'5". He is an excellent point guard. However, because the CBA doesn't pay well he has to hold down a second job to pay his bills.

2. In the next story Robin is a cheerleader. Without reading the story what do you know about Robin?

Robin goes to college at the University of Miami. As a former basketball player who hurt his knee, being on the cheerleading squad was a way for him to stay close to the game. His role is to be at the bottom of the cheerleader pyramid, holding up the women who do gymnastics from the top of the pyramid. He himself has no gymnastic or dance skills.

3. *On his first day on the job, Stu was nervous and shook hands with his boss using his left hand. Did Stu do anything wrong?*

While Stu was nervous, he did not do anything wrong. Stu recently sprained his right shoulder so his right arm was in a sling up against his chest. The only hand he had free to shake his boss' outstretched hand with was his left hand.

Preconceptions and making assumptions are a natural part of pleasure reading. Do not do that on the job.

Business Writing

Very early in my career at Citibank, I wrote a memo explaining why I wanted to change the way the customer service center forecasted future months' call volume from a simplistic approach to a more sophisticated statistical approach. When I completed my five page memo I was very proud. I thought it was the one of the best things I had ever written. I followed the approach I learned in school.

About a day later, the Vice President I wrote the memo for returned it to me and said, "I started reading this and have no idea what it's about so I am returning it to you."

I was crushed. About a year later, after getting a better handle on how to write effectively in the workplace I gave it another shot and the same Vice President said yes to my idea and we implemented the forecasting model for incoming phone calls.

In school I learned writing techniques that included: build to a conclusion, paint a picture with your words, have a powerful ending, etc. This was fine for writing fiction or for making a case in an essay on a test. When writing in the workplace, throw all that out.

The basic strategy for writing in the workplace is simple. *Time is money.* So first, descriptive writing (painting a picture in words) is considered wasteful writing. Both for extra time spent writing the document, and for the extra time required by the reader to read the document. If you want to write that there was a messy desk, just write that there was a messy desk. Do not paint a picture by saying, "There were papers, file folders, discarded food wrappers and more placed seemingly at random all over Jay's desk. If I had dime in my hand I would not have been able to place it directly on the surface of the desk. I would have had to place it on top of a pile of papers or trash and hope, when I came back 15 minutes later, that it wouldn't be buried even deeper in more junk, never to be found again."

At work, the write-up would simply be:

"Jay's desk is very messy. I understand now, why he has trouble finding client files."

This shows not only proper workplace writing, but helps demonstrate what I meant in the prior section about "reading between the lines." The last sentence about never finding the dime again is an example where a writer wants his reader to "read between the lines" to come up with the conclusion that finding required work items could be a problem for Jay given the mess on his desk. At work, if there was concern about Jay finding items at his desk, the memo would be written straight forward like the example shown. If the memo only stated, "Jay's desk is very messy"; then the problem is the mess, do not read into that statement that there has been a problem with Jay finding client files.

The second *time is money* rule for writing in the workplace is that the person you are writing the memo to, needs to be able to determine quickly, the importance of your memo so he/she can allocate the proper amount of time to reading it. In my Citibank example, the Vice President was very busy so when he couldn't get a feel for what the memo was about after reading the first paragraph or two, he decided not to invest the time needed to read, digest, and think about the full five page memo. I needed to get across what the memo was about and the importance of what I was writing about immediately.

That is why writing to build to a conclusion, making your case by building to a big finish is not the proper way to write memos or studies or anything in the workplace.

Writing in the workplace can be demonstrated by the diagram that follows.

Purpose of the memo

Support information: most important

Support information: next most important

Support information: least important

The business memo should open with purpose of your memo. For example: "The current method being used to forecast incoming call volume to the Phone Center is inefficient. It results in more staff expense and poorer service being delivered to our customers, than if a more accurate forecasting method, multiple regression analysis, was used."

What would follow next is support to backup the claim that was just made. You would start with the most important support information, and end with the least important support information. You do not start small, and keep building your case to a climactic conclusion. If you do not get the attention of the readers right away and give them cause to continue reading, they will never make it to the end of your memo containing your climactic conclusion.

As you can see, your writing needs to be direct, organized from most important to least important, and use as few words as possible to make your point. In school your writing assignments often came with "using at least 1,000 words explain <whatever the topic of the

writing assignment was>." Your goal was often to write descriptively to add words to reach the minimum goal. In work it is just the opposite. If there was a word goal attached to a work assignment, it would be "using XX words or <u>less</u>, describe your <whatever the topic of the work writing assignment was>." Your goal would be to write straight forward, not descriptively, so you could reach your goal of an effective memo using as few words as possible.

This is yet; again, a difference between how writing assignments are positioned in school versus how writing assignments are completed effectively in the workplace.

Right and Wrong for Business Writing

WRONG – Like a school assignment; using more than 1,000 words write .....
RIGHT – Use as few words as possible

WRONG – Paint a picture using your words
RIGHT – No painting pictures, be direct

WRONG – Allow the reader to reach his or her own conclusion
RIGHT – Tell the reader what conclusion they should reach right up front, then back it up

Business Letter Components

1. Date

2. Company name and address (company stationary is acceptable)

3. The date you are writing the letter

4. A salutation (e.g. Dear Sir or Madam)

5. A first paragraph stating the purpose of the letter

6. Support information (from most important to least important)

7. A closing (e.g. sincerely)

8. Your name with space for your signature between the closing and typed name

9. Phone number and/or e-mail address (optional)

Sample Business Letter

The sample business letter is on the next page.

January 10, 2013

Jay Goldberg, CEO
Name of Company
Street Address
City, State, Zip

Name of Person Sending Letter To, Title
Name of Company
Street Address
City, State, Zip

Dear Mr./Ms. Last Name,

Contents of Letter

Sincerely,

Signature

Name Printed
Title
Phone Number (optional)
E-mail address (optional)

cc: (other people sending letter to; if needed)
encl: (if attach anything to letter indicate what it is, if needed)

Business Memo Components

1. To: Person sending memo to

2. From: Your name

3. RE: (or Subject:) A short sentence regarding the topic of the memo

4. Date: The date the memo is being written

At the bottom of the memo use cc: for all other people you are sending the memo to where you want others to know those people received the memo; cc means carbon copy.

Note – it is considered a common courtesy to cc: anyone who is named in a business memo even if there is no reason for that person to receive that memo. This lets everyone know what others are saying about them first hand and stops rumors.

Business Memo Format

The business memo format should be used at all times with all correspondences, even hand written notes.

To: Randall F. Crowl

From: Jay Goldberg

RE: Work Readiness

Date: 01/10/13

==

Content of memo mentions Duncan Kassel.

CC: D. Kassel

Hand Written Notes

Bad hand written note:

Bob

The problem we talked about is still open.

Why is this note bad?

What if the note falls on the ground; which Bob gets it?
Is it an old note or a current note?
Bob may be working on numerous problems which one is this?
Who sent the note?

Good hand written note:

To: Bob Jones
From: Ian Goldtown
RE: Customer problem - Worldwide INC.
Date: 1/12/06

Bob

The problem we talked about is still open.

So take an extra few seconds to put the handwritten note into memo format to eliminate all potential problems.   Also keep in mind that had written notes must be legible (easily read by the person you are giving the note to), otherwise they are useless.

EXERCISE WS8

Write a hand written note to your instructor informing him or her of the ranking the top three things you have learned so far in this course that will help you in the workplace. Please use the proper format and proper structure for this assignment.

Understanding Basic Math

In school students are often "hand-held" through math. Many teachers will acknowledge that math is difficult. Hogwash, math is based on logic. If all teachers approached math with the attitude that it is easy, then more students wouldn't feel it was okay if they didn't excel in math. But, that's enough of my soapbox.

In school students get dependent on machines for doing their math (calculators, computer programs, etc.). You would think we would have all learned how bad an idea relying on machines is from the *Terminator* movies. But no, we still rely on machines to perform simple math problems. Don't get me wrong, that would be fine if everyone understood numbers, but many people do not.

Let me give you an example. Let's say you are working a cash register and a customer buys five items and one item was for $100. Then, the total after scanning the price tags shows $101.25. Unless you're working for a store that sells a lot of items for less than thirty cents, and doesn't charge sales tax, something may be wrong. Possibly the $100 product was keyed into the system incorrectly either at the cash register (you), or by the person who entered the prices into the computer (a co-worker). When an error like this happens it often results in products being sold below store prices. Since that negatively impacts the store's profits, that could eventually lead to lower pay raises and employees losing their jobs. Therefore, you need to be able to do basic calculations in your head without relying on "machines", so when an error shows up you can catch it, and question it.

In this case, if you estimated the total amount of the sale in your head, you would know that the total price charged the customer appears to be wrong. Your next step would be to look at the customer's receipt before handing it to him/her. It's possible that an item is on sale. It's also possible that there was an error. Another possibility is that the customer switched tags so that the item printed on the receipt does not match the item the customer is holding.

Whatever the situation is, without understanding numbers, you would not have been able to spot the potential error.

If you spot an error, never accuse the customer, or a co-worker, of doing something wrong. Your workplace should have procedures on how to handle situations like this. If you are not sure what to do, call for a supervisor and explain the situation without blaming anyone. Then allow your supervisor to handle it. Be sure to learn the procedure so the next time you can handle it yourself (unless you are informed that supervisors always handle situations like these).

Here's another example. Your supervisor tells you that a product the company sells for $10 dollars is going on sale for 30% off. He/she then hands you new price tags that show the reduced price and asks you to place them on the products. The price tag says $5.

You need to understand math enough to know that 30% off $10 is not $5. That is half (50%) off. You must be able to catch that error and correct it before placing the new price tags on the items.

Your supervisor handed you the wrong tags. More than likely they were for another product. However, with a big sign that says 30% off on top of the display of those items, if you do not catch the error you will be held accountable. If you fight it by saying you were just doing what you were told, you not only will still be held accountable, but would have just told management through your actions that you are not capable of a role in the company that involves anything more than following orders. You'll remain a "private" in that "corporate army."

By the way, just because you get blamed doesn't mean that your supervisor didn't have his/her head handed to him/her as well. So by not catching the error, you also put your supervisor in a bad position, and this is the person who determines your pay raises. This also means "what's bad for my supervisor could be <u>very</u> bad for me." Being taken to task is not a pleasant experience for your supervisor. You could have, in fact <u>should</u> <u>have</u>; caught the error. So your lack of math knowledge turned you from hero (catching the error so your supervisor avoids an unpleasant experience) to resident of your supervisor's doghouse (not catching the error causing your supervisor to endure an unpleasant experience).

Let me give you one more example. The original price for an item was $10. It has already been marked down 50%. Now your supervisor tells you to mark it down another 50%. Would you know what to do? Well logic tells you that the item is not going to given away for free, so you are not going to take 100% (50% +50%) off the price and mark it down to zero. At least I hope not. So the correct way to mark an item down twice is to do it in two steps. First it was $10, so you take 50% off making it $5. Then you take 50% off the new price ($5), making the price after both discounts are applied $2.50.

You need to understand basic math functions: addition, subtraction, multiplication, division without having to rely on a calculator. Don't get me wrong. Use them. However, if you make a mistake because you entered in wrong numbers, you need to be able to recognize you made an error so that you can correct it. You do this by estimating. For example if a customer buys five items with the following prices:

- $5.12
- $2.98
- $1.22
- $3.86

- $2.01

I would know that the total before taxes would be around $15. I would know this because I would have added $5 + $3 + $1 + $4 + $2 = $15.

I did this by rounding each transaction to the nearest whole dollar ($.01 to $0.49 is rounded down, while $0.50 to $0.99 is rounded up).

When the total came out to $15.19, I would have known that everything appeared right.

However, if the total came out to $12.19, because I accidentally entered $3.86 as $0.86, I would have known that the total appeared low and checked the receipt.

Know one thing, errors that favor the business are almost always caught and if not, result in lost customers. However, errors favoring the customers are often not caught resulting in the business losing money. There are ethical people who will mention if there is an error in their favor, but not all people act ethically in that situation (which can result in the employee being fired, or docked pay, but they do not think about that).

There are some businesses that honor incorrect prices that favor customers when products are tagged incorrectly by one of their employees. The business will honor that sale and then immediately correct the price tags on the remainder of products. But, how happy do you think management is that the business sold a product at a lower than expected price because of a mistake by an employee? If that happened because an employee relied on a calculator and had no idea the result was wrong because he/she doesn't understand numbers, how well do you think that excuse will fly? Well, I'll tell you; not very far.

Here is another example. You work on a machine in a manufacturing plant. The machine is supposed to produce 100 products an hour. The machine starts at 7:00 AM every day. You work the second shift and get in at noon. You look over and see only 250 items completed so far that day. Using your math skills, you know that there should have been 500 items (5 *100; 5 hours with 100 items produced per hour). So you inform your supervisor that something is wrong. Since you caught the problem early and production is only 2.5 hours behind it can be made up that day and the customer order can still be filled on time. If it wasn't spotted until it was time to pack the order (let's say two days later), the customer order would have been delayed resulting in the customer receiving the order late. If receiving orders on a timely basis was crucial to that customer, that customer could decide to no longer do business with your company. That would mean fewer profits and that could mean fewer jobs or reduced hours, or lower wages. So if you caught the production problem early, your basic math skills would have saved the company from a potentially harmful result.

Quick Multiplication

There are some tricks you can use to multiply without using a calculator. Break the problem down into its component parts and then add those pieces together. Some examples follow:

Problem: 33 x 99

Step one: multiply 33 x 100 = 3300
Step two: subtract 33 (problem was 99, not 100) =
3300 - 33 = 3267

Problem: 56 x 12
Step one: multiply 56 x 10 = 560
Add two more 56's to that total = 560 + 112 = 672

Problem 15 x 220

Step one: multiply 220 x 10 = 2200
Step two: take half of the result above (5 x 220 is half of 10 x220)
half of 2200 = 1100
Step three: add the parts together = 2200 + 1100 = 3300

Problem 124 x 80

Step one: multiply 124 x 100 = 12,400
Step two: multiply 124 x 20 = 2,480
Step three: subtract 2,500 (to use an easier number) from 12,400 = 12,400 – 2,500 = 9,900
Step four: add 20 back in (subtracted 2,500 instead of 2,480) =
9,900 -20 = 9,920

Fractions and Percents

To change a fraction to a percent, divide the numerator by the denominator.

To change a decimal to a percent, multiply it by 100

1/2 (numerator/denominator)

1 dived by 2 = .5

.5 x 100 = 50%

3/8 (numerator/denominator)

3 divide by 8 = .375

.375 x 100 = 37.5%

5/2 (numerator/denominator)

5 divided by 2 = 2.5

2.5 x 100 = 250%

Percent change

Comparing old to new:

1. Subtract the old value from the new value.
2. Divide the difference by the old value

So if you earned $40,000 last year (old value) and earned $50,000 this year (new value):

$50,000 - $40,000 = $10,000
$10,000/$40,000 = 25%

So you earned 25% more this year as compared to last year.

Comparing new to old:

1. Subtract the new value from the old value
2. Divide by the new value

So in the prior case:

$40,000 - $50,000 = -$10,000
-$10,000/$50,000 = -20%

So you earned 20% less last year than you earned this year.

Therefore, when doing percent changes, it is important what you are using as the base for comparison (e.g. current as compared to past – first example; or past as compared to current, second example).

EXERCISE WS9

1. In 2011 a baseball player had a batting average of 290, had 30 home runs and 100 RBI. In 2012 that same player improved to a batting average of 300, hit 40 home runs and knocked in 120 RBI. What was the baseball player's percent improvement in 2012, over 2011 in each of these three categories? (HINT – 2011 is the base)

2. A business owner earned $80,000 in profits in 2011. Revenues (sales) were $200,000 and costs were $120,000. If costs are expected to be $130,000 in 2012, and revenues are expected to be $225,000, what is the percent increase in profits expected to be in 2012? (HINT, Profits = Revenues – Expenses). What is growing at a faster rate, revenues or expenses? (HINT – you must calculate profits for 2012 before you can answer the questions)

3. The regular price for books is $2.50. However, there is a 20% discount if you buy 100 or more. What is the discount price for buying 100 or more books? What is the total product cost if you buy 200 books? What is the total product cost if you buy 10 books?

4. The regular price for desks is $100. However, there is a 10% discount if you buy 10 or more. What is the total product cost if you buy 60 desks? If the customer is given an additional 10% off at the register, what will the price now be for the 60 books?

5. Your original price for music CDs is $14. What is the sale price if you mark it down 10%?

6. Your original price for computers is $1,000. What is the sale price if you mark it down 30%?

7. Your cost for puppies is $100. What is your selling price if you want to make 75% on each puppy?

8. The original price for a book is $30. It has been discounted 10% already. Your supervisor asks you to mark it down an additional 10%. Does that make the sale price $24 or $24.30?

9. True or false. As long as I have a calculator, computer and point of sale terminal, it is okay if I do not understand numbers; these devices will always give me the correct results.

10. True or false. Math is very difficult for many people so I know all my supervisors will understand and not hold me accountable if I do not catch simple math errors at work.

Advanced Workplace Skills

In video games there are special codes that allow you to advance faster, or have more fun by using items, or have powers not available without those special codes. Well, in work, there are skills you can develop that do the same thing. By mastering these skills you will see your compensation grow faster because you will be more valuable in the workplace, and you'll advance to jobs that will be more fun and rewarding since the jobs will make more use of your advance skills.

The "special codes" (advanced workplace skills) that follow will help you become very valuable in the workplace.

Problem-solving skills

Steps you can take to help you come up with solutions for solving problems follow:

1. Understand the problem – this means more than just understanding the obvious. Write down the impact the problem has on everyone affected by the problem.

2. Determine the cause of the problem – knowing the cause of the problem helps ensure that the solutions fix the root cause.

3. Identify the current solution – the current solution is not working; know what it is and why it is not working so your new solution is not just a re-hashing of the old, ineffective solution.

4. Come up with possible solutions – here is where you can be creative; first write down anything that comes to mind, even if it does not initially make sense, or you cannot see how to implement it. For example, if the problem is that not enough people know about the store you work for, you could write down, "go to the busy corner of fifth and main, get a bullhorn, and talk about your store." Just be sure that the possible solutions solve the problem and are not re-treads of the existing solution that is not working.

5. Identify real-life solutions for the possible solutions – look at your list of possible solutions and try to think of a way to implement them. You may not be able to do

this with all of your possible solutions. For the example in step 4, a real-life solution could be to place a billboard at the busy corner of 5th and main, or a sign on the bus that picks people up at the 5th and Main bus stop, as well as other heavily trafficked spots.

6. Rank the solutions – after coming up with possible real-life solutions, rank them. If a real-life solution does not make much sense at this point, eliminate it from your list.

7. Present the solutions to your supervisor – inform your supervisor, either in writing or verbally, of the solutions you've come up with for the problem. Present them in order from best to worst. Allow your supervisor to pick the one he/she likes best, even if it is not on the top of your list. Your supervisor will have other criteria (such as cost, time frames, prior experience, etc.) which could change your order.

8. Follow through – if your supervisor uses you to implement the solution to the problem (e.g., come up with the wording for the billboard), be sure to complete that assignment fully in a timely manner.

9. Monitor the results – an area where some employees and even supervisors fall short is that they do not track the results of what they implement to fix a problem. For example, if a billboard is placed at 5th and main so that more people know about the store you work for, there needs to be a way to determine if the billboard is doing its job. You cannot assume because more people come to the store that it was because of the billboard. It may be a sale that is going on in the store, or that a new business opened across the street so you are getting some of their overflow customers. So there needs to be a way to monitor the effectiveness of the solution. If you can think of one, discuss it with your supervisor and implement it, and you will be a very valuable employee indeed. In this case, asking a couple of questions of customers in the store and tracking the results will go a long way towards knowing the effectiveness of the billboard. For example you can ask the customer, "How did you find out about our store?"

Problem-solving worksheet

Sales in the restaurant you work for, a diner, has declined by 30% over the last three months. It is also down 30% over the same three month period last year. The drop off is not due to the economy. Other restaurants in the area have not seen a reduction in sales. In addition, a new diner which opened six months ago appears to be growing its business significantly.

1. What is the problem? _____

_____

_____

2. What are some possible consequences of this problem? _____

_____

_____

3. What are some possible causes for this problem? _____

_____

_____

4. What are some steps you could take to try to determine the real cause(s) of this problem?

_____

_____

_____

5. Choose one of the causes you listed in question 3 and indicate three solutions you could take to help solve the problem.

_____

_____

_____

_____

_____

6. Rank your three solutions in order from most likely to fix the problem to least likely to fix the problem.

1. _____

_____

2. _____

_____

3. _____

_____

7. How would you track whether or not your top solution (#1 above) was working (note – not just that sales increased but that your solution is the reason sales have increased)

_____

_____

_____

Creative thinking

Creative thinking is often called thinking outside the box. Mastering this skill is a sure fire way to make yourself valuable in the workplace. Why? Unlike other workplace skills, which get the same results from every worker, the results from the creative thinking process varies by worker.

Creative thinking is a way for you to stand out in the workplace. If management values your creative thought process in solving problems, management knows if you leave, the person who replaces you will not come up with the same creative solutions that you did.

Creative thinking comes natural to some, and must be honed and developed by others. If you are someone who could see himself/herself writing a good detective story one day, you probably have good creative thinking skills. If you read or watch a good "who did it" book or movie and marvel at how the writer put together the clues to solve the fictional case, you may have to work on these skills.

As an example, let's use one of my favorite movies, *Armageddon*. In the movie a giant asteroid is hurtling towards earth and if it hits, it will destroy all life on the planet. After looking at, and dismissing, all of the obvious solutions, they decide to send astronauts to drill in the asteroid to a depth where a nuclear bomb will split the asteroid and the two main pieces will the bypass earth.

Knowing that drilling is too tough to learn in the time they have, the Bruce Willis character recommends that they send his teams of deep-core drillers to the asteroid to do the work.

That combination of drilling on the asteroid and using non-astronauts to go into space is an example of thinking outside the box, hence a creative solution.

A Strategy for Continuing Education

When it comes to taking continuing/community education courses many people react in the moment; they look at the course offerings at the local venue, and decide to take a course that will be fun or helpful.

For career purposes, the better way to approach continuing education is determine what subjects will help you grow in your career, and look for courses in a variety of venues that offer the courses you want.

This is subtle difference, but a big one. The first is going with the flow, the second is goal oriented.

For example, you may need Excel and Access knowledge to be eligible for a promotion, but only see a course for Excel at the local venue and take that course. Then you sit back and wait for a course in Access in that venue. That course may not be offered there for a year and a half, if at all. Here it was good that you got knowledge in Excel, but your goal should have been both Excel and Access to put yourself in a position to get promoted.

This also means that you need to look at the higher level positions in the company and determine the skills needed to put yourself in a position to advance in the company. Remember, it is not what you think will be helpful, it is what management thinks will be helpful.

One strategy is to ask someone in management or in human resources what they recommend you learn to help you advance in the company. It is best to do this after you have had enough time in the company to demonstrate that you have strong work readiness skills. If you do this at that time, management could keep an eye on you since they know you are a very good employee who is looking to stay with and advance in the company.

On the other hand, if you do this too early, before demonstrating your value as an employee, management may feel you are being too aggressive, or that you are not satisfied performing the job you were hired to do. Also, if you have time on the job and have not performed your work readiness skills well, management may feel that you should concentrate on performing better in the workplace before you worry about getting a promotion.

Next, understand that businesses market their product and services to get customers. Most do not sit back and wait for customers, on their own, to find out what the business sells.

This means that you must let your supervisor (and human resources) know that you are taking a course in a subject matter that will help the business. Don't oversell, but be direct and let the people in charge of promotions know you are taking steps to put yourself in a position to get a promotion.

Continuing education worksheet

List three areas (specific topics or courses or programs) you would like to pursue through continuing education (either formally though a degree or certification program or informally through a community education course) to help you grow in your job or in your career.

1. _____

   How will this area help your career? _____

   _____

2. _____

   How will this area help your career? _____

   _____

3. _____

   How will this area help your career? _____

   _____

Report Generation and Analysis

This advanced skill uses the other skills written about previously in this book. For example, you know you have to write your report using the business writing approach; that you need to spell everything out since the readers will not be reading between the lines; that your math skills will come in handy during the analysis; that new skills you obtained through continuing education could also help you throughout the process; and that following the problem-solving steps and using your creative thinking skills will help you come up with solutions to any problems uncovered by your report.

This is all while managing you time effectively, being sure to not just undertake the task, but complete the report, following any company or department directions for writing and distributing your report, and updating associated procedure manuals if changes are made to any procedure or policy based on the recommendations in your report.

Charts and Graphs

Charts are an easy way to display a lot of detailed information in a report. Be sure to have column headings that clearly indicate the information being reported in that column. If you use any abbreviations in the column headings, use an asterisk (*) and at the bottom of the chart indicate the full title.

Here is a sample chart:

Jay's Fantasy Football Roster Breakdown

*Position	How many	Percent of Roster
QB	2	16.7%
RB	3	20.0%
WR	3	20.0%
TE	2	16.7%
K	1	8.3%
DEF	1	8.3%

*QB = quarterback, RB = running back, WR = wide receiver, TE = tight end, K = kicker, DEF = team defense

In addition to charts, graphs are another way to effectively show detailed information. Using a spreadsheet program such as Excel can turn charts into graphs. A graph that could have been used in the previous exercise is:

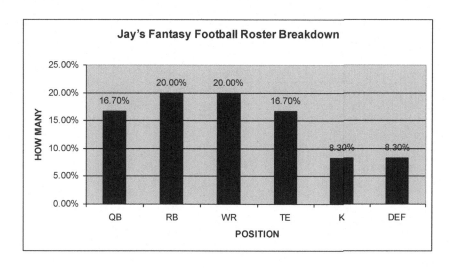

As you can see the graph contains the same information as the chart, the number players by position.

<table>
<tr><td colspan="5">EXERCISE WS10

You are assigned to determine how effectively your supervisor's secretary is answering the phone. This includes the time it takes for the calls to be answered, as well as what the secretary says while on the phone. Your supervisor states that the goal is to have all the calls answered with no more than four rings and for the secretary to never make the company look bad to the person calling.

So your supervisor sets you up to monitor (listen in) on all of the secretary's calls for one day. You ask your supervisor if the secretary knows you will be monitoring and he/she says, yes, and wants the secretary informed as to what you find.

There are ten calls. This is what you find:</td></tr>
</table>

Call #	# Rings Before Answered	Comments	Professional & Courteous
1	3	Nothing negative	Yes
2	2	Nothing negative	Yes
3	5	Nothing negative	Yes
4	4	Nothing negative	Yes
5	2	Said supervisor not back from lunch yet	Yes
6	3	Nothing negative	Yes
7	1	Nothing negative	Yes
8	4	Said supervisor too busy to take any calls now	Yes
9	2	Nothing negative	Yes
10	3	Nothing negative	Yes

Use the business memo format and business writing techniques and etiquette to write a report to your supervisor (use the name of your instructor as your supervisor's name). The secretary's name is Pat Jones. Also include a chart summarizing the 10 calls by number of rings.

EXERCISE WS11

Q1. Use the information below to fill in the form that follows.
(The plant is open 24 hours a day, be sure that the information for time is entered precisely)

Jack Smith is finished cleaning machine ABC at 8:50 AM, and machine JAY at 10:15 AM. Jack also sets machine ABC at 8:55 AM and machine JAY at 10:20 AM.

Mary Jones completes the test for machine XYZ at 7:00 AM and machine ABC at 9:30 AM.

Lisa LaDonna verifies that the model 15 blades are the right size at 2:15 PM, she counts 100 blades. She then verifies that the model 25 blades are the right size at 3:30 PM, she counts 200 blades.

Cassie Douglas finishes assembling the model 15 blades at 5:30 PM. There are 100 of them.

Arthur Batman starts his quality control of the model 15 blades at 8:30 PM, and passes 95.

Q2. How many model 15 blades did not pass the quality control inspection?

Harold's Collectible Knives, Inc.
Task Checklist

Enter first name and last initial upon successful completion of each task

Date:_____

FABRICATION Blanking the blades	Name	Time	COMPLETION Knife assembly	Name	Quantity
Machine XYZ cleaned			Model 15 blade proper size		
Machine XYZ set			Model 15 blade spinning		
Machine XYZ tested			Model 15 blade bracketing		
Machine ABC cleaned			Model 15 final assembly		
Machine ABC set			Model 25 blade proper size		
Machine ABC tested			Model 25 blade spinning		
Machine JAY cleaned			Model 25 blade bracketing		
Machine JAY set			Model 25 final assembly		
Machine JAY tested			# passed quality control model 15 model 25		m15 ____ m25 ____

PEOPLE SKILLS

Communication Skills

Communication refers to both verbal and nonverbal communication. What you say and how you say it is very important. I remember a Seinfeld episode where Kramer had a line in a Woody Allen movie. The line was "These pretzels are making me thirsty." Each of the four main characters has their own spin on how the line should be said, and based on how the character says the line, the emotion communicated to the listener changes. From matter of fact, to the appearance of great thirst, to severe annoyance, to anger at the pretzels; the message communicated changed based on the delivery of the line.

Likewise you can get messages across just by your actions. For good examples, watch an old Marx Brothers movie or catch Penn and Teller's act. In both cases there is a person who does not talk, but gets across what he is thinking just on his actions and facial expressions.

Verbal communication

Being able to communicate with your co-workers, supervisors, and customers is a workplace skill that is valued by employers. Therefore, do not use slang, computer lingo, or street talk when talking or writing. For example, using computer lingo, if I finished talking to you and then said, "TTYL", you may or may not know that I meant that I'll "talk to you later." Worse, what if I wrote you a note and started it, "IMHO", and then went on to contradict what you wrote me. You might get the impression that I was correcting you rather than just stating my views on the subject ("IMHO" means 'in my humble opinion"). Also, if one of your co-workers is provoking you and your supervisor comes over to ask you what is going on, don't say, "I was chillin' when my homey came over and started fronting." Just say, "I wasn't doing anything when Bob came over and started provoking me." Obviously you should also avoid slang that many will take offense too, even if you do not believe you are using it in an offensive manner.

When communicating verbally in the workplace, speak clearly, and choose your words carefully. There are other things to remember while communicating in the workplace. Including:

1. Don't take how people react personally. Their reactions are usually about the impact of what you communicated, and not directed towards you personally. For example, if you had to communicate to a co-worker that your supervisor said everyone had to work late, his/her response may be angry, but the anger is at the situation and is not directed at you.

2. Do not make up facts, or even guess at facts. If you do not know an answer, just say so.

3. If you are unsure of what someone means, don't assume, ask questions until it becomes clear to you.

4. Be patient. Often someone you are talking too will be saying something you already know. Allow that person the opportunity to say what he or she wants so that he or she can have the satisfaction of knowing that he or she was heard.

5. Be open to other people's points of view. Everyone has different life experiences. Do not automatically discount other people's opinions. You just may find that others have interesting perspectives worth thinking about.

6. Understand that the person you are conveying information to may have difficulties that arise from your discussion. Do not downplay something that the person you are speaking to may find difficult regarding what is being discussed. Instead, acknowledge it, and then offer suggestions to help ease their pain.

7. Avoid arguments. Concentrate on what you and the other party agree on first, to establish common ground, and then move towards solving differences. Be understanding of everyone's position in the discussion by looking at the situation from the other person's point of view.

8. Be sure to listen to what others are saying, do not step on their words or tune them out.

9. When using examples, personalize the examples so that it is easier for the other party to relate to what you are saying.

Verbal communication worksheet

Understanding your communication strengths and weaknesses is the first step towards becoming an effective communicator in all scenarios. Use the worksheet that follows to indicate your strengths, weaknesses and a plan to improve your overall communication skills.

1. Which three of the nine communication skills listed previously are your strengths (write the number)

_____   _____   _____

2. Which three of the nine communication skills listed previously do you need to work on, or be aware of, the most (write the number)

_____   _____   _____

3. How do you plan to improve, or be more aware of, the three areas you indicated in question 2? _____

_____

_____

_____

_____

_____

_____

_____

Non-verbal communication

One of my favorite books is *Dune* by Frank Herbert. Besides being a fascinating story, an aspect I found very interesting was the communication between characters in political situations. Besides the dialog, Frank Herbert also sets up the scenes by writing about the personal signals involved in many of those interactions.

Believe it or not (George isn't at home, where could I be – sorry, that tune just sticks in my head from George's answering machine in a Seinfeld episode), *Dune* opened my eyes to reading the motivation behind personal signals at work. I was fresh out of graduate school with my MBA working on a project in the Systems and Technology Department for the Merchant Credit Card Division of Citibank. There was an Assistant Vice President (AVP), who was not in charge of the area, who, at times, would come to work in a t-shirt with a sweat stain. Now, this was a conservative bank, at a time when everyone showed up in suits and ties. This AVP was not a slob, was not unsophisticated, and was not unaware of how he should dress. So using my new found "Dune" skills, I figured out what his purpose was in coming to work on occasion in a t-shirt with a sweat stain. He was saying nonverbally, "If I can show up like this to work and get away with it, I'm very important to management and not someone you should ever cross."

Now, I do not recommend you try this at your place of employment; this was an extremely rare situation.

As an aside, one day I asked the AVP if he ever read *Dune*, and he said a very energetic, "Yes, it's one of my favorite books."

Now I'll go on to the topic. Be aware of the personal signals you are broadcasting. You may say the right thing but if your body language is saying something else, you will be sending mixed signals. You can also use those always present personal signals to your advantage. By reading the personal signals of the individual you are talking too, you can tell if he/she comprehends what you just told him/her. A puzzled look goes a long way in letting you know you will have to find different words to explain what you just said again. I do that all the time when I teach my entrepreneurship course. If I see looks of acknowledgement, I go on to the next topic, on the rare occasion I see some looks of confusion, I go over the topic again, presenting it in a different way.

Personal signals

Below are some personal signals and what they generally indicate when communicating with others.   Despite television shows like *Lie to Me*, I do not believe this is an exact science, so consider what follows as a rule of thumb more than a given.

✓ Direct eye contact, but not staring (shows interest)
✓ Long stare without head movement (annoyance)
✓ Rolling of eyes (frustration)
✓ Avoiding eye contact (uncomfortable, wants situation to end)
✓ Winking (friendly acknowledgement)
✓ Tight lipped smile (hiding something)
✓ Normal laugh (relaxed)
✓ Forced laugh (nervous cooperation)
✓ Teeth grinding (tension)
✓ Biting lip (tension)
✓ Hand over mouth (suppressing something)
✓ Nodding yes (agreement)
✓ Head shaking no (disagreement)
✓ Looking down (disinterested)
✓ Slight tilt of head (shows you are listening)
✓ Head tilted down (criticism)
✓ Chin up (pride)
✓ Slow head nodding (listening intently)
✓ Fast head nodding (agree, get on with it already)
✓ Crossed arms (defensive)
✓ Leaning forward (shows interest)
✓ Leaning back (to reflect and take time to think)
✓ Leaning on chin (shows concentration)
✓ Cupping chin (boredom)
✓ Clasp hands behind neck or body (extreme confidence)
✓ One hand on back of neck (disagreement)
✓ Grasping upper arms (insecure)
✓ Palms up (submissive)
✓ Palms down (in control)
✓ Pointing finger at someone (aggression)
✓ Clenched fists (determined resistance)
✓ Interwoven clenched fingers (negativity)
✓ Rubbing hands (anticipation)
✓ Hands in pockets (disinterest)
✓ Constantly shifting position (not relaxed)
✓ Stroking nose (exaggeration, possibly lying)
✓ Scratching neck (disbelief)
✓ Yawning (fatigue)
✓ Scowling (anger)
✓ Tapping fingers (impatience)

In addition to using these personal signals to read your audience, know how others may be interpreting you when you use some of these personal signals.

Personal signals (nonverbal communication) worksheet

1. Understanding the personal signals you use, often naturally without even thinking about what you are doing can go a long way to ensuring that the personal signals you actually use in the workplace match the message you are communicating and convey how you truly feel about the situation. Use the worksheet that follows to indicate three personal signals (use the prior list of personal signals) you know you use appropriately to help you convey what you are saying or feeling.

1. _____

2. _____

3. _____

2. Now list two personal signals that you use that seem to come up automatically and often get you into trouble because they either convey the wrong message or give away what you are feeling in a situation where that is inappropriate and may get you into trouble despite your words.

1. _____

2. _____

Obviously, these are two personal signals you need to be aware of and try to eliminate.

EXERCISE PS1

Robots for Ronnie Inc. (RFR Inc.) is a growing management consulting company in the field of Robotics. While the company has an excellent reputation in the area of using robotics to solve manufacturing problems, the staff has problems communicating with its customers. To help solve these problems, RFR Inc. hires you to observe staff communications with customers. What follows are the first four communication sessions you observe. Indicate whether or not these sessions represented good or bad communication skills and then explain why you choose good or bad. (FYI – "Robots for Ronnie" is a song by Crack the Sky)

Q1. The Senior Vice President (SVP) of RFR Inc. wants to know what customers think of their new Robot, Model ABC. The SVP asks an employee to obtain feedback from customers on how well the robot is doing in their places of business. The employee asks the following to ten customers, "Could you please tell me about your experience with Robot ABC?" The employee does his/her homework and knows exactly what the robot is being used for at each of the ten businesses and adds a specific comment to the end of the question. When a client responds with a bad experience, since the employee knows what the robot is being used for, the employee acknowledges the customer's difficulty, and helps the customer overcome their issues.

EXERCISE PS1 (continued)

Q2. An employee is given the task to inform a group of sales representatives about Robot Model ABC. The employee was up all night working. The presentation starts at 7:30 AM the next morning. During the presentation, the employee gets across all important details of Robot ABC, including its features, uses, and why it is better than the competition's similar model. The presentation was given very straight forward with little to no emotion, a few yawns, and at times was delivered very slowly.

Q3. An employee is asked to give a presentation of how Robot Model ABC functions at a convention of Powdered Metal Manufacturing Plant owners and managers. This employee has excellent presentation skills, and knows the product very well. Throughout the presentation the employee uses examples of how the robot can be used. All of the examples are long and very detailed. The examples are in the medical and theme park (e.g. Disneyland) industries. There were no powdered metal examples.

Q4. On day three of your assignment, there is a recall of Robot Model XYZ. An employee is placed in charge of picking up the customers robots. When a client asks the employee why the robot is being recalled, the employee stares at the client a long time (head held still), then points a finger at the client and says, "Call customer service, they can give you the details."

Getting Along with Co-Workers

Here is a recommendation I trust you will follow; treat your co-workers like "friendly neighbors."

When you move into a new neighborhood, your neighbors are already there. You don't choose them and you have no power on how long they will remain your neighbors. The same is true in the workplace. When you get a new job, there are already people employed by the company. You don't choose them, and you have no power on how long they will stay with the company. Your best strategy is to get along with all your co-workers. If you do, you will be a positive force in your workplace, and that goes a long way on increasing your value to your employer. It also shows that you can get along with all kinds of people, which demonstrates that you have the ability to manage diverse teams of employees. Therefore, getting along with your co-workers is not only the ethical (right) thing to do, it is the smart thing to do to increase your job security, and keep you in the running for supervisory positions.

Blueprint for getting along with co-workers

If you keep in mind the concept "friendly neighbors" you'll be okay. The best strategy with neighbors is not to get too personal, and that is true with your co-workers.

(1) Leave "water cooler talk" to what was on television last night, not what you heard your co-worker did last night. Gossip is usually wrong, and often hurtful to the person being discussed. Keep away from office gossip, and if you hear something, certainly, do not pass it on. It is possible that your co-worker will consider gossip about him/her harassment. Worst case he/she could consider it a hostile workplace. If your co-worker talks to his/her supervisor, or the Human Resources Department, you don't want to be part of the group that gets called on the carpet to explain the situation. You definitely don't want to be the center of the "gossip storm." If you are a "gossip-hound", stand in line at the supermarket, read the headlines of the magazines that line the aisles, and gossip about celebrities at the water cooler. Don't cross the line no matter how tempting, and spread gossip and rumors about your co-workers.

(2) Don't get dragged into your co-workers' personal problems, and don't share your personal problems with your co-workers. If your co-workers start to talk to you about something too personal, just say, "I'm sorry to hear that. I'm sure you'll be fine." Then get back to work. Asking questions and expanding on the comments will just lead to more

details and future conversations. The same goes for you. Separate your friends from your friendly co-workers and keep your conversations about your personal problems to the people that care about you; your friends.

(3) If a co-worker is complaining about work, don't join in. You would be surprised what is overheard and gets back to management. Instead say something like, "I know you're going through a tough time now, but I believe in you and you're going to be fine." In general be positive and supportive, not negative or a "Doubting Thomas" or a "constant complainer."

(4) If a co-worker is doing something wrong on the job and it is negatively impacting the quality of the work, don't allude to it; don't talk behind his/her back. You have to be discreet and direct. One approach is to say, "I have been doing <that function> differently, can you show me how you have been doing it." After he/she shows you, explain how you have been doing it. Hopefully it will become clear that your way is the proper way and your co-worker will change. If your co-worker continues to perform <that function> incorrectly, inform him/her that you will be talking to your supervisor to clear up the proper way to complete <that function>. Then tell your supervisor how you have been doing <that function> and ask if it is correct. If your supervisor informs you that it is correct, say that some of your other co-workers are not performing the task that way and may need a refresher in how the procedure is done. Then leave the next move up to your supervisor.

Notice how there was no arguing with your co-worker on how <that function> should be done. Also, you approached your co-worker to verify the way you were performing <that function>. Finally, you told your co-worker that you were going to talk to your supervisor (not going behind a co-worker's back), and you approached your supervisor to help clarify a job function for yourself, not to discuss how your co-worker was performing <that function>.

(5) Do not take credit for something another co-worker does. When you do a good job and it is recognized, take full credit. If you do something as a team and are given credit, share the credit with your team members. If you get credit for something that someone else did, shine the light on your co-worker. Believe it or not ("George isn't at home" – there goes that song from Seinfeld in my head again, sorry). Let me start again, believe it or not you will score big points for being honest. A supervisor values an employee he/she can trust. Supervisors also value an employee that can share credit with team members.

(6) Don't be overbearing. You may have done things differently in your old job, or you may have liked the way the workplace was run better in a previous job, or you may not like the way a new supervisor is running things. Do not keep talking about the way things used to be. Accept change. However, if you truly believe you can identify ways to improve the workplace, arrange a meeting with your supervisor and talk to him/her about it. But do not preach or complain to your co-workers, and accept the final decision your supervisor makes.

(7) Treat your co-workers like team members, not competitors. That means helping them when needed, and not being afraid to ask for help when you need it. When asking for help, be sure you ask the right person. The person you ask needs to be an expert in the area in which you need help. If you ask the 12th ranked salesperson for help with your sales

technique, you may not get the best answers. The person to ask is the top ranked salesperson. Remember, if a co-worker teaches you something incorrectly, that is not an excuse for doing something the wrong way in your supervisor's eyes, unless, of course, your supervisor told you to ask that person for help. After receiving help, be sure to thank your co-worker for his/her help.

(8) Perform your job functions well. In most workplaces employees' job functions are dependent on the work of others. Therefore, if you do not perform your job functions timely and accurately, it could make it difficult for some of your co-workers to perform their job functions timely and accurately. Then, depending upon the management style in the workplace, even though you might be the cause for the below-par performance of others, management could hold everybody accountable. You could be directly impacting the compensation and career growth of some of your co-workers. So performing your job well not only is important to the business, and to you; but also to your co-workers who rely on your work. So if you are making mistakes on the job, and your co-workers become annoyed with you, do not get angry thinking they are getting involved in something that is solely your business; it is their business as well.

(9) Be even-keeled at work because you will be dealing with a wide range of people. This is not just the obvious of dealing with people of varying religions, races, ethnicity, sexual orientation, gender, age, disabilities, etc.; but also dealing with people with varying personalities, values, political views, and outlooks on life. Work is not the place to get into heated discussions or to show your prejudices (which you shouldn't have anyway). So avoid conversations on those heated political conversations and polarizing topics with your co-workers.

EXERCISE PS2

Jack works with and lives next door next to Juliet and Sawyer. Last night he heard loud talking coming from Juliet and Sawyer's home, looked out his window, and saw Juliet leaving in a huff and driving off. Jack gets into work two hours earlier than Juliet. When he got up the next morning, Juliet's car is not in her driveway. Later in the day Kate, a woman Jack has a crush on, approaches Jack and says "Juliet is in a bad mood today, I wonder if she is having problems at home with Sawyer?"

Q1. How should Jack answer that question?

Because of the Holiday rush, Hugo has been working very hard, including long hours and little time for breaks. His buddy and co-worker, Charley, stands up, throws his hands in the air, and says, "This is bull. I need a break and I'm taking a break." In the room there are lots of head nods and a few others get up to walk to the vending machines with Charlie. As he is leaving, Charlie turns to Hugo and says, "Come on Hugo, don't you agree this is bull? Let's go."

Q2. How should Hugo answer that question? Should Hugo go on break with the others?

EXERCISE PS2 (continued)

Desmond has been the top-rated employee at Lost Island, Inc. for the last three years. He is the only one who knows how to punch the numbers into the Keeping Things Right Machine. Desmond has his eye on a promotional opportunity and believes it is his knowledge of the Keeping Things Right Machine that will eventually get him that promotion. His main competitor for the promotion is Ben. Ben finishes all his assignments early and his supervisor told him he could go home and still get paid for the day. Instead, Ben approaches Desmond and asks him if he can teach him how to punch in the numbers. Desmond is just about to punch in the numbers, so the timing is perfect.

Q3. What should Desmond do?

Jin believes strongly in alternative energy, particularly solar energy (energy from the Sun). Locke, on the other hand has relatives that work in the petroleum industry. Jin and Locke eat lunch together in the employee cafeteria. There are not friends outside of work, but enjoy eating lunch together. Today, Jin gives a speech about the evils of petroleum, the benefits of solar energy, and invites Locke to a rally that is taking place on the weekend, when neither is scheduled to work. Jin has no idea that Locke has relatives that work in the petroleum industry.

Q4. How should Jin respond to Locke's request?

Claire worked very long and hard on a study that is going to be included in the department's monthly report. In the monthly report all information is included as one write-up from the department with no names attached to the individual studies in the report. While putting the report together Claire asks Sayid if he could provide her with some data from his work area. Sayid runs the numbers and hands them to Claire. Claire then analyzes the data, finds some interesting trends, and includes some insightful written analysis in her study. After the department's monthly report is published, the President of the company walks past Sayid's desk, stops, and says, "Sayid, that was a great analysis of your numbers, keep up the good work and you'll go places in this company."

Q5. How should Sayid respond?

Teamwork

The sum of the parts is greater than the whole. That statement is more than just an old wives' tale. It is true. That is why teamwork is important for all businesses. If everyone is working together, then any problem in the workplace is a problem that is important to all workers. Yes, even you. And solutions to problems can come from any worker.

Therefore, to be a valuable employee, look at your place of work as your team, and your co-workers as your teammates. Do what you can to support your teammates and to ensure that your team wins. In this case, winning means the business is making profits by satisfying its customers, thus keeping everyone employed.

Working with the Team Leader

The Team Leader can be a unique person for employees to deal with. When the Team Leader is a supervisor, then the lines of command are obvious. However, often a co-worker will be put in charge of a team. When that happens, you suddenly find yourself having to follow the lead of an individual who is not in charge of your pay raises or your performance review. In fact, this could be someone who has less experience than you, or is at a lower pay scale that you. That doesn't matter. A team needs a leader to be successful and that co-worker was chosen to lead. For the tasks related to the team, you <u>must</u> treat that co-worker as your supervisor. If you do not, it is you who will look bad, not the Team Leader. This is not sports. The Coach (Team Leader) will not get fired if the team does not succeed, and the Owner (Supervisor) can fire the players (workers) rather than Coach (Team Leader) for the team's failure.

If you find yourself in the role of Team Leader, the following will help you be a successful Team Leader:

1. Set goals for the team
2. Provide all team members with a chance to state his/her ideas
3. Get feedback on the ideas presented from the team members
4. Choose the best ideas yourself after hearing all comments, but make it appear as a group choice
5. Assign roles for all team members so they know what to do
6. Use the word "we" when talking about the team, not "I"
7. Recognize individuals for their ideas and accomplishments

8. Whenever possible, do not force individuals who do not get along to pair up; split them up
9. Do not be hesitant to take control; that is your job
10. Take your role seriously; do not kid around with your friends on the team, if you do others may not take you seriously

Another important fact is that Team Leaders get credit for team accomplishments, and they deserve that credit. Managers in baseball, don't hit, don't pitch, and don't field, but get credit when the team wins by putting their players in a position to succeed. It is the same with Team Leaders. Even if the Team Leader's contributions to the work seem to be minimal, the Team Leader ran his/her team in a way that good solutions and work was produced. That is valuable to employers; is recognized; and deserves to be recognized. Despite what people think, not everybody can manage the New York Yankees and win because of their big payroll and star players. Sometimes handling the best of the best is more difficult than rallying a group of highly-motivated over-achievers.

Of course good Team Leaders will share the recognition with his/her team members and note individuals who made major contributions by name. However, that is out of your control. Know that the Team Leader's supervisor understands that the Team Leader could not be successful without contributions from his/her team, and will look at the Team Leader's lack of sharing recognition for the team's accomplishments with his/her team members as a negative. A good supervisor will not show that to the Team Leader's team members, because that would undermine the Team Leader; but know that the greedy Team Leader is not fooling anyone, and is most likely, being chastised or "coached-up" for that behavior behind the scenes.

Team leader skills worksheet

Understanding your team leader skill strengths and weaknesses is the first step towards becoming an effective team leader. Use the worksheet that follows to indicate your strengths, weaknesses and a plan to improve your overall team leader skills.

1. Which three of the ten team leader skills listed previously are your strengths (write the number)

_____   _____   _____

2. Which three of the ten team leader skills listed previously do you need to work on, or be aware of; the most (write the number)

_____   _____   _____

3. How do you plan to improve, or be more aware of, the three areas you indicated in question 2? _____
_____
_____
_____
_____

How to be a good team member

I am a big proponent of playing team sports. When a team wins a championship, everybody feels good, from the star of the team to the last player off the bench. The Super Bowl MVP (most valuable player) may get to go to Disneyland, but the guy who only played one play gets the championship ring as well.

You don't have to be the star to enjoy it when your team wins.

Therefore, the key to being a good team member at work is to understand your role, do it the best of your ability, help your teammates, ask for help when you need it, treat all team members and the Team Leader with respect, make accomplishing the goal of the team important to you, and feel good about your team's accomplishments no matter what your role was in helping the team reach its goals.

Being a good team player is important to management. Often, talented workers are not good team players and that holds them back from advancing in their careers. The worker that needs to be the center of attention, have the spotlight always shinning on him/her, always has to get his/her way, etc.; is not an ideal employee even if he/she is brilliant in those circumstances. Your workplace is like baseball or football, not golf or tennis. You do not work in a vacuum. You work with others and have to be a good team player, sometimes leading (when given the responsibility to do so by your supervisor), but more often being a good follower.

Value of Diversity in the Workplace

Since the workplace is based on teamwork, the more diversified the team members, the stronger the team.

If a team has team members who can look at a challenge from a variety of backgrounds and viewpoints, the team stands a better chance of coming up with solutions that address all aspects of that challenge.

This includes a mix of workers of different genders, age, ethnicity, race, sexual orientation, etc. The company wants to do business with all customers. If a team is assembled to fix a problem, it is best if the people working on the solution can fairly represent the company's customers.

For that reason, companies that employ a large staff, often have a goal of assembling a diversified workforce. Many ill-advised workers may feel the diversification is due to pressure from forces outside the company. That is a foolish viewpoint. Workplace diversification is strength for a business.

Below are nine positive attitudes that are important for teamwork. Rank them in order from 1 to 9. Use one for your strongest attribute and nine for your weakest attribute. Use each number only once.

Positive attitude	**Rank**
Work well with others	_____
Take pride in team accomplishments	_____
Provide team spirit	_____
Deal with team members openly and honestly	_____
Keeps all agreements, is very trustworthy	_____
Help team members to get to know each other	_____
Good at resolving conflicts between team members	_____
Keep the team leader well informed	_____
Accepts change easily	_____

When working on a team project, remember your strengths and use them; and be aware of your weaker areas and manage them.

EXERCISE PS3

This is a teamwork exercise with no correct answer, as long as your team's answer makes logical and business sense. Arguments could be made for different combinations of answers. In order to pass this exercise you must participate in the team discussion, follow the appointed team leader's rules for running the team respectfully, participate in the team's oral presentation, show interest throughout the team exercise, and demonstrate with your words and personal signals that you are on board with the team leader's final decision. If you are not doing this exercise in a group, and just reading along, think about what you would choose and how you would respond if the team leader went in a different direction.

You work for a very profitable business in the medical research industry. While in the past the company has had some public relations issues in the form of protests; overall the drugs developed by the company has saved tens of thousands of lives.

EXERCISE PS3 (continued)

Past protests have run the gamut from the high price for the company's drugs when they first hit the market, to the use of animals in research, to making the company's drugs more readily available to people in need in poor countries, to not concentrating on developing cures for diseases that are not widespread such as Creutzfeldt-Jakob Disease and Collagen Disorder, to not helping with U.S. unemployment because the company has its production facility overseas.

To help with the bad press, and because the company is a socially conscience enterprise, it has decided to start a working Not for Profit Corporation (a business that does work, not a foundation that gives money to other not for profits). You have been selected as part of team to help decide what area the not for profit should work in, and what three tasks that not for profit should staff up to undertake. The only parameter that senior management has placed on the group is that the not for profit needs to be in an area from one of the recent protests.

Before the team leader is announced, senior management distributes the form that follows and asks each team member to write down his or her initial thoughts, to help start the group discussion. So you fill out the form.

Area for the Not for Profit Corporation (circle one):

A) Helping low income individuals and families in the United States be able to afford new drugs

B) Helping animals

C) Helping people in foreign countries get needed drugs

D) Helping people with rare incurable diseases

E) Helping the local economy

For the area you choose, list three specific tasks the Not for Profit Corporation can perform.

1. _____
   _____
2. _____
   _____
3. _____
   _____

EXERCISE PS3 (continued)

After completing this task, senior management assigns a team leader. The team leader is responsible for choosing the final decision for the area for Not for Profit Corporation and the three tasks that the Not for Profit will undertake. The team leader opens the floor up for discussion …

After the team discussion, the team leader makes the final decision regarding the area and three specific tasks. The team leader then organizes the presentation that will be made to management (instructor) making sure every team member has a role in that presentation.

EXERCISE PS4 (NASA Teamwork Exercise)

There is a fairly well know NASA exercise that is used in employee and classroom teamwork training. Below is the exercise. While there are real answers and they will be presented after the conclusion of the team presentations, you will not be graded on whether or not you get the answers right. However, for classrooms with more than one team, the teams should compete with each other for fun. The team that gets the top three items according to NASA wins the championship. If there is a tie, the team that has the lowest number after adding the ranks of their eight items is the champion.

Like the previous team exercise, in order to pass this exercise you must participate in the team discussion, participate in the team's oral presentation, show interest throughout the team exercise, and demonstrate with your words and personal signals that you are on board with the team's final decisions. **You will be observed throughout the entire exercise including how you react after the real answers are disclosed.** *Remember, this is a presentation being made in the workplace; act accordingly throughout. In addition, you will also be judged on the method the team chooses to select the answers and you must present a logical reason for each item chosen in your answer.*

Scenario:

You are a member of a space crew originally scheduled to rendezvous with a mother ship on the lighted surface of the moon. However, due to mechanical difficulties, your ship was forced to land at a spot some 200 miles from the rendezvous point. During reentry and landing, much of the equipment aboard was damaged and, since survival depends on reaching the mother ship, the most critical items available must be chosen for the 200-mile trip.

What follows are the 15 items left intact and undamaged after landing (continues on next page). As a group you must decide on eight items to take with you. However, if you leave out any of the three most important items according NASA (space agency) you all die.

EXERCISE PS4 (continued)

Get busy you have to be on your way in 30 minutes!

_____ Box of matches
_____ Food concentrate
_____ 50 feet of nylon rope
_____ Parachute silk
_____ Portable heating unit
_____ Two .45 caliber pistols
_____ One case of dehydrated milk
_____ Two 100 lb. tanks of oxygen
_____ Stellar map (map of the stars)
_____ Self-inflating life raft
_____ Magnetic compass
_____ 5 gallons of water
_____ Signal flares
_____ First aid kit, including injection needle
_____ Solar-powered FM receiver-transmitter

Assignment:

Decide on a method for selecting the 8 items that allows everyone's opinion to be heard in the short time frame.

Finalize your list of 8 items. Indicate which three items in your list you believe are NASA's top three items.

When called upon, present your results. Everyone in the group must have a role in the oral presentation. Include the following in your presentation:

> Method used to decide which items to take.
> The 8 items you are taking with your reasoning why.
> The 3 items the group thinks were NASA's top three.

Meeting Supervisors' Expectations

For those of you who have forgotten the definition of congruent, it goes like this: if A is the same size as B; and B is the same size as C; then A has to be the same size as C (or A is congruent to C).

At work I have proved in the section, Workplace Basics, that what's good for the business is good for you (more profits, more job security and more money available for employee salaries). It is the same with your supervisor. What is good for the business is good for your supervisor. Therefore, using the congruent theory, what is good for your supervisor is good for you.

In short, your boss <u>wants</u> you to succeed. Your boss is on your side, even if it does not appear that way to you. The better you perform in your job, the better it is for your boss, and the better it is for the business.

This concept works on many different levels.

- ✓ Your supervisor wants you to succeed because your failures are his/her responsibility.

- ✓ Your supervisor wants you to succeed because if you fail and have to be let go, he/she will have to spend valuable time training a new employee and have to accept a learning curve for that new employee, which will reduce productivity (work output). And it is the supervisor who will be held accountable for any work that is not getting done on time.

- ✓ Your supervisor wants you to succeed because a large part of his/her job is getting you (and your co-workers) to succeed, and if he/she cannot, he/she risks getting a poor performance appraisal and a lower than hoped for raise.

- ✓ These are in addition to the basic premise that the better everyone performs at work, the more profits the business earns, the more secure the supervisor's job is, and the more money available for supervisor salaries.

Workers who believe that their boss is "out to get them", are either wrong, or have to take a look in the mirror. From the first two sections, Workplace Basics and Workplace Skills, you are aware that even if you are excellent in your job functions, that is not enough to be considered an asset (a plus) in the workplace. Workplace behavior is important. In fact, poor workplace behavior is the biggest cause of a worker who is performing his/her work very well, feeling like his/her boss is "out to get him/her." If you are good at your job and an asset in the workplace, your supervisor will like you.

For example, if you do your job extremely well but are at the center of workplace gossip, or constantly complain about the company to co-workers, or show up late often, or date and dump your co-workers, or tell inappropriate jokes, or forget to leave your personal problems at the door; you will have problems with your supervisor. Something like this is usually going on when workers feel that their boss is picking on them. Workers look at one item, completed work. Supervisors look at the big picture. Keep in mind that in addition to managing the work produced by his/her staff; <u>it is a supervisor's job to manage the workplace</u> to ensure that there are no problems, and that everyone feels comfortable enough to produce to the best of their abilities. Again, this is not something your supervisor chooses to do; it is not a power trip; it is part of his/her job. Your supervisor is being paid to ensure that the workplace operates smoothly. If it is not operating smoothly, he/she could receive a poor performance appraisal, and a lower than hoped for pay raise; even if all work is completed on time and is of high quality.

EXERCISE PS5

Answer the following questions, good cause for concern or not really a cause for concern regarding the following situations between a worker and a supervisor. If you answer good cause for concern, please explain why.

A company employs 200 phone representatives. Worker A is one of the top 20 phone representatives (in the top 10%) in terms of job performance. At the lunch for the top phone representatives, Worker A meets, and then starts dating Worker B who was also one of the top 20. After a month Worker A starts dating Worker C who was also one of the top 20 phone representatives. Feeling uncomfortable, Worker B immediately finds a new job and quits the company. While dating Worker C, Worker A is flirting with Worker D, another of the top 20 phone representatives. After their last discussion, Worker A gets the feeling that the Phone Center Supervisor may not be on his or her side.

    Q1. Cause for concern?   Yes   Not really   If yes, why?

Worker A is the highest rated employee in the top rated department in the Company. Worker A is also a Miami Dolphins fan. Worker B is a New York Jets fan. Last night on Monday night football the Dolphins beat the Jets to get into the playoffs while also knocking the Jets out of the playoffs. Worker A comes to work and good naturedly teases Worker B about the Dolphins defeating the Jets. The Supervisor witnesses this short, good natured exchange. Later, Worker A finds out that the Supervisor is a big-time New York Jets fan. Suddenly, Worker A starts worrying if he/she has done damage to his/her career.

    Q2. Cause for concern?   Yes   Not really   If yes, why?

A supervisor's responsibilities on the job are many. You need to understand that your supervisor is being paid to manage and direct you. Supervisors delegate work to his/her staff, not by seniority, not by which worker he/she likes or dislikes. It is not personal. Your supervisor delegates and splits up work by how he/she believes the overall work he/she is responsible for will get completed best. Your supervisor is not only responsible for his/her work, but is responsible for your work, and your co-workers' work as well.

This may mean that some of your co-workers, who are not as efficient as you, seem to get the easier assignments. That is not because your supervisor likes them better and favors them with an easy work day. It is because he/she feels that that is the assignment that best fits their skills. Supervisors look at giving tough assignments to an employee as a badge of honor for that employee, not a punishment. If your supervisor did not think you could handle the tougher work assignment, you would not get it. After all, your supervisor is responsible for that work as well. This also means that you are thought of more highly in the company and will, most likely, get higher raises, and have a better chance at a promotion. By the way, workers exaggerate about salaries and raises. So if a co-worker tells you he/she got a raise and it was higher than your raise, that isn't necessarily the truth.

This should also tell you that your supervisor will get recognition for the work done by his/her staff. That is because a supervisor is suppose to delegate work to his/her staff, and delegate in a way that results in all work being completed on time and all work being of high quality. That is what management is all about (at least one thing management is all about).

I remember doing an analysis of survey data while I worked for the Lower Manhattan Region of the New York Banking Division at Citibank. At the time, doing that analysis was not part of my normal responsibilities. However, Division (no, not Division from Nikita; Division here was the central management staff that presided over all the New York Banking Regions); was not interpreting the data from the surveys correctly, and in doing so, was putting my Region in a worse light than we should have been put in. My supervisor gave me permission to do the special analysis. When the analysis was a big hit with my Regional Business Manager, my boss was right there with me sharing in the praise. He did shine the light on me, but he received credit as well. And I agreed with that. After all, it was his call to let me do the special study.

There is also a side of your supervisor's job responsibilities that his/her staff often does not see. Supervisors are usually responsible for providing written status reports, explaining/implementing new company policies, managing his/her department's budget (money), training and developing his/her staff, managing the workplace, solving problems, analyzing the way work is being done to see if there are better ways to do it, providing support to other supervisors and senior management in the company, and much much more.

Your supervisor has little time, and no motivation to "be on your back for no reason." So again, if you think your supervisor is "out to get you", that will only be true if you are not performing to expected levels of work (quantity and quality), or are a disruptive force in the workplace.

Strategy for Meeting Supervisor's Expectations

There are steps you can take to consistently meet your supervisor's expectations. They are:

1. Accept the fact that your supervisor is control of your work life and treat him/her with respect at all times (when present, and when not there).
2. When told how the workplace operates, such as not taking your break at your work station (could appear to customers that you are available to them, could be disruptive to co-workers, etc.), abide by the rules of the workplace.
3. When given a task to do, do it to the best of your ability, and ask questions if you need help.
4. If you do not complete a task up to your supervisor's standards, take responsibility, do not blame others, and certainly do not blame your boss.
5. Take criticism well. Your supervisor is on your side and is only trying to help you (and his/her work unit), improve. It is not personal.
6. When you do something not up to standard (or wrong), show that you are eager to learn the better (right) way, and make the improvements (corrections) immediately.
7. Always keep your supervisor advised of what is going on, even if the message is not an easy one to tell him/her.
8. Do not get pig-headed. If your supervisor asks you try to do something a different way, give it a try with an all-out effort (not half-heartedly).
9. Always be honest with your supervisor. That includes conversations regarding work, the work environment, and by putting in an honest day's work on the job.
10. If you see something wrong, or if you see a way something can be done better, let your supervisor know, and then be willing to accept your supervisor's decision on how to proceed (do not argue or become stubborn or get an "attitude" because your idea was not used).

Meeting supervisor's expectations worksheet

Please classify the 10 steps listed for meeting supervisor's expectations as comes easy to me; understand it but need to work on it; or don't really see it will have to change my thinking, by placing the number of the statement in the appropriate comment category.

COMMENT	STATEMENT NUMBERS
comes easy to me	
understand it but need to work on it	
don't really see it will have to change my thinking	

Please indicate your plan of action for items in the "understand" or "don't really" categories:

_____
_____
_____
_____
_____
_____
_____
_____
_____
_____
_____
_____

Communicating with Supervisors

Communicating with supervisors is easy. In a way, many of us have been practicing since we were children. As a kid, your mom (and/or dad) was your supervisor.

When your mom told you how to do something, you were expected to do it that way or you risked being punished. The same is true with your supervisor. You have to be able to follow both written and verbal instructions. And not just follow most of the instructions, follow all of them. If at home you didn't follow all the instructions, you may have lost your radio/television/Internet/video game system/Xbox/cell phone rights depending upon the technology of your youth. At work you will get poor performance reviews which will lead to small pay raises (if any), and quite possibly losing your job.

That leads to the next step. If your mom (or dad) gave you instructions, and you didn't understand them and did them anyway and messed it up, it was back to a Stone Age day (no technology for you). You, hopefully, quickly learned to ask questions to avoid having to spend a boring night. It is the same when communicating with your supervisor. If you do not understand something, your supervisor will expect you to ask questions. So ask them to clarify everything you are not certain about regarding instructions (or anything else). Here is a great tip. When asking questions always have a pad of paper to write down what your supervisor is telling you when answering your questions. This is for two reasons. The first is that it will impress your supervisor that you are serious about doing a good job (positive personal signal). The second, and more important reason, is that while supervisors expect to be asked questions when their staff does not understand something; they do not like being asked the same questions over and over again by the same staff members. By writing down the answers, you will have notes to refer to in case you forget, and that could avoid you having to ask the same question to your supervisor a day or two (or week or two) later.

Try to minimize the number of times you need to interrupt your supervisor. Whenever possible, review an unfamiliar task in its entirety in advance of performing it so you can accumulate all of your questions and go to your Supervisor one time instead of a each time a question arises.

When you took a test in school, your mom (and/or dad) expected you to tell them your score on the test. If you got a bad score but told them, your consequences were usually less than if you hid the score from them and they found out on their own later. Worst case was when they got shocked by a bad grade on your report card because they did not know you were doing poorly. It is the same with your supervisor. <u>Good or bad, you will be expected to communicate (verbally, or in writing) the results of your work</u>. This may also include any obstacles you encountered while completing the work, and recommendations on how work procedures can be improved.

I don't know about you, but once in a while I'll call a customer service number to report a problem and a rude customer service phone representative will say something that he/she should not have said, and hang up. How foolish. I just call back because the problem still exists and report the comment and hang up. It is then very easy for that customer service phone representative's supervisor to find out who answered my call. <u>So don't try to avoid difficult situations or tasks</u>. Take them on.

Growing up at home, remember what happened if you answered the phone and forgot to give you mom or dad an important message? Right, you'd get "Flintstoned" again (no technology, back in the Stone Age). The same was true if you gave you mom or dad a message, but left out important details, such as the phone number of the person who called. Well, the same is true with your supervisor. <u>Be sure to write down all messages for your supervisor accurately and completely, and give him/her all messages</u>.

Following this advice to meet your supervisor's expectations, and communicating honestly and directly with your supervisor will go a long way in making you a very valuable employee to your employer.

Oh, and if you were one of those kids who got away with everything at home and avoided being punished, well your trip ends now. Your supervisor doesn't love you; doesn't look at you through the eyes of parent; and doesn't buy into the "my baby can do nothing wrong" crap. Thinking you can fool your supervisor is the perfect way to get fired, and end up jumping from entry level job to entry level job, never seeing your income grow.

EXERCISE PS6

Worker A was suppose to finish a report by the end of the day, however the analysis became more involved than initially thought. At day end, when Worker A goes to the Supervisor's office, the Supervisor is not in. Worker A, decides to go home, come in early and finish the report.

Q1. Is this good or poor communication? Why?

Worker A is given a new task. The new task comes with written instructions. At the very beginning of the instructions there is a contraction. Rather than going to the Supervisor's office to find out what should be done here, Worker A makes a note of the contradiction and continues to read the instructions, finding three more contradictions. Now with all four contradictions written down, Worker A knocks on the Supervisor's door.

Q2. Is this good or poor communication? Why?

Understanding Expectations

One of the best ways to know what is expected of you on the job is to look at your job description. Job descriptions are documents that deal with a job position not an individual. Anyone who works in that job will be expected to perform the functions contained in the job description. This is important because at first you may only be expected to do some of those functions. Later when you are asked to do something new, you may be surprised, or upset, but if you had read your job description you would have known that the new function was part of the responsibilities for the job you were hired to perform.

This happens quite often. Work assignments are shifted; a new supervisor re-arranges how things operate, etc. Many workers feel that they are being asked to do something that they were not hired to do because they never read their job descriptions. Others may believe that the new task is more difficult so they should be paid more money. Usually, there was always a chance that these new, more difficult, work assignments were going to come their way. Depending upon the needs and staff size of the company, you may be called on to perform all or some of the tasks required of the job for which you were hired. Read your job description.

By the way, job descriptions can change. As new tasks, functions, products, technology, etc. are introduced into your workplace, job descriptions are revised to account for the new work. So you are not only hired to perform the tasks in the job description at the time you were hired; but to perform the tasks in your job description as it changes over time.

Performance Appraisals

Obtaining feedback on how well you are performing your job is a good thing, not a bad thing. One of the responsibilities of your supervisor is to generate a performance appraisal on you. How much money you get for a raise and your opportunities for a promotion to a job with more responsibility and more money are centered on your performance appraisal. Therefore, do not wait until your formal performance appraisal to see how well your supervisor thinks you are performing in your job. By obtaining feedback prior to your official appraisal, you will have time to correct issues before it becomes written into the records.

To do this, however, you have to be able to take criticism. If your supervisor tells you where you need improvement, he/she is doing you a favor. Yes, the criticism is a favor your supervisor is doing for you. By telling it to you in advance you can improve your job performance. If you do not get the criticism in advance, it will just come out anyway during the official performance appraisal.

Also keep this in mind. If your supervisor is not criticizing you, that means one of two things. It either means that your supervisor thinks you are perfect (congrats on that!), or that your supervisor believes that telling you what is wrong is meaningless because you are doing the best you can and cannot improve your performance (bummer!).

So you need to look at criticism the right way. That you are not the perfect employee (who is), and your supervisor believes in you (otherwise he/she won't bother to criticize you).

Personal performance appraisal pledge worksheet

If I have not had formal feedback from my supervisor during the last 6 months, I will ask my supervisor how well I am performing my job. Please initial _____

When my supervisor criticizes me, I understand it is to help me and I will not react poorly to that criticism. Please initial _____

After receiving criticism from my supervisor, I will generate a plan to improve my performance. Please initial _____

If I cannot think of a plan or need help determining how to improve my performance, I will ask my supervisor for his or her input or suggestions. Please initial _____

Ability to Handle Change

In many businesses, management and workplace procedures change often. You need to be able to adapt to these changes smoothly and without complaining. Remember, the goal for change is to improve the businesses profits, so that everyone can remain employed. Sometimes, however, there is a negative impact in the short run to get the long term benefit. In the NFL, a team may move away from a middle of the road veteran quarterback and insert a rookie with more long term potential. Often that leads to a worse record in year one (than if the team stayed with the middle of the road veteran), but bigger rewards down the line after the rookie gains experience and realizes his potential.

Therefore, do not get caught up in the idea that there is only one correct way to accomplish your tasks and to run your workplace; or that there is only one person who can manage you or your department.

If after giving new procedures time to see if they will work, you believe they are ineffective (not because it results in more or harder work for you, but that it is causing problems in the workplace or for customers); talk to your supervisor and explain why you believe the new procedures are causing problems. The key is talk, not argue. After getting your day in court, allow your supervisor to make his or her decision, and accept what he or she decides. In any event, embrace change, do not resist change.

Ability to Handle Stress

Many work environments are all about deadlines and employee productivity. Accept this as a fact, not a power trip from a power-hungry boss, or management trying to make life difficult for its employees. Deadlines and productivity measurements (used to track whether or not deadlines are on track to be met), are set to ensure that the company's customers remain satisfied and continue to do business with the company; or to keep costs in check. In either case the result is more profitability for the business which keeps everyone employed.

However, deadline-drive workplaces, at times, result in a hectic, stressful work environment. You need to be able to adapt. Most likely, the company you work for has been in business for awhile. Therefore, others have been able to meet the demands of the job, and thrive in the work environment. Look around you; I'm sure some of your current co-workers fit into that category. So if others have been able to adapt and succeed, you can too.

Business Basics

Since your ability to live your life and meet your life goals are tied very closely to the business for which you work; I thought it would be a good idea to write briefly about some basic business concepts. These are functions that most businesses undertake, either formally or informally.

Business Plan

A business plan is a living, breathing document that needs to be researched and written before a business starts. It contains strategies the business will follow and has projections for what it will cost the business to operate.

Not having a business plan is one of the main reasons businesses fail. Without a plan, it is difficult to know if the business is performing as expected, better than expected, or worse than expected.

The business plans I write for clients have the following sections:

1. Executive Summary
2. Industry – Historical Analysis
3. Industry – Current Trends
4. Industry - Conclusion
5. Strategic Plan
6. Marketing Plan
7. Management & Organization
8. Finances
9. Risks
10. Supporting Documents

The purposes of a business plan are:

- To look at the feasibility of establishing the business in the first place
- To set initial strategies so that management can track how the business is performing, so that, if needed, changes can be made in a timely manner
- To help the business owner determine his or her business strengths and weaknesses
- To get funding, whether a loan or an investor

Below is a list of common reasons why businesses fail. Some of the items on the list may help you better understand why management chooses to act as it does.

- No business plan
- Poor management
- No strategic planning process (a continuation of the business plan process)
- Undercapitalization (not enough money)
- Poor cash flow (money on hand to pay bills when they are due)
- Ineffective or nonexistent marketing
- Not knowing what competitors are doing
- Poor customer service
- The owner being a friend, not a boss to the employees
- Uncontrolled growth

Strategic Planning

Strategic planning is a four step process.

Step one is to generate a baseline strategy. SWOT analysis (business' strengths, weaknesses, opportunities, and threats) is a common tool to use for step one.

Step two is to develop a plan to:

- take advantage of/utilize strengths
- overcome/eliminate weaknesses
- find/capitalize on opportunities
- minimize/avoid/neutralize threats

A common process that is used to develop this plan is to generate a list of objectives, strategies, tactics and goals.

- Objectives are what you are trying to accomplish
- Strategies are the processes that will be implemented to accomplish the objectives
- Tactics are the specific steps that are needed to be done within each strategy
- Goals are specifics that need to be met to be assured of the success of the undertaking; without goals there would be no way to know if the strategies are accomplishing the objectives

Step three is to assign the tactics, with associated goals, to specific employees. Many times a tactic can involve multiple tasks. It is when these tasks are assigned to different people that team leaders are often required to help coordinate all the tasks. Sometimes that team leader can be a supervisor, sometimes a co-worker. Meeting the goals is often the basis for productivity and quality and timeliness measurements for individual workers and for work units, departments or the company as a whole.

Step four is to periodically review the progress and strategies and make adjustments and changes as needed.

Marketing

There are four main components to marketing:

- Price – this refers to the pricing strategy used by a business.
- Product – this refers to the full offering, not just the products and /or services sold to customers. For example: warranties, excellent customer service, money back guarantee, etc.
- Promotion – this refers to the tools used to inform customers and potential customers about the company's product and/or services. Promotion includes everything from commercials, to brochures, to web sites, to billboards, to blogs, to press releases, and more.
- Distribution – this refers to the methods and places where a company's products and services are delivered to its customers.

Sales

Sales drive businesses. Without sales, the business would not earn revenue, and therefore, would close. There are many different sales techniques and businesses often strategize on the best sales methods, sales approaches, and sales scripts to maximize closing sales. If you are in a sales position, and have your own approach, learn and try the company way first. You may pleasantly surprised at how well the company's sales process works.

A common phrase at many businesses is that everyone is a salesperson. What this means is that everyone will find him or herself in a position where they meet or know someone who could use their company's products or services. Therefore, be prepared. That means, at a minimum, have the contact information for someone in the company you can refer that person to.

However, since your economic health is tied to the success of the company you work for, you could be a little more proactive. This doesn't mean that you should aggressively go after sales. However, well informed entrepreneurs and sales people have what is called an elevator pitch.

An elevator pitch:

- Opens with a hook in the form of a statement or question that piques interest
- Consists of about 175 to 225 words that can be said in about 30 seconds
- Is spoken with passion and energy
- Ends by asking for something (a business card, a referral, an appointment)

You could development a stock answer to the question, "What do you do for a living?" that has a little bit of a sales twist. You can accomplish this by incorporating a little bit about the company's product and services into your answer, and conclude with, "I can give you the name and number of someone in the company who can help you if you like."

If you find out that the person you gave the contact information to does indeed call the company, don't be shy about informing your supervisor that it was you who pointed that customer to the sales department (or whoever's contact information you gave to the person with whom you were speaking).

EXERCISE PS7

Answer the following questions true or false

Q1. A business plan is important for all businesses.

Q2. If someone asks you about your company and job you should never bring up what your company sells and never give that person contact information for someone in your company.

Q3. Businesses need to goals so that they can determine whether or not their business strategies are working. This may mean measuring how much work you complete since the goals could be related to work completed.

Q4. If you and your fellow co-workers treat customers poorly, that could lead to the business failing.

Q5. As long as they are making some money on each product, it doesn't matter what price the company decides to charge on each product; profit is profit there is no strategy to setting prices.

What if You Were the Boss

EXERCISE PS8

This whole chapter is an exercise. Please read what the follows and perform the exercise at the conclusion of the write-up.

Congratulations! You have just been promoted to Team Leader. Your Manager, Stuart Advocate, calls you into his office and has the following to say:

"As you know, we had to let go of Steve Oneyear. While production is okay there are too many signs that the workplace is deteriorating and we may lose our best workers. Since you have been taking management courses at night, I have decided to give you an opportunity to see if you can handle the job. In addition to your course work, your excellent work record in terms of job performance and attendance, and your ability to get along with your co-workers were major factors in my decision to offer you this opportunity. In fact, we are counting on your knowledge of your co-workers to fix the current problem. I suggest that you develop a plan of action for each worker to follow to ensure that the workplace will run smoothly so we can keep our best workers. Oh, by the way, production is fine, but not optimal. So while working on the plans of action, include recommendations for training assistance for each worker to help him or her become more productive in their job. If you develop a solid plan of action, and I see some improvement in 90 days, your promotion will become permanent. A 15% pay raise, the potential for bonuses and an additional paid week's vacation will come with the permanent promotion."

As you return to your work station you start thinking about the first five workers for whom you will develop a plan of action. You know them very well. What follows are your thoughts on these five employees:

Mike Dee

Mike is a very productive employee. He is also very well liked. Mike has a great sense of humor although at times Mike gets into arguments regarding some of his jokes. However, Mike does have a unifying effect on the team. He arranges and invites everyone out as a group to eat dinner once a month, and has gone to lunch with everyone in the group. Mike also takes pride in his work and the work for the unit as a whole; and his pride is contagious.

Mike does, at times, come in late to work, but has never missed a deadline. However, while Mike's numbers on his reports are always accurate, he does not always highlight the key trends in his written analysis, and does not use charts and graphs in the report to help the reader visualize the trends easily. Therefore, Mr. Oneyear was constantly re-writing Mike's analysis, which may or may not have been the cause for some delays in other areas under Mr. Oneyear's control.

Josephina Prof

Josephina is the most productive employee on the team. She is single and attractive. While she does not go out of her way to socialize at work, there are often co-workers, almost always men, stopping by her desk trying to get into long conversations with her. She always tries to get rid of them quickly, so she can get back to work, but that isn't always successful. Two weeks ago, Josephina was called into Mr. Oneyear's office. Since then, she hardly even acknowledges her co-workers when they walk by, let alone talks to them. Because of the way Josephina is now treating her co-workers, you have overheard gossip "that Josephina now believes she's too good for the rest of us." In fact, one of them pointed out that "the only person Josephina has ever gone to lunch with is Mike Dee." A second chipped in, "Yeah, but that was only when she wasn't mad at him over one of his jokes." You happen to know she does go to lunch with co-workers other than Mike, since you had lunch with her just last week. Another rumor going around the office is that Josephina is looking for another job. You have a gut feeling that this one is true. Too bad you think; you would consider promoting her to your old job if she knew word processing.

Larry Lip

Larry is a good worker, but Larry is a party animal away from work. While Larry shows up on time and never calls in sick, it often takes him longer than his co-workers to get into his work assignments. His productivity is okay, but you know it could be better. Also, at times, it seems as though Larry just rolls out of bed and shows up for work. You know this because Larry has to work in close proximity to his co-workers and many have commented that Larry is wearing the same clothes as he was wearing the prior day. You can relate. Boy, how you hate working with Larry on those days. It's a challenge to the senses. In fact, you often thought about calling in sick on days where you were scheduled to work with Larry, but, of course you never did. But you begin to wonder if others had the same thought and actually do call in sick from time to time when scheduled to work with Larry. In addition, you are anticipating a problem with Larry. He has expressed a desire to advance in the company and has been taking the same management courses as you. You just know he will be disappointed that he didn't get the opportunity afforded you. Larry has also expressed interest in becoming Frankie Cash's back-up. However, Mr. Oneyear turned down his request to attend trade school because Larry would have to miss a half a day of work once a week for eight weeks to complete the training.

Jeannine Comeback

Jeannine is a new employee. She is married and has school-aged children at home. She demonstrates excellent potential and is fitting in well with the team. You have noticed that Jeannine does need to improve her computer skills to improve her overall job productivity. Jeannine was trained by Mr. Oneyear and often talked about how brilliant he was and how he knew the best way to do everything. Jeannine is also someone who writes down every step in a work procedure and performs those procedures while continually looking at her notes. You know you are going to make changes in how some of the tasks she just learned will be performed. You wonder if she will resist your changes. Another thing you noticed is that Jeannine is constantly going to the supply cabinet for new supplies. She seems to go through items such as pens, pencils, pads of paper, and scotch tape faster than anyone else. She is even on her second calculator and third pair of scissors. Knowing that if you get the promotion that you will be in charge of the budget, and therefore, held accountable for supplies, you wonder what's up with that.

Frankie Cash

Frankie has a highly specialized job and gets paid very well for his work. He does his work flawlessly. Due to the nature of his work, Frankie is the only worker required to wear safety equipment. Frankie often comments that he feels self-conscious being the only person walking around with gloves and a helmet. You have noticed that when Mr. Oneyear is not around, Frankie often worked without wearing his helmet. Frankie's skill is unique and there is no one else in the company who can perform his job. Mr. Oneyear, realizing this, often looked the other way when Frankie broke the rules. In fact, one time when Mr. Oneyear talked to Mike about coming in late in front of everybody in the room, Mike responded, "Hey, you don't get on Frankie when he comes in a half hour late so don't get on my back for coming in ten minutes late." Frankie is also very set in his ways and is not shy about speaking his mind on any topic, no matter who is around, no matter whether bringing up an inappropriate for the workplace topic from out of nowhere, or whether inviting himself into a private discussion. Often, after hearing Frankie's comments, you just shale your head and cannot believe the insensitive things Frankie says. And Frankie doesn't limit his comments to co-workers. On a couple of occasions he entered into uncomfortable conversations with customers. And Frankie's job contains no customer contact component. Frankie is also in the middle of the group that hangs around Josephina's desk.

EXERCISE PS8

Use the forms starting on the next page to record your detailed plan of action and training needs, for each employee. There is also a form to use for the topics you will cover in your first group meeting with these five employees (address the management change; discuss any items from the write-ups you believe should be brought up to the group). For the group meeting include the topic and a brief statement regarding the specifics you will cover on those topics.

Employee: Mike Dee

Training Plan

Plan of Action (what will you cover in your one-on-one meeting with Mike Dee)

Employee: Josephina Prof

Training Plan

Plan of Action (what will you cover in your one-on-one meeting with Josephina Prof)

Employee: Larry Lip

Training Plan

Plan of Action (what will you cover in your one-on-one meeting with Larry Lip)

Employee: Jeannine Comeback

Training Plan

Plan of Action (what will you cover in your one-on-one meeting with Jeannine Comeback)

Employee: Frankie Cash

Training Plan

Plan of Action (what will you cover in your one-on-one meeting with Frankie Cash)

Topics to cover in your first group meeting (a meeting with all 5 employees in attendance). Include topics and brief write-up on the specifics to cover for each topic.

CUSTOMER SERVICE

PART I

Customer Service Practices

Focusing on the Customer

I don't know about you, but before sitting down to start the learning process, I like to eat a good meal. So give me a sec while I call this great burger joint around the corner and order some food. Thanks.

I'm back. Developing good customer service skills is one of the most important things you can do to increase your value to your employer. But before you hone your customer service skills, understanding what constitutes good customer service practices, and why those practices are important to your employer, is vital.

Hey, time to pick up my food. Be right back (I know from the section *People Skills* that if I wrote "BRB" it would be wrong in a business environment).

Back again, and I can't wait to eat my burger and fries. Hey wait, they forgot the fries. You know; great food or not, I'm angry. From now on I think I'll get a pizza instead.

Let me call them and give them a piece of my mind. Want to listen to my call? Sure, why not.

"Hello, great burger joint around the corner, this is Jay, I just picked up my order and you forgot my fries." <great burger joint employee is responding> "No, I can't run back over now to pick them up, I've already wasted enough of my readers time!" <great burger joint employee is responding> "Let me get this straight, so next time I order I will not only get a free side of fries, but a free appetizer as well. Cool." <great burger employee is responding> "No problem, see you soon. Bye."

This example shows two things about customer service. The first is that bad customer service can cost businesses money. After not receiving my fries, I was ready to get pizza instead of burgers from now on, and even if that didn't last forever, it certainly would cost the great burger joint around the corner some sales. From *Workplace Basics*, we know how important it is that the business you work for makes profits, so bad service leads to less money available for businesses to pay its employees.

The second is that if a customer has a problem, and that problem is satisfied quickly and satisfactorily, the business will, more often then not, not lose that customer. So having employees with good customer service problem-solving skills is very important to businesses. In this case, the apology (implied before I said "no problem") and the free appetizer ensured that I continued ordering from the great burger joint around the corner rather than switching to pizza.

One last, important note is that as an employee you can suggest solutions to customer problems that involve giving away merchandise (e.g. giving away a free appetizer), but you cannot make your own independent decisions to do so. Follow the company policies. In this case, if you independently decided to give a free appetizer, and that was against company policy, it would be unethical and that comes with potential consequences (fired, looked at as theft) even if done in what you feel is the best interests of the business (circumstances are irrelevant).

Good and bad customer experience worksheet

Look at your life as an example, after all when not at work, you are a customer.

Think of a situation where you experienced **bad** customer service:

What happened?

_____
_____
_____

How was it handled?

_____
_____
_____

How did you feel about it?

_____
_____
_____

What was the result?

_____
_____
_____

Would you deal with that party again?   Yes   No

Think of a situation where you experienced **good** customer service:

What happened?

_____

_____

_____

How was it handled?

_____

_____

_____

How did you feel about it?

_____

_____

_____

What was the result?

_____

_____

_____

Would you deal with that party again?   Yes   No

Now, a final question; is there anything that the business in the first example could have done to make the situation better; thus keeping you as a customer? If yes, what could the business have done? If no; why not?

_____

_____

_____

Customer focus

Since satisfying customers is a key to a business earning good profits, everyone who works for the business needs to understand what service levels will satisfy their customers, and what levels of service their customers expect.

When a business gets all of its employees (including you) understanding this, that company is a customer-focused company and has a very good chance of being profitable, which keeps everybody who works for the company employed.

Therefore, to keep your job, you need to be customer-focused.

Notice that I said to be customer focused a company needed to understand what its customers want and expect, <u>not</u> that it always had to do what its customers want or expect.

That is because there is always a trade-off between what customers want and the cost for a company providing everything that a customer wants. For example, I would love it of my cable company had a combination service person/tech assigned just to me, so whenever I called I would get through immediately and not have to listen to elevator music or sale pitches for upcoming pay-per-view events while on hold. Also, if I was having a problem, or moving, I would not have to put aside a whole day because the company said a tech would be coming to my house between noon and six at night. I would love to be able to say, meet me at my house at five in the evening.

However, it would cost the cable company too much money to provide a service person/tech for every customer. Besides, while that is what every customer would like, it is not what every customer expects. Customers expect a wait time on calls and expect a time frame for appointments. So it is up to the management at the cable company to decide what those wait times and time frames will be so that the <u>majority</u> of its customers will stay with the cable company (e.g. not switch to satellite), at a cost where the cable company is making profits (thereby keeping everybody employed).

So understand that every employer is faced with this trade-off decision. In this case, it is likely that shorter wait times and shorter appointment time frames would result in more customers staying with the company. However, at what cost? If the cable company has to hire ten more phone representatives to shorten the wait time on the phone, those costs will have to be made up in money earned from customer retention and/or higher fees charged to customers for the better service.

Customer service is vital to the success of a business, but every company has to perform an analysis on how much to spend on customer service based on the money earned by the company on its service delivery. This makes service delivery that doesn't cost the company anything (such as treating customers with respect, using a warm and friendly greeting, etc.) extremely valuable. Therefore, if you are an employee who can deliver this "free" superior customer service, you become extremely valuable.

Customer perceptions

A segment of customer focus that often gets ignored is erroneous customer perceptions. If the customers believe there are problems, it doesn't matter if those problems are real or perceived, they must be addressed. Only the resolution to those problems differ; not the effort in solving the customer issues. Very often, the solution to a customer perception issue is consumer education.

What follows is a true case study from the 1980's. Only the names have been changed to protect the innocent "ba; ba-ba; ba; (slight pause) baammm" (think *Dragnet* theme music)

Case study

Metrobank was one of the largest banks in the New York City marketplace. With high volumes of customers per branch, particularly during lunch time, Metrobank management was concerned that their customers may not be experiencing levels of service that was satisfactory to them, in order to keep them as long-term customers.

In order to get an understanding of how their customers felt about the service being provided by Metrobank branches, they surveyed a statistically significant portion of their customer base, concentrating on customers that had visited a branch within the last 30 days (of the survey date).

While they found some positives, they also uncovered some complaints. The most predominant ones were:

- Customers were not happy with the line waits at the branches, particularly at the teller windows. They indicated that the average line wait was about 15 minutes and indicated that a line wait of about 9 minutes would be acceptable.

- Customers felt that the tellers were often busy doing work other than helping customers, and that they should prioritize their time better, particularly when they see a long line wait during lunch hours. They based their responses on the fact that (1) they would often see the tellers at teller stations either doing work other than helping customers (e.g. talking on the phone) or taking care of personal business (e.g. eating lunch) and (2) that there were often many unmanned teller stations.

In order to study the situation further, Metrobank implemented a shopping program to determine what the tellers were actually doing and performed time and motion studies to dimension the teller line wait problem.

What they found was:

- Tellers were very productive in their jobs; they spent almost no time taking care of personal business. In fact, they often ate lunch at their work stations so they could help serve customers during their lunch hour.

- Individuals making phones calls from their teller work station was almost always work related. Sometimes they were even branch customer service reps (not tellers) that were working with a customer on a problem at a teller station to solve a customer issue and perform a transaction so that customers would not have to wait on a second line.

- On average, teller line waits were about 8 minutes not 15 minutes as indicated by the customers. In fact, only about 5% of all teller line waits were at or in excess of 15 minutes; and only about 10% were in excess of 9 minutes.

However, while the actual news was good, there was still a lot of customer dissatisfaction that, through prior experience, represented a great risk to Metrobank in terms of losing customers.

Case study worksheet

If you were Metrobank management, given that the problems appeared to be more perception than reality, would you do something to solve this problem?

Yes   No

If yes, what are some solutions you would recommend?   If no, why wouldn't you do anything?

_____
_____
_____
_____
_____
_____
_____
_____
_____
_____
_____
_____
_____
_____
_____
_____
_____
_____
_____
_____
_____
_____
_____
_____
_____
_____
_____
_____
_____
_____

Intentionally left blank so that you must turn the page to see what actually happened.

The main three solutions implemented by Metrobank were:

- Metrobank invested in automated line wait equipment for every branch with even a hint of a traffic problem. The line wait equipment: (1) accurately calculated customer line waits at teller stations so the bank had a warning system in place in case line wait got out of hand (2) indicated the time of day and an approximate line wait to everyone as the entered the roped off teller line wait section thus ensuring that individuals were more accurately attuned to actual teller line waits and (3) had a clock that the customers looked straight at as they were in position to be called as the next customer to a teller station.

- Metrobank put up curtains in all teller work stations. Now, when a customer service representative or teller was working on the phone or if a teller was eating lunch at his/her station so he/she could help out during his/her off-time, they could close the curtains so that the customers could not see what he/she was doing. In addition, large branches having more work stations than would ever be used; could close the curtains at those stations so the branch did not look as if it had a lot of tellers missing all the time.

- To ensure that teller line wait remained in the satisfactory range for its customers, Metrobank initiated a floating teller pool (tellers worked at different branches each day depending upon where they were needed) to help with any real issues caused by teller absences or specific customer traffic patterns based on the day of the week or day of the month (for example a major employer in the area may have pay days on the 15th and 30th so there was a lot of traffic in that branch that day). Many of the floating tellers were part time workers who only worked four hours a day from 11:00 to 3:00 to cover lunch time hours.

- In addition, Metrobank included a note on all customers' bank statements telling them that they listened to their complaints and have made changes in the branches to help reduce teller line wait.

Follow-up customer research indicated that the measures implemented by Metrobank helped solve customer dissatisfaction. The measures employed by Metrbank solved the customer perception issue.

Your customer focus worksheet

This exercise can be done two ways. The first is to determine your personal, customer focus. The second is to determine the business you work for's customer focus. For option one, answer the questions for yourself. For option number two, answer the questions for your employer.

What follows are 30 items. The scale for this exercise is:

3 = most important
2 = next most important
1 = least important

There are 30 statements that follow. Give 10 items a "3", ten items a "2" and ten items a "1". I know this will be tough, that you may feel all 30 items are "most important." However, performing this exercise will show you, when push comes to shove, the service areas that you (or your employer) prioritize. There is a method to this madness and the 30 items will be grouped into categories later to help define your service priorities.

Question #	Rating	Service item
1.	_____	Actively seek out customer perception of the product/service provided
2.	_____	Keep complete and accurate records
3.	_____	Respond to a customer request the first time

4.	_____	Review fulfillment of customer requirements as originally stated by the customer
5.	_____	Meet all customer deadlines
6.	_____	Respond to incoming customer communications immediately, with at least an acknowledgment of receipt of said communication
7.	_____	Tell the customer what you can do for them, not what you can't do for them
8.	_____	Know what your company standards are for delivering customer service
9.	_____	Work longer hours when needed to solve customer problems
10.	_____	Constantly stay in touch with customers, not just when trying to make a sale or dealing with a customer question or problem
11.	_____	Proactively offer a response to a customer need or problem (rather than waiting to be asked)
12.	_____	Ask for customer input when developing or improving products or services
13.	_____	Able to solve customer problems without always having to ask supervisors for help
14.	_____	Listen intently to customers' requirements
15.	_____	Ask customers for feedback on their customer service experience with the company
16.	_____	Develop and implement vehicles to monitor customer satisfaction
17.	_____	Analyze customer complaints or problems, and learn from those issues
18.	_____	Give high priority to quality in product, service, and customer service

19.	_____	Know what the company is trying to achieve for its customers
20.	_____	Know what the company's business objectives are
21.	_____	Provide the same high level of service to other employees as you do to your customers
22.	_____	Stride to have shorter resolution times to customer issues
23.	_____	Have a positive attitude, and be open to customer comments, good and bad
24.	_____	Be polite at all times to internal and external customers
25.	_____	Strive to be error-free
26.	_____	Provide service that exceeds customer expectations
27.	_____	React with a positive attitude to customer complaints
28.	_____	Are open to change when that change will help customers
29.	_____	Looks at the company's product and service delivery from the customer's point of view
30.	_____	Know how well you are performing in terms of the company's expectations so that you can improve your service delivery when needed

Now write your results in the table on the next page (some questions will be in more than one category).

Question	A	B	C	D	E
1	xxx	xxx	xxx	xxx	
2	xxx	xxx	xxx	xxx	
3	xxx	xxx	xxx	xxx	
4	xxx	xxx	xxx	xxx	
5	xxx	xxx	xxx	xxx	
6	xxx				xxx
7	xxx	xxx	xxx	xxx	
8	xxx				xxx
9	xxx	xxx	xxx	xxx	
10	xxx	xxx	xxx	xxx	
11		xxx	xxx		xxx
12		xxx	xxx	xxx	xxx
13	xxx	xxx	xxx	xxx	
14	xxx	xxx	xxx	xxx	
15	xxx	xxx	xxx	xxx	
16	xxx	xxx	xxx	xxx	
17	xxx	xxx	xxx	xxx	
18	xxx	xxx	xxx	xxx	
19	xxx	xxx	xxx	xxx	
20	xxx	xxx	xxx	xxx	
21	xxx	xxx	xxx	xxx	
22	xxx	xxx	xxx	xxx	
23	xxx	xxx	xxx	xxx	
24	xxx	xxx	xxx	xxx	
25	xxx	xxx	xxx	xxx	
26	xxx				xxx
27	xxx				xxx
28	xxx				xxx
29				xxx	xxx
30	xxx	xxx	xxx	xxx	

Add up the totals for each column and record the results in the table below:

Column	Total*	Factor	Result**
A		3	
B		5	
C		5	
D		6	
E		22	

*add up the numbers (1, 2, or 3) in each column (A,B,C,D, E)

** calculate the result by dividing the Total (from *) by the Factor
(for example if the Total for A is 6, then divide 6 by 3 and the result is 2; all results should be between 1 and 3)

Next write the results into the diagram below:

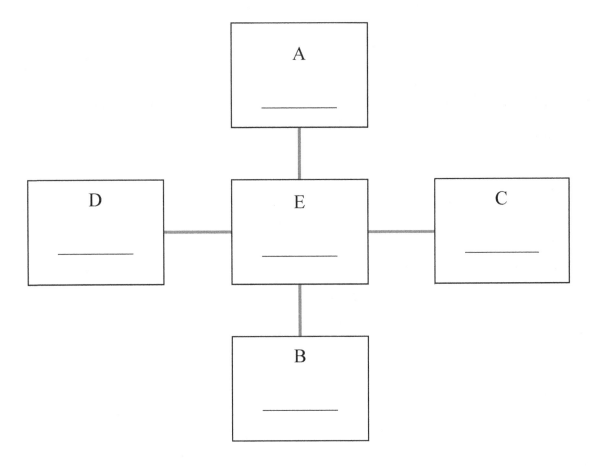

Explanation of the chart designations (areas of customer focus)

- Focusing on products and services (A)
- Delivering quality (B)
- Building the positives (C)
- Dealing with the negatives (D)
- Across the board (E)

Next copy the numbers from the chart above to the chart on the next page and you will know your (or your employers) customer service focus. The highest numbers are your areas of main focus. Your (or your company's) mission is to be very aware of situations that arise in the areas that are <u>not</u> your main focus, since performing well in those situations may not come as naturally for you (or your employer).

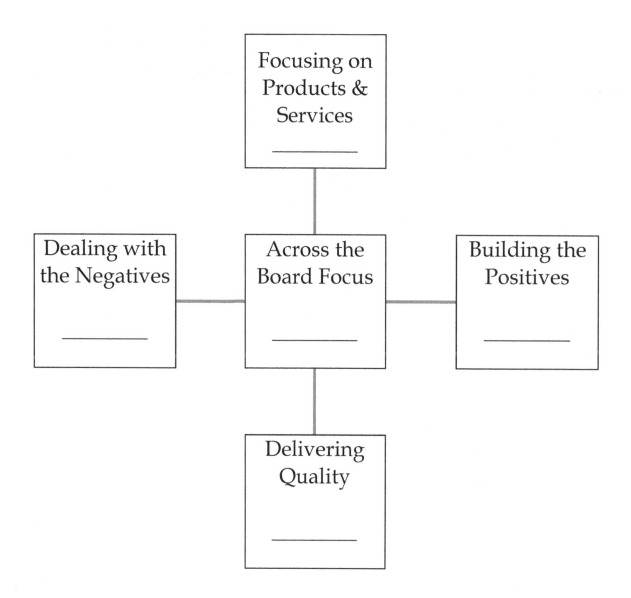

Areas of customer focus

Focusing on products and services includes:

- Good product design
- Manufactured products are up to spec (quality control)
- Developing a comprehensive package of services
- Product/service continues to meet the needs of the marketplace (solicit customer comments about the product/service)
- Make changes to the product/service to meet changing needs of marketplace

Delivering quality includes:

- No product defects
- High quality product/service

- Meet all deadlines
- Streamline processes

Building the positives includes:

- Developing customer relationships
- Being responsive to customers' needs
- Anticipating customer needs
- Professional appearance and communication

Dealing with the negatives includes:

- Solving customer problems quickly and effectively
- Correcting errors
- Rebuilding customer trust after problems/errors occur
- Keeping a cool and professional head when dealing with angry, frustrated and worried customers

Across the board includes:

- Has an impact on all four of these service areas.

EXERCISE CS2

Please answer the area of customer focus each situation represents (focusing on products and services; delivering quality, building the positives, dealing with the negatives)

Q1. Harvey is a top notch attorney and always provides the very best defense for his clients.

Q2. Donna is very intuitive when it comes to what the law firms clients need. She is always one step ahead of everyone.

Q3. Louis, who is great with numbers, takes it upon himself to review the law firm's accounting reports. And it's a good thing since he often finds and corrects errors.

Q4. Mike, who is a very quick study due to his excellent recall skills, has just added copyright law to the firm's service offerings.

Q5. Rachel writes legal briefs and prides herself on never having any errors and always filing her briefs on time.

Identifying Your Customer

One of the least understood concepts of customer service by employees is that their fellow co-workers can be their customers as well as the people who purchase the company's products and/or services.

In a restaurant, the waiter/waitress is the worker who deals directly with the customers. A large portion of his/her income is based on tips. So it is easy to understand how providing exceptional service leads to higher earnings (more tips) for the waiter/waitress. However, the dining experience for the customers is not controlled entirely by the waiter/waitress. If the chef is slow in preparing food, if the restaurant manager overbooked the restaurant so a customer with reservations had to wait before being seated, if the bus-person cleared half the table while others were still eating, or if the food is bad, the waiter/waitress will get lower tips even if he/she does his/her job exceptionally.

In this case the waiter/waitress is a customer for the chef, manager, and bus-person. These workers need to treat the waiter/waitress in the same manner that they would treat the customers of the restaurant. They need to understand the needs and expectations of the waiter/waitress and provide service to the levels established by management. While being an excellent cook is obviously part of a chef's job, so is satisfying his/her customers, which includes both the customer eating his/her food <u>and</u> the person serving the food to the customers.

Let's look at another example. Jane Doe works in the accounting department, entering adjustments to clients' accounts. John Ray is a telephone customer service representative. If Jane makes a mistake in data entry, it is John who will receive an angry call from the customer. So John Ray (telephone representative) is a customer of Jane Doe's (accounting), and what Jane Doe in accounting does, has an impact on customer satisfaction, even though she never deals directly with customers.

Everyone's job has an impact on customers and co-workers. Your goal needs to be to satisfy both the external customers (people who purchase the company's products) and internal customers (co-workers who rely on your work).

Know your customers

Whether internal or external, understanding your customers' needs goes a long way towards improving your ability to satisfy those customers. One method to help you understand your customers' mindsets is to ask and answer a set of simple questions.

1. What products and services, and support, do your various customers need?

2. When do your various customers need their products and service delivered? (This helps set work schedules and work task priorities.)

3. Where do you need to provide the products or services you provide to your various customers?

4. How do your various customers use the products and services you provide to them?

5. Why do your various customers use or need the products and services you provide?

6. The interconnectivity between "the how" and "the why" helps you identify how satisfied your customers will be with your products and services; and ensures that your products and services continue to meet your various customers' needs.

7. Who is the decision-maker for purchasing your products and services, and for determining how satisfactorily your product or service meets your various customers' needs (e.g. determining the quality of the product or service delivered to the customer)?

8. How much are your various customers willing to pay for the products and services you provide? How often do your various customers use your products and services? How much of your products and services do your various customers use?

EXERCISE CS4

Answer the 8 questions for know your customer for the following customer:

You work for a printing company and your customer is a law firm that has a standing order for their law firm's custom stationary to be delivered to them by your company every Wednesday. The order is 10,000 pieces and they pay $1,500 for the stationary that uses top shelf paper. The order is dropped off between 9:00 AM and 9:30 AM and is reviewed by the manager of Purchasing Department who signs off on the delivery.

Q1. What product and services are used by your customer?
Q2. When do they need the products and services delivered?
Q3. Where do your customers receive their products?
Q4. How do your customers use your products?
Q5. Why do your customers need this product?
Q6. What is the interconnectivity between the how and the why? (bonus question)
Q7. Who determines if your product meets your customer's standards?
Q8. How much of the product do they use and how much do they spend on the product?

Your job's impact on customers

It has been estimated that on average, about 23% of all employees deal directly with external customers, but on average 75% contribute to the customer's experience while never interacting directly with the customer. So even if you never interact with external customers directly in your job, there is an excellent chance that your work still directly impacts your company's customers' experience, good or bad, with your employer.

Some examples:

- The employee who writes the instructions for putting together or using a product

- The manager who hires and trains customer service representatives

- The employee who codes the web site customers use to conduct business with the company

- The employee who decides the price to charge for the company's products and services

- The manager who sets the policy for returns

- The manager who decides the pay levels within the company (dictates employee turnover and employee skill level which directly impacts the experience and knowledge of the employees that customers interact with)

- The manager who determines the marketing budget and strategy (this can determine if customers even find the company to be able to use a product or service that they need or would enjoy)

- And many, many, more

Service Measurements

Now that we all know that customer service, to both internal and external customers, is vital to everyone keeping their jobs, how does a company know if the service that is being provided is good enough to keep (and grow) the business' customer base?

The answer is by using service measurements, both from a department and company perspective, and from an individual perspective.

Many companies have quality and timeliness indicators. These include timeframes and the percentage of work that meets that time frame. For example, a company may have an indicator that states that 95% of all customer problems will be resolved within two days. Then the company puts a process in place to measure how long it takes to solve customer problems. The company hires employees who will record when every problem first comes in, and record when every problem resolution letter or email is sent out. This is not done to create a "big brother" atmosphere at work. It is done because that company's experience and/or research shows that a quick two-day resolution is the time needed to satisfy and maintain the majority of that company's customers who experience problems (note – the two day timeframe here is an example, not a standard resolution time).

However, timeliness is only half the battle. The other half is quality (e.g. proper resolution explained in a manner that the customer can easily understand). To measure quality the company might randomly select problem resolution letters or emails and have them reviewed by a supervisor. The company might also keep track of the number of repeat problems (when customers contact the company a second time for the same problem after a resolution letter or email was previously sent to them).

The key here is for you to expect that the work you do will be tracked, and that it is being tracked so that management can respond in a timely manner when they see that service delivery is at a point where it will negatively impact the company's profits and therefore, your job security. This may mean more paperwork and recording of data than you feel is necessary, but that extra work is there to protect your job.

A more personal service measurement is when your employer tracks your work. This is done so that when problems are found (e.g. there have been too many repeat problems) the company can find the cause of the problem and fix it. For example, the company may find that one worker is the primary cause of the increase in repeat problems and decide that that employee needs to be re-trained. Also, if the repeat problem is found to be from many employees, a further analysis may determine that a standard response letter or email for a specific problem needs to be re-worded.

Without tracking individuals, companies would only be able to determine when bad service exists, but would not be able to pinpoint and correct the problem.

So expect to have your specific work tracked. That could be the number of calls answered per hour, the type of problems you have worked on, the number of sales made, etc. Also know that these numbers are used to help identify and fix problems and to identify where employees need additional training help.

In addition to tracking actual work, many companies involve their customers in the service tracking process. Surveys, where customers report on actual experiences with the company are one way this is done. Another is called "shops." This is where a company hires someone to be a customer and report on their experience with the company.

Examples of Service Measurements

Customer Service Call Center	• Number of rings before a call is answered • Percent of time all trunks are busy • Percent of calls abandoned (caller hangs up before call is answered) • Call monitoring for proper greeting, proper procedure (one stop service, correct information given to customer, etc.) • Test calls to ensure proper information is being given out for specific scenarios • Percent of time phone representatives are off-line • Number of times a phone representative is late to work • Employee productivity measurement
Sales Call Center	• All of the above plus number of sales by product, number of up-sells, sales per hour, etc.
Back Office	• Problem resolution time frame • Correspondence sent out on time (e.g. customer statements, etc.) • Accuracy, clarity of customer correspondences • Quality control checks on correspondences (correct correspondences sent to proper customers) • Accuracy of accounting records • Delivery deadlines met • Employee productivity measurements

Retail Outlet or Service Center	• Average line waits by type of function
	• "Shops" to determine if the employees are either selling correctly and professionally or are providing customers with the proper information or problem resolution
	• Employee productivity and sales measurements
Manufacturing	• Proper safety procedures followed
	• Product inspection (sample finished product to accept/reject batches of work)
	• Machine inspection (to ensure working correctly and to ensure proper maintenance was completed
	• Quality review of packaging and customer orders
	• Measure production output and time frames
	• Employee productivity measurements

Customer Service Phone Center

A customer service phone center offers an excellent window into the entire service process.

First, one of the keys to an efficient phone center from a customer's point of view is to minimize the wait time on the phone before speaking to a phone representative. To do this it is important that the business makes efficient use of its phone representatives. So customer service phone centers run on a tight time schedule to ensure that there are enough phone representatives available to handle the expected call volumes whereby callers do not spend too much time on hold. Therefore, when management gets on a phone representative's back because he/she shows up late, or doesn't allow a phone representative to pick his/her own lunch time, or doesn't allow more than one person to leave on a bathroom break at a time, it is not that the supervisor is treating his/her staff like kids or that the supervisor is a control freak; it's that the supervisor is trying to minimize hold times for the callers.

To show you how quickly a phone center can get out of control, let's say a co-worker of yours comes in 15 minutes late (I know you wouldn't come in late). During those 15 minutes callers are on hold longer than usual because the phone center is down one staff member, so 10 callers hang up because they have to leave to go to work. These 10 <u>dissatisfied</u> customers are now going to call back later in the day adding unexpected call volume to that time frame. Let's say that all ten call during their lunch break. Now the phone center is understaffed during lunch because it was staffed for ten less calls than it gets. So during lunch time callers will be on hold longer than expected and some of them will hang up because they have to eat. This creates more dissatisfied customers and adds more unexpected call volume to another time period in that day or the next day. That in turn will create even more dissatisfied customers and create future time periods where there will be more calls and longer hold times than expected. As you can see, this fifteen minute tardiness can result in a problem that lasts for days, and many dissatisfied customers. Now add in the fact some workers could come back late from lunch or take a bathroom break at a bad time, etc. and you see why phone center managers have to manage their employees' time very closely. So if you work for a phone center, expect your time to be managed closely and do not blame it on your supervisor's lack of respect for you or his/her personality. Know that it is because of the nature of phone centers.

However, call wait times are not the only service delivery that is important to customers when they call a company's phone center. Being able to get their question answered without being transferred from person to person, not being placed back on hold for long periods, the tone of the phone representative, etc. are all important to the callers.

Therefore, most phone centers have quality and timeliness indicators for both the phone center as a whole and for individual phone representatives.

For the phone center as a whole, the service indictors could be the percent of callers placed on hold, the average hold time, the percent of callers on hold that were on hold for over two minutes, the number of calls by hour by day (to help with staffing), the type of calls being received, the average talk time per call, surveys to determine customers' experiences and expectations, and more.

These indicators help management with staffing schedules; help management know how well service is being delivered to its customers; and provides red flags to indicate when poor service could start impacting the company's profits (and worker's jobs).

For individual phone representatives, service indicators could be the number of calls answered per day, average talk time, the percent of time the phone representative was plugged into the phone system and available to take a call, the number of calls transferred to someone else, the types of calls handled by each phone representative, and more.

These indicators help phone center management ensure that the phone center is operating efficiently and where to go to solve problems and improve service delivery.

One area where phone representatives often get mixed signals is when they are told to resolve all customer problems and then are expected to keep to an average talk time. Many phone representatives feel that if they have to spend a lot of time with a customer to resolve his/her problem, that he/she should do so. What phone representatives have to understand is the big picture. While they are providing superior customer service to one customer on a long call, three or four other callers are experiencing bad customer service because of the long hold times due to the unavailability of that phone representative to answer more calls. So use good judgment when extending call times beyond the norm, and try not to extended calls unnecessarily.

EXERCISE CS5

You start your own computer repair business. You have three employees who perform all computer repair work. You know that customers do not like being without their computers for more than a day or two. In fact you advertise that you not only fix all problems, but fix them faster than your competition.

In addition, since this is a brand new business, in six months you plan on hiring a manager to assign work, solve the most difficult computer issues; and to contact all customers twice a year to help nurture an excellent customer/company relationship, remind them of the services your company provides, and gently probe them to see if they have any current computer issues that your company can help them with. You hope that you will be able to promote one of your three current employees to that position down the line.

Q1. List three service measurements you would implement to help track the amount, quality and timeliness of the work being done by the company or by individuals.

Q2. List two service measurements you would implement to help you track who would be the best person to promote to manager down the line.

Customer Service Profitability

The reason that businesses put money, manpower and resources into customer service is that superior customer service makes a company more profitable.

Old thinking is that customer service is a necessary expense. Current thinking is that providing excellent customer service is a way for a business to differentiate itself in the marketplace, thereby maintaining and growing its customer base.

Therefore, most companies measure and track their service delivery, and often obtain input from customers to see how their service delivery could be improved.

Below are some real life examples:

- Research by GTE Telephones showed "perceived service" companies can charge 10% more.

- Detroit Diesel canvassed 40 distributors, whose 250 suggestions cut deliveries from five days to three days.

- Within the first three years of its customer service measurement program, American Express cut transaction costs by 21%.

- In 1991 a large UK engineering company responded to customers' requests and issued clear spare part lists with prices. Parts sales rose by 34%.

- Citibank's strategic plan for differentiation in the marketplace (to grow market share) went from dealing with countries rather than individuals to technology (they were the first to offer cash machines) to offering superior customer service.

- Citibank's credit card division performed a customer service profitability model that showed that: (1) customers satisfied with the service provided by Citibank used their Citibank credit card about twice as often as customers dissatisfied with service provided by Citibank (those customers used other options such as cash or a different credit card) and (2) 80% of customers who had problems with their Citibank credit card but were satisfied with the service provided when Citibank fixed their problem, returned to be satisfied customers with product usage at levels the same as customers that never had a problem and were satisfied with the service they received from Citibank.

Dissatisfied customers defect, and spread negative word of mouth about the company which reduces the company's revenue. Satisfied customers continue to use a company's products and services, and spread positive word of mouth about the company which increases the company's revenue.

PART II

Customer Service Skills

Service Attitudes

Many service providers have the wrong idea about customer service. They place burdens and expectations on their customers unfairly. What follows are the "Top Ten Truisms of Customer Service." While this "top ten list" may never make it to the *Late Show with David Letterman*, it is an important list just the same. If you understand these ten truisms, you will become an extremely valuable employee of any business.

1) Customers expect a lot of service. As a provider of customer service, it is not your job to define your customer's need, but to satisfy those needs.

2) Customers contact a provider of customer service to have their problems resolved. They don't want excuses; they just want their problems resolved. If there are problems in your workplace that are prohibiting you from resolving their problems (e.g. computers are down, staff is out sick, etc.) they don't care, and why should they, that's your problem, not their problem.

3) Customers expect to be able to get an answer to all their questions from the person to whom they are speaking. Customers do not care if the person they are speaking to is a new employee, is in another department, etc. They want an answer. So if you are the right person, be prepared; if you are not, know who the right person is and patiently and politely send your customer to him/her. However, be sure that the person you send your customer to can, indeed, resolve his/her problem.

4) Customers feel it's their right to contact the company that they transact business with, whenever they want. While this may cause extra call volume, this is a good thing for the business since it means that customers are becoming comfortable with, and dependent on it. This results in customer loyalty, which leads to more sales, which leads to more profits, which leads to job security and more money available for employee salaries.

5) Customers hate waiting on long lines whether on the phone or at a place of work. Having customers wait long is like telling them that you do not value their time. Customers have better things to do than wait. Try this. Look at your watch's minute and second hand. Now put down the book and without counting, pick it up when you think two minutes have passed. Now look at your watch again. Waiting makes time pass slowly.

6) Customers know that they are important. Without customers the business would close and you would be out of a job. So they are correct. Therefore, customers do not care that

providers of service have many customers to deal with. When they have problems, they expect you to deal with them, not to be busy with other customers.

7) <u>Customers expect to be able to get quick resolutions to their problems.</u> After all, they chose to do business with your company, and they had every right to expect that <u>no</u> problems would occur. If one occurs, it is the company's fault (customers never believe it was their error, even when it clearly is, and they have paid for the right to feel that way with their purchase), so the company should fix it right away.

8) <u>Run-around is one of the most hated of all bad customer practices and usually results in losing a customer.</u> That is why it is important that you know your job so you can resolve all problems that you are suppose to be able to resolve (or are given the responsibility to resolve) and that you know the responsibilities of your co-workers so if you must refer the customer to someone else, you are referring him/her to the right person (one who can resolve the problem). If the customer interaction is over the phone, when you transfer the call, stay on the line and inform the person of the details that the customer has already told you so he/she does not have to repeat everything all over again. If possible, do this in a three-way call with the customer also on the line. Introduce the customer to the new representative and explain the situation briefly at that time. The same thing goes for an in person visit. If possible (same building, is okay to leave your work area) walk the customer over to the person you are referring him/her to, introduce the customer to your co-worker, and briefly explain the situation.

9) <u>Customers will often try to go over the head of the person with whom they are speaking without giving that person a chance to solve the problems.</u> Like it or not, this is their right. However, your supervisor may not like taking calls/having customers referred to him/her from customers who have problems that their providers of service can resolve. A good way to handle a situation like this is to say, "I have no problem with transferring you/sending you to my supervisor whenever you want, but I would appreciate the opportunity to satisfy you by resolving your problem first." If this doesn't work, transfer the call/refer the customer. If the interaction is over the phone, do not hang up to avoid transferring the call. The customer will just call back (still has to get the problem resolved), and in most cases, the call can be traced to you. Sometimes this happens and the employee never finds out, and wonders why he/she never receives good pay raises. Other times, the employee who hung up is called into his/her supervisor's office to explain why he/she hung up on the customer.

10) <u>Customers will often call/show up with problems that they could easily resolve themselves.</u> For example, a customer may continually show up/call for help programming his/her cell phone. And he/she may keep contacting your company to program the same feature! Once again, it is their right to do so. In fact, it may be this service feature (calling in for help) that has kept them a customer of the business and may have even resulted in a lot of referrals. As a provider of service, you cannot choose what services your customers should take care of themselves and which services you are fine with performing for them. Customers decide what they need help with and your job is to help them with all of their needs.

EXERCISE CS6

Please answer the following questions true or false. Then explain why you choose true or false.

Q1. If you are working with a customer and cannot answer his or her question it is okay to pass them off to another customer service representative whether or not that other employee knows the answer the answer since with that employee there is at least a chance that the customer can get his or her question answered.

Q2. If there is a serious customer problem going on at work resulting in a lot of customer calls about that problem, and a customer calls you with a simple question such as how to use a product feature, you have a right to tell that customer to try doing it the best he or she can and if they cannot figure it out to call back tomorrow. After all the other callers on hold have serious problems.

Q3. If a customer does not like the way a conservation with you is going and asks to speak to your supervisor; your response should be that you are the only one who can help the customer so they should relax and be respectful and allow you to fix his or her problem.

Q4. Customers who expect all their problems will be fixed with one simple phone call are customers the business should cut loose. After all, it will be impossible to always satisfy them.

Q5. Customers need to understand that phone representatives have no control over how long they wait on the phone before a call is answered so they have no right to start off their call with you complaining about that long wait.

Active Listening

When you get into a conversation with one of your friends, you spend about half the time talking and half the time listening to what your friend has to say. Often you interrupt your friend because you believe you know what he/she is going to say, or because you just have to get in a comment at that specific point in time. While this is okay for friendly chats, it is not how you should conduct your conversations with customers, management, and even co-workers when he/she is explaining a work-related item to you. Even in friendly chats, I have found that when I interrupt the person I was talking to because I thought I knew what he/she was going to say, often my friend tells me that I got it all wrong. When that "friend" has been a woman I'm in a relationship with, I've heard that I got it all wrong with great emphasis and major consequences!

When interacting with customers, supervisors and co-workers who are explaining work-related topics to you, instead of using normal conversation skills, use active listening skills.

Instead of the 50% talking, 50% listening, active listening involves only 20% talking and 80% listening. Also, do not interrupt the other person. Allow him/her to finish his/her thought. Do not jump to conclusions or assume. Save your questions until after he/she has completed his/her thought. To help you with this, have a pad of paper and a pen handy. Take notes on important points. Do not rely on your marvelous, but sometimes failing memory. Jot down your questions so you can ask them at the appropriate time.

In addition, when using active listening skills in person, your personal signals (nonverbal communications) count. You need to convey to the person you are talking to that you are paying attention and are interested in what he/she is saying.

To summarize:
- Normal conversation = 50:50 (talking to listening)
- Active listening = 20:80 (talking to listening)
- Active listening deals with other's views & feelings
- Active listening requires a lot of concentration before responding
- Active listening is needed to:
    - help understand others
    - eliminate emotions from the message
    - be able to identify real concerns
    - keep attitudes and prejudices out of way
    - help decode hidden messages

- All of the active listening characteristics previously listed, leads to taking the appropriate action

Normal Conversation vs. Active Listening

NORMAL CONVERSATION	**ACTIVE LISTENING**
Passive	Make eye contact
May forget quickly	Keep concentrating
Doesn't fully register	Summarize to ensure everything registers
May not show you are concentrating	Display behaviors to show concentration
No notes	May make a few notes

Active Listening Building Blocks

- Attention: good posture, make eye contact, attentive silence, lean forward, smile, nodding yes, do not cross your arms or legs
- Cues: invitation to talk, infrequent but open-ended questions (e.g. tell me about your problem, what happened next)
- Reflection: repeating brief (key) phrases, paraphrasing using your own words, summarizing

Active Listening Stumbling Blocks

- Judging: criticizing, prejudices, name-calling, assumptions
- Controlling: giving orders, moralizing, threatening, know-it-all, advising (as opposed to solving)
- Avoiding: diverting, reassuring only (when there is a real problem)
- Selective Listening: hearing what you want or expect to hear, not what is actually said

---

EXERCISE CS7

This is an exercise to build the active listening skill of <u>attention</u>. The exercise is done in pairs. The exercise will be done twice with each person taking turns being the speaker and the listener.

Q1: The speaker takes about seven minutes and talks about his or her favorite movie. The listener sits and listens. The only thing the listener can say during the seven minutes are invitations to talk (please continue, go on, etc.). The listener needs to show with his or her body language (posture, eye contact, etc.) that he or she is very interested in what the speaker is saying. After the seven minute session is over, the speakers lets the listener know if her or she believed that the listener was truly interested in what the speaker was talking about. Then the speaker should say why he or she felt the listener was or was not interested. Remember to perform this exercise twice with each party taking turns at being the speaker and listener.

EXERCISE CS8

This is an exercise to build the active listening skill of <u>repetition</u>. The exercise is done in pairs. The exercise will be done twice with each person taking turns being the speaker and the listener.

Q1: The speaker takes about ten minutes and talks about his or her favorite television show (must be a new topic, not the same talk as last time). After every two or three sentences the speaker stops talking and the listener tries to repeat what was said word for word. The speaker must talk at a normal conversation pace, not slowly to help the listener. If the speaker forgets to stop, the listener should put up his or her hand to stop the speaker (FYI - a nonverbal personal signal). The purpose of this exercise is to get the listener to listen very closely to what someone is saying, close enough that he or she can repeat what was said. It is not a memory exercise and will not be graded as such. This is also an excellent exercise to help build the foundation for waiting until someone completes a thought before talking. Remember to perform this exercise twice with each party taking turns at being the speaker and listener.

EXERCISE CS9

This is an exercise to build the active listening skill of <u>summation</u>. The exercise is done in pairs. The exercise will be done twice with each person taking turns being the speaker and the listener.

Q1: The speaker talks in three minute spurts and talks about his or her favorite book, comic or magazine (must be a new topic, not the same talk as last time). There will be three three-minute intervals for each speaker for this exercise. After each three minute interval, the listener will summarize what the speaker just said. The listener should NOT repeat what was said word for word; and should not add any of his or her thoughts, views or comments on what the speaker communicated. The listener should just summarize the key facts. After each summary (please note that a summary is shorter than the original), the listener should ask the speaker if the listener got the key facts correct. If the listener says "no", ask him or her what was missed, and continue with the exercise. Remember to perform this exercise twice with each party taking turns at being the speaker and listener.

Helpful hint: Here is an example of a summary from a statement:

"My favorite book is *Dune* by Frank Herbert because I found the correlation between the spice in the book and oil today very interesting. I was an economics major in college and amongst other things; Dune is a novel about economics."

The summary might be: *Dune* is Jay's favorite book because of how it's relevant to today's economy.

EXERCISE CS10

This is an exercise to put the three previous skills learned together to provide a <u>comprehensive active listening skill set.</u> The exercise is done in pairs. The exercise will be done twice with each person taking turns being the speaker and the listener.

Q1: The speaker will talk for about 10 minutes and talks about his or her favorite band or favorite type of music (must be a new topic, not the same talk as last time). For this exercise the listener will use all three skills performed in the previous three exercises. The listener will listen to what the speaker is saying; showing attentive personal signals (including invitations to talk) and will listen closely and speak only when the speaker completes a thought. When the listener speaks it will be to summarize what was said, using a key word or phrase in the exact way that the speaker said it to the listener. Remember to perform this exercise twice with each party taking turns at being the speaker and listener.

The skills learned in these four exercises not only work well on the job with customers and supervisors (and co-workers who are talking about a work topic), but will also work in social situations to make good impressions on the people you meet.

Conquering Communication Barriers

Unfortunately, you don't get to choose the person to whom you are providing service. Also, in some instances your work environment may be less than ideal. Therefore, there are often barriers to communicating with a customer. It is important that you recognize these barriers so you can work around them to provide quality service to your internal and external customers.

Communicator's weakness

The customer who is informing you about their problem may have some communication shortcomings. They may:

- use an inappropriate tone or approach
- be unable to use communication skills adequately
- lack sufficient knowledge to communicate their problem effectively
- be a poor listener
- have a predetermined solution to their problem that is not a realistic solution

Receiver's weakness

The customer service representative who is listening to a customer's problem may have some communication shortcomings. They may:

- be reluctant to receive information
- not be paying attention to the customer
- be unfamiliar with the content or subject matter
- be unprepared to handle customer problems
- possess or be affected by some of the items expressed previously

Language

Language can be a barrier to effective communication. The vocabulary of both the individual communicating a problem and the individual listening to the problem can be problematic. Also, when discussing your solution to a customer's problem, be sure not to use jargon, especially not jargon internal to your company (e.g. "Go to the bank and speak to the CSR" should be "Go to the bank and speak to a customer service representative"). Finally, make sure that there is no ambiguity, rambling or double meanings in your communications with your customers.

Psychology

Individual personalities can also be barriers to effective communication. Emotions (fear, shyness, aggression) and frames of reference (bias, prejudice, experiences, assumptions, etc.) often shape communications. In addition, the current mood and life pressures on both the individual with a problem and the individual who is listening to the problem impact communication.

Business

Communication is also impacted by the policies, systems and structure within the company for which you work. For example, customers that experience long telephone wait times will have a different attitude on the phone than customers that waited a very short time on the telephone before their call was answered.

Situational

The environment in which you work, and the surrounding circumstances, may also be barriers to effective communication. For example, the time of day when a call is answered could be a factor in communications (e.g. during a hectic lunch hour). Also the temperature in the workplace, the noise volume in the room you work in, the number of intrusions and interruptions, etc. can impact communication.

A few specific examples of barriers to communication

- Your customer's primary language may not be English. Your business wants to sell to all potential customers to maximize profits. This could make communicating a challenge. Do not get frustrated. Know your co-workers. You may have one who can communicate with your customer better. If you do not, do your best.

- Your customer and you may have different levels of education, and use different words in normal conversations. Use your active listening skills (attention, repeating, summarizing) to ensure that your customer understands you, and that you truly understand your customer.

- Avoid using jargon, even when dealing with internal customers. It becomes very easy to use words that are common in your workplace, but are not part of the general public's vocabulary. If I were to tell you that every business owner should enroll in "S.E.E.K.", you would have no idea what I meant. Instead, if I said that every business owner should enroll in the Palm Beach County Resource Center's entrepreneurship training program where participants learn while creating work product for their businesses, you would have a better idea what I meant. While saying

"S.E.EK." saves me a lot of words, there would have been no comprehension from the person to whom I was speaking.

- Be sure you speak in clear language to avoid any double-meanings or uncertainty in your statements to customers. Double-meanings are great for jokes, but customer service is serious business!

- Unfortunately, personalities are part of every exchange with customers. Some people handle stress well, while others do not. Some people react calmly to problems, while others do not. And some people just rub other people the wrong way for no real reason. These situations can get in the way of communicating with your customers. You cannot allow that to happen. Be aware of these situations when they arise. Know that they are unavoidable in customer service roles, and that they happen to everyone. Therefore, do not take these situations personally. Be professional and ignore the personality conflicts and concentrate on understanding and resolving your customers' problems.

- Sometimes business policies can hinder your communications with customers. Know those policies because it will help you understand how to deal with those situations. For example, a customer may have bought an item at "final sale prices" and that may mean no returns. If the customer didn't know that and tries to return the item, it could lead to a misunderstanding and an escalation of the problem if you did not know that policy either.

- Often work conditions add to the difficulty in communicating with customers. If there is construction going on in your office, the noise could make it hard to hear customers you are talking to on the phone. So, while you may not normally use headphones when talking on the phone, you may need to use them until the construction is completed.

- Customers may have experience a long wait, or the run-around before getting to you. Therefore, they could start off demanding and impatient. Get beyond their impatience and solve their problems.

To summarize: the best way to ensure that communication between your customer and yourself goes well is to be prepared by knowing your job well, using your active listening skills, using a friendly tone at all times even if your customer is not, and assuming that you will have to overcome communication problems or communication shortcomings.

Personal Signals

Personal signals were covered in detail in the chapter Communications in the *People Skills* section. Personal signals are non-verbal communication. They are your voluntary and involuntary facial and body movements that are in play as you communicate with others.

So be aware of the personal signals you are broadcasting. You may say the right thing but if your body language is saying something else, you will be sending mixed signals. You can also use those always present personal signals to your advantage. By reading the personal signals of the individual you are talking to, you can tell if he/she comprehends what you just told him/her. A puzzled look goes a long way in letting you know you will have to find different words to explain what you just said again. I do that all the time when I teach my entrepreneurship course. If I see looks of comprehension, I go on to the next topic, on the rare occasion I see some looks of confusion, I go over the topic again, presenting it in a different way.

For an in depth look at personal signals, including a list of some positive and negative personal signals, see the *People Skills'* chapter on communications.

EXERCISE CS11

Whose Line is it Anyway personal signal exercise

Q1: Just like the television show where the catch phrase is where everything's made up and the points don't matter. That's because this is an improvisational exercise and there is no grade so the points don't matter.

Wait for instructions from your instructor; and have fun.

Communicating with Customers

What follows are some skills that will help you become a superior provider of customer service, which will result in you becoming a valuable asset to your employer. As you read through this section, think about situations where you have interacted with businesses whose employees made some mistakes regarding these skills. Then think about the image these employees gave of their companies.

Choosing words

You call my company DTR Inc. and want to talk to me. The employee who answers the phone responds, "Mr. Goldberg is still on his break. I'll have him call you when he gets back."

What impression does this response give you?

Let's try another. Again, you call my company to talk to me. The employee on the phone responds, "Mr. Goldberg is not back from lunch yet. I'll have him call you when he gets back."

What impression does this response give you?

We'll try this one more time. You call, this time the employee who answers says, "Mr. Goldberg is busy, can he call you later?"

How would you feel if you got this response?

I don't know about you, but in the first case I would have the impression that Mr. Goldberg is taking an extended break. In the second case, I would get the impression that Mr. Goldberg was expected back from lunch earlier and is late reporting back to work from lunch. In the third case, I would feel that Mr. Goldberg does not value me as a customer. After all he is busy with something else, but I have a problem, and he should be dealing with me; at least enough to talk to me quickly.

Choosing words worksheet (done during lecture)

How would you re-word what the employee said to correct these negative impressions?

What was said: Mr. Goldberg is still on his break.

Corrected: _____

What was said: Mr. Goldberg is not back from lunch yet.

Corrected: _____

What was said: Mr. Goldberg is busy, can he call you later?

Corrected: _____

I'll give you my take on these statements in a bit. However, I want to add two more employee/customer interactions for you to consider.

A customer who had a serious problem calls you. The Problem Resolution Department completed working on the customer's problem an hour ago, and in addition to putting in a fix on the customer's account ensuring that the situation would not happen again, they refunded money to the customer's account.

When the customer calls you inform that customer that he or she is getting a refund and that the Problem Resolution Department made changes to the customer's account so that the problem should not occur again.

See anything wrong here?

Obviously, I do or I wouldn't ask the next question. How would you change that response?
_____
_____
_____

Let me give you another example of "words gone wrong."

A customer calls in with a major problem. After taking in all the information, the employee responds, "You should be hearing from us within five days."

How would you change this response?
_____
_____
_____

Now that you had time to think about the prior examples of employee/customer interactions, let's see what was done incorrectly by the employee.

When interacting with customers (both internal and external) it is very important to watch the words that you use. Words like, "still, yet, busy, should" need to be avoided. For example:

Mr. Goldberg is "still" on his break gives the impression that he is late coming back from break. That is not a positive image to create for the customer.

Mr. Goldberg is not back from lunch "yet" gives the impression he is late coming back from lunch. That is not a positive image to create for the customer.

Mr. Goldberg is "busy" can he call you later gives the impression that what he is doing is more important than spending time with the person who wants to speak to him. That is not a positive image to create for the customer.

In all these cases the best response is a simple, *"Mr. Goldberg is unavailable; how may I help you?"*

One of the biggest no-no's in customer service is the use of the phrase, "Your problem 'should' be resolved now." Should is a wishy-washy, weak, leaving room for not coming through word in these cases. If I were the customer, use of the word "should" would get me angry and invoke a response like, "Should, should, what do you mean should? It better be resolved." The proper response is, "Your problem is now resolved."

So in the previous example, the wording needs to be "so that the problem *will* not occur again." Please, don't use "should not occur" again.

The same is true with timeframes. You "should be" hearing from us within five days." Again, say, "You *will* be hearing from us within five days."

While some of you will just need to watch your words, others will have to be careful not to give too many details. These are customers, not personal friends.

For example, "Mr. Goldberg left early to meet with his divorce attorney." Unless we're buds and you think the caller is someone I could be interested in dating, this is too personal a response for the caller. In fact, even if you think I could be interested in the caller it is too personal. Again, just say, *"Mr. Goldberg is unavailable, may I help you?"*

Another doozie I've heard is, "Mr. Goldberg can't talk to you now; he's in an important meeting with Senior Management working on a major problem that a very important client has encountered. Can he call you back as soon as he's out of that meeting?" Huh? First of all it is a horrible idea to tell a customer that the company has a major customer problem. It's none of their business. Second, what is this customer; chopped liver? This customer will feel he/she is as important as any other customer so his/her problem should get the same immediate attention as the supposedly "very important client." Once again, a simple, *"Mr. Goldberg is unavailable, may I help you?"* will suffice.

Even the word, "may" can, at times, be a weak word. For example, I apologize for the inconvenience this "may" have caused you. In this case, "may" is a terrible word. If the customer was not inconvenienced, he/she will not care if the word "may" is used or not. However, if the customer <u>was</u> <u>inconvenienced</u> "may" sounds like you are belittling what he/she went through. So always say, *"I apologize for the inconvenience this has caused you."* This works for both customers who were and who were not inconvenienced.

EXERCISE CS12

Point out why the following statements are not appropriate for the workplace (some contain more than one reason why it is a poor statement). Then re-write them so that they are appropriate and do not reflect poorly on the company or the individuals involved.

Q1. Mr. Dean is not back from his meeting with his son's criminal attorney. I don't know when he will be back, but I'll have him call you as soon as he can.

Q2. I'm glad you called us about your that problem. As it turned out it impacted about half of our customers. But, we should have it under control now.

Q3. Ms. Dean is busy talking with Roland from the Tet Corporation. That is our most important client. So I'll try to help you the best I can. If I cannot help, please be patient and I'll have Ms. Dean call you as soon as he can.

Q4. I know we missed your deadline. Therefore, our next delivery will be free. I am sorry for the inconvenience this may have caused you.

Q5. Jake had to leave early and to take his pet, Oy, to the vet. Can I help you?

Q6. I am sorry that you haven't heard from the billing department yet, but they are backlogged. However, you should hear from them within the next 24 hours.

Q7. Mr. Dean is not in yet. Can I help you?

Classifying customer statements

Active listening is a key skill in helping you determine if a customer (internal or external) statement to you is a comment, a question, or an objection. Many providers of service turn a one minute customer session into a ten minute hassle by misinterpreting a comment as an objection. Others breed customer dissatisfaction by misinterpreting a question as a comment and, therefore, never addressing that question. Perhaps worst of all is when a provider of service (or a salesperson) misinterprets an objection as a statement. In a service scenario, the customer interaction will never end satisfactorily for the customer until the objection has been addressed. That's hard to do if the provider of service never "hears" the objection. In a sales scenario, if the salesperson does not "hear" a customer's objection he/she cannot overcome it, and he/she will not make the sale.

Let's look at some examples.

1) "Your prices are higher than I thought they would be"

This is an objection. You must first address the fact that the customer believes the prices are too high before proceeding. A response could be, "I hope that won't be a problem. Our products are the best in the business. May I show you some?" If you never address the objection, the customer will never consider purchasing your products.

2) "My computer is broken"

This is a statement. If you interpreted this as an objection (something you had to overcome to continue with the customer) you may have responded with a statement such as, "We have an excellent track record with our computers. We have the best service record in town." The customer might then respond, "Not with me…" and then either get into an argument with you over your company's service record, or worse, say, "Not with me, maybe I'll check out your competition!"

If you correctly classified this as a statement, your response would have been, "Tell me what's wrong so we can get it fixed right away." This avoids a long, unnecessary discussion.

3) "How do I use this feature"

This is a question. If you do not answer it by showing the customer how to use the feature, your customer will not be satisfied.

EXERCISE CS13

Identify whether the following are statements, questions or objections.

Q1. I think your service is the best in the business
Q2. Why was I charged a service fee
Q3. Your selection of pipes is insufficient
Q4. You delivered the wrong product
Q5. When will you have Boston Terriers in stock
Q6. I need the product immediately
Q7. I refuse to pay that bill

Overcoming objections

Use the following four-step process to overcome objections:

1. Use your active listening skills to hear what the customer is saying.

2. Provide an immediate response that addresses the customer's objection.

3. Talk in a concise, clear and positive manner.

4. Don't provide unnecessary information and conversation.

Proper Telephone Technique

There are certain procedures that are fairly universal when answering a telephone call from a customer. They are:

1. Greet the caller by stating the name of your company, your name and "how may I help you."

2. Use a friendly, cheerful tone when answering the phone.

3. Never place a caller on hold without first giving the caller a chance to respond. In other words, do not follow up the greeting in number one with "hold please" and then place the caller on hold.

4. While talking with a customer on the phone, ask them if you can place them on hold (e.g. "I need to look that information up on my computer, can I place you on hold for a moment?")

5. Do not leave the customer on hold for a long time. Check back with the customer every minute or two to provide a status (e.g. I am still working on your problem; I will have your answer shortly).

6. If you did not do this earlier: Look at your watch or a clock and write down an exact time (including seconds). Then sit and do not look at the clock, do not count or do anything else to help track how much time passes. Then look at your watch or clock again when you believe two minutes have passed. This will give you an idea how customers are experiencing the time.

7. It is also important to take notes when performing customer service functions. After one day we forget 46% of what we heard, after 7 days we forget 65% of what we heard, after 14 days we forget 79% of what we heard.

Managing Customers

Customers are people. You come across all kinds in life, and you will on your job as well. What follows are suggestions on how to handle different types of customers. While this will help in the workplace, it can also help you in every day life.

<u>The demanding, determined customer who is speaking very strongly and wants immediate action.</u>

Steps to follow:
1. Use your active listening skills to identify the problem correctly.
2. Even though the customer may be worked-up, remain friendly and courteous.
3. React only to the problem, not the customer's tone. The customer is not mad or angry at you, just at the situation. Do not take it personally.
4. Ask the customer questions about the situation, and using your active listening skill of repetition, repeat some of the customer's key words back to him/her.
5. After you understand the customer's problem, use your active listening skill of summation, to re-state the problem in short, to-the-point sentences.
6. Communicate your understanding of the importance of this issue to the customer.

<u>The laid-back customer who has a serious problem, but is an ineffective communicator causing you problems in getting all the details.</u>

Steps to follow:
1. Draw the customer out by asking a lot of questions.
2. Use your active listening skill of summation often and ask the customer to comment on your summary.
3. Make the customer feel comfortable by remaining warm and friendly throughout the entire conversation (if you are getting frustrated by the customer's lack of communication skills, do <u>not</u> show that frustration).

<u>The chatty customer (also known as the "Energizer Bunny customer" because they go on and on and on) who views you as both a person who will solve his/her problem, and a person to engage in general conversation.</u>

Steps to follow:

1. Only ask questions about the customer's problem and ask specific questions (not general, open-ended questions). For example, "Tell me why your stereo is not working", not, "Tell me what's wrong."
2. Talk in long bursts and leave little time between statements, making it harder for the customer to jump in to interject personal comments.
3. Be careful not to be rude. You may think that the person has no concern for you since he/she is stopping you from doing your job, but you cannot let that show. He/she is a customer and customers are the reason you have a job. So stay friendly and courteous.
4. Provide very short responses to off-topic questions. Be sure not answer in a way that leaves the door open for a long comment by the customer. Remember; do not be rude by ignoring the customer. Let's say the customer is buying a music CD and asks you who you like. Answer with a popular band who the customer is likely to know (an unknown will result in follow-up questions) and finish by asking a yes-no question that has no where else to go. For example, "I like U2, do you need anything else today?"

The furious customer who does not cross the line in terms of language (does not curse), but is coming close and does have a legitimate problem.

Steps to follow:
1. Apologize for the problem. Remember do not use the word "may" when apologizing. Say, "I apologize for the inconvenience this has caused you."
2. No matter what, remain friendly and courteous. Again, the anger is about the situation even though it appears to be focused on you.
3. Use your active listening skills to identify and to restate the problem. In this case it is very important that you identify the correct problem or the customer's anger will grow.
4. Be sure that you have resolved the customer's problem, and that you have communicated the solution effectively to the customer.
5. Once the problem is resolved, repeat step one. Apologize again.

If a customer crosses the line and curses, you can tell him/her that you do not have to listen to that and if he/she continues you will call security (or report the customer to your supervisor). That usually works, you get an apology and the rest of the conversation is often much easier. If the customer continues to use foul language, call security, or report the customer to your supervisor. Also, if a customer shows any physical aggression, do not even try to handle it yourself. Call security or the police.

Consumer Rights

As a provider of customer service you should be aware of the rights of your customers. What follows is information taken from the Consumer Protection Act.

"Be it enacted by the Senate and House of Representatives of the United States of America in Congress assembled, that this Act may be cited as the "Consumer Protection Act of 1997.

STATEMENT OF FINDINGS AND PURPOSES

Sec. 2 (a) The Congress finds that the interest of consumers are inadequately represented and protected within the Federal Government and that vigorous representation and protection of the interest of consumers are essential to the fair and efficient functioning of a free market economy. Each year, as a results of this lack of effective representation before Federal agencies and courts, consumers suffer personal injury, economic harm, and other adverse consequences in the course of acquiring and using goods and services available in the marketplace.

(b) The Congress therefore declares that-

(1) A non-regulatory governmental organization to represent the interest of consumers before Federal agencies and courts could help the agencies in the exercise of their statutory responsibilities in a manner consistent with the public interest and with effective and responsive government. It is the purpose of this Act to protect and promote the interest of the people of the United States as consumers of goods and services which are made available to them through commerce or which affect commerce by so establishing an independent Agency for Consumer Advocacy.

(2) It is the purpose of the Agency for Consumer Advocacy to represent the interest of consumers before Federal agencies and courts, receive and transmit consumer complaints, develop ad disseminate information of interest to consumers, and perform other functions to protect and promote the interest of consumers. The authority of the Agency to carry out this purpose shall not be construed to supersede, supplant, or replace the jurisdiction functions, or powers of any other agency to discharge its own statutory responsibilities according to law.

(3) It is the purpose of this Act to promote protection of consumers with respect to the-

(A) safety, quality, purity, potency, healthfulness, durability, performance, repair ability, effectiveness, truthfulness, dependability, availability, and cost of any real or personal property or tangible or intangible goods, services, or credit;

(B) preservation of consumer choice and a competitive market;

(C) price and adequacy of supply of goods and services;

(D) prevention of unfair or deceptive trade practices;

(E) maintenance of truthfulness and fairness in the advertising, promotion and sale by a producer, distributor, lender, retailer or other supplier of such property goods, services, and credit;

CERTIFICATION SCENARIOS

Jerry works for the company If It Wasn't True It Would Be Funny, Inc. Every day something goes wrong. In fact, most days, many things go wrong. However, that isn't the worst part. It's the way the people that work at the company react to these events. It's like they have had no training in basic workplace skills.

Today, when Jerry stops bye Joe's house to pick him up on his way to work, Joe walks out in his PJs and tells him he forgot to set his alarm, he was out late partying last night and was going to blow off the day by calling in sick rather than coming in late. Jerry reminds him that this is an important day since they have a lot of work to do to be sure that they fulfill Much Ado About Nothing's order by the end of the day. Joe just smiles and says, "That's their problem, it has no impact on me." Jerry then chips in, "Isn't this your seventh sick day this year? We only get six." Joe shrugs and says, "I don't know how many sick days we get." Oh, Jerry thinks that crazy Joe D.

When Jerry arrives at work, 10 minutes early, he is pleased to see that Carol is already at her desk busy working. Carol, a new mother, looks alert. Like him, Carol takes her job very seriously. Jerry greets her by asking, "how's the new baby?' Carol responds, "Fine, thanks. Our regular daycare provider cancelled at the last minute so I had to drop her off at my mom's on the way to work. Jerry, you have to come out and see the baby." Jerry, responds, "My weekends are pretty booked, but from the pictures I can see she's breathtaking."

For his first task of the day Jerry has to work with Kenny. Kenny thinks he's a funny guy. He is always telling jokes, many of which use curses and are sexual in nature. Not only does Jerry find the jokes in bad taste, but he finds Kenny's "comedy act" in general very unfunny. Worse, Kenny doesn't believe in using deodorant so working with him is a challenge to the senses. Jerry often finds himself rushing through his work when paired with Kenny. Today, he notices the plant supervisor, Russell, watching Kenny very closely. During his last performance review with Russell, Jerry's only negative comment came in regards to the work he performed with Kenny. Russell commented that Jerry's work was a little sloppy when working with Kenny and he was surprised because, otherwise, his work was near perfect. When Jerry mentioned this to Carol, she said that she received the exact same feedback from Russell regarding her work with Kenny.

After Jerry finishes his work with Kenny, Russell calls him over and gives him a new assignment. Russell tells him that the company expects an OSHA audit sometime in the next few weeks and he is giving Jerry a special task. He wants Jerry to walk around the plant and note unsafe conditions and practices. This is the assignment Jerry hoped to get. There is an opening in the company for a Safety Supervisor and Jerry took an OSHA training course at night to help put him in a position to get that job. It appears, given that Russell assigned him this task, that management has taken notice.

As soon as Jerry starts his safety tour, he observes that no one is using the machine affectionately nicknamed Kramer. Jerry then asks one of the workers why the machine isn't being used. The worker informs Jerry that the machine is out of order, so if used, it could be dangerous. Jerry then asks the worker, "How does everyone know not to use that machine?" He tells Jerry that everyone on the floor has been notified not to use the machine. So Jerry follows up with, "What if someone forgets; and what about next shift?" The worker responds; "That's their problem, not mine." Ah, Jerry thinks, what else should I expect from (making a fist with his right hand), Newman. Okay, Jerry thinks, this is problem number one.

At the far corner of the room Jerry notices a frayed cord attached to the fax machine. Elaine is standing next to the fax machine drinking water she got from the water cooler. Immediately, Jerry remembers Elaine telling him that their supervisor, Russell, asked her out on a date. Elaine turned him down flat, but you could tell Russell was still pinning after her.

In a flash, someone rushes past Elaine and bumps her elbow causing her to spill her water. As the water is making its way towards the frayed cord, Elaine, enraged, chases the person who bumped her elbow shouting, "Come back here. If you think I'm going to clean that up, think again." Jerry notes this as problem number two.

Jerry continues his walking tour and enters the break room. There he notices his good friend George banging on the candy machine because, George says, the machine took his money and didn't give him his candy bar. Right next to the candy machine is a garbage can. Above the garbage can is a fire extinguisher with the label A,B,C. Jerry next witnesses George throwing his lit cigarette into the garbage can. The only thing in the can besides the cigarette is one piece of paper. Smoke immediately starts to rise from the garbage can. George, noticing the smoke, runs out of the room yelling, "Fire, fire." Jerry notes this as problem number three.

Jerry then starts to walk back to his work station. Doing so, he passes through the work shop again where he notices Puddy working. Puddy has band aids all over his fingers. Puddy is using a machine that has very rough surfaces. Jerry further notices that Puddy is not wearing protective gloves. That's why Puddy has all those cuts. So Jerry asks Puddy why he is not wearing gloves. Puddy tells him, "Wearing the gloves is optional." Jerry looks again at Puddy's hands and says, "Soon your hands will be so cut up you won't be able to work; and still you don't wear gloves?" Puddy responds simply, "That's right. " Then adds, "That's what Worker's Comp is for." Jerry shakes his head and moves on. This time Jerry thinks a policy needs to be changed.

As Jerry approaches his work station he falls and bangs his head resulting in a large cut (laceration) with lots of bleeding. As Jerry is being taken from the room by the ambulance crew he sees Cosmo cleaning up his blood spill using his bare hands. Boy, Jerry thinks, even as I'm going to the hospital I see a fifth problem.

It is Louie's first day on a new job. On his way to work he runs into traffic and a drive that took him 25 minutes when he came in for an interview, takes him 50 minutes because of the traffic. The result is that he gets into work at 8:25 AM instead of his scheduled time of 8:00 AM. He explains what happened with the traffic to his new boss, who asks, "What road do you take to work?" Louie responds, "I95." His boss then counters with, "I95 is always backed up this time in the morning on work days." Louie replies, "Geez, I'm sorry." His boss just walks away.

When Louie meets with Human Resources his first task is to fill out paperwork for his benefits. When finished, he is handed the company's Employee Handbook. The head of Human Resources then tells him to read the Handbook while she gets his benefits paperwork processed.

She returns in 30 minutes and asks Louie if he read the manual. He didn't, but he answers, "Yes," thinking he could read it at another time. She then asks if he has any questions. Louie answers, "No."

So the head of Human Resources picks up the book, turns to the first page, and notices that Louie did not sign the form indicating that he read and understood the Handbook. She asks him why he didn't sign that form. Louie answers, "I forgot. I'll sign it now."

Before handing the Handbook back to Louie, the head of Human Resources makes it clear that if Louie doesn't understand anything in the Handbook, please, let's discuss it now.

Louie, with impatience clearly coming through in his response answers, "Just give me the Handbook so I can sign the form."

The Head of Human Resources gives the Handbook back to Louie, who signs the form stating he read and clearly understands everything in the Handbook, while clearly knowing that he never read the book.

Louie is then taken to his new office. It is a cubicle (temporary, free-standing walls). His cubicle is in the middle of the room and has walls that are four feet high, high enough to give him privacy when seated at his desk, and low enough for his supervisor (and others) to see into his cubicle when walking past it. On the wall of the cubicle he hangs the Sports Illustrated swimsuit calendar.

He then notices that his cubicle is next to Latka, who is from the Caspiar. Louie is a patriot and does not want to work next to an immigrant. He immediately sends an email to his new boss asking to be moved as far away from that guy as possible. In fact, that reminds him of a cartoon joke he has in his briefcase. It is poking fun at Muslims, but there is no bad language, and even has a hidden dig at Jewish people. Louie walks over to the copier and makes 20 copies and puts them in all the employee mailboxes on this floor.

Later in the day Louie walks over to Elaine's desk. He has been meaning to introduce himself to her all day. Alice is Louie's assistant. He controls her pay raises and writes her performance appraisal. The first thing Louie notices is that he finds her very attractive. The second thing he notices is that she has an engagement ring on, but no wedding ring. Louie asks her about her wedding plans. When he hears she has no firm plans, Louie tells her that she should go on a date with him just once, and she will never set a wedding date. When she turns him down, he somewhat kiddingly reminds her he is in charge of her raises and performance reviews so maybe she should reconsider.

Before leaving for the day, Louie is introduced to Simka, a co-worker at the same job level as Louie himself. Simka was told to meet with Louie by her supervisor to tell him about the client he will be serving. It was Simka's client but she has been overloaded since taking on Alex's clients, the person Louie was hired to replace. Boy, Louie thinks, Simka is really cute. After talking about the client, Simka is set to leave for the day. She extends her hand to shake Louie's hand goodbye, but instead Louie says, "come on, we're going to be working closely on this account for awhile, I think a hug goodbye is in order." He then gives Simka a hug.

When Louie comes in the next day he sees a note on his desk telling him to report to his supervisor's office at 8:00 AM. Louie looks at his watch and it indicates that the time is 8:25 AM. There was traffic on I95 again so it took Louie 50 minutes to get work. On his way to his supervisor's office Louie stops bye Elaine's desk, winks and asks, "Given any more thought to our date?" and then thinks, this is going to be a wonderful day.

When Louie gets to his supervisor's office he sees that the head of Human Resources is there along with Simka.

Louie knocks on the door and immediately his supervisor asks him why he wasn't at his office at 8:00 AM.

Maybe this isn't going to be such a wonderful day in the life of Louie after all.

Olivia walks past the desk of her co-worker, Charlie, and can see by the look on his face that he is very upset. She asks him, "What's wrong?" Charlie tells Olivia that he gave what he thought was an excellent ten page report to their supervisor, Broyles, and he looked at it briefly, and handed it back to him saying I don't have the time to read this." Olivia then asks Charlie if she can read the report. Charlie responded, "That would be great!"

The report started as follows:

"There are major problems in the workplace. Before stating what they are, let me inform you how this situation came about.

It all started five years ago before you were put in charge of this department. Back then ...."

The report then goes through the history spending about seven pages on the past before stating the problems. Furthermore, Olivia notices, there are generalizations, not specifics in the report as it relates to the problem, and the report contains no possible solutions to the problem. However, the report did highlight some real problems that definitely needed to be addressed.

So Olivia asks Charlie if it would be okay if they worked together to write a memo to Broyles, to alert him about the problems and that they include some suggestions to fix the problems in the memo. Charlie answers, "Why not; we need to try to get Broyles to see what is happening."

Before writing the memo, Olivia and Charlie needed to come up with some possible solutions to the problems.

Olivia says, "Why don't we start now; there is no time like the present." Charlie agrees.

Unbeknownst to Olivia is that Charlie has to get a package out to a customer, Nina, by 2:00 PM so that it could be guaranteed for delivery the next day. Since it was 1:00 PM, and the packaging task would only take Charlie 30 minutes, he feels he can push that task back a bit to attack the solutions to the problems since solving the problems is very important, and working on the solutions is a lot more fun and meaningful than the manual labor associated with the packaging task. In fact, Charlie thinks, packaging the product isn't my normal work anyway, I was only doing it because Lincoln is on vacation.

As they begin to brainstorm ideas, Charlie immediately starts throwing out possible solutions. Some make sense, some do not. Some of his solutions rely on processes that Olivia believes are breaking down and causing the problem. However, Charlie is on a roll and Olivia cannot get a word in edgewise to slow him down. Finally Charlie does slows down, and says " I need to take a break" and heads to the vending machine on the fourth floor.

When Charlie comes back from break he looks at his watch and sees that the time is 1:50 PM. He immediately tells Olivia he has something he needs to do and they should meet up again in 30 minutes.

During the time Charlie is away, Olivia does some work to provide a solid background so that the solutions they both come up with will make more sense.

Charlie comes back 30 minutes later right after he finishes packaging the product for delivery to Nina. They continue the work on the memo and it goes very well. In fact they talk to Peter and Walter, who run the phone monitoring program, to get more detailed information to help dimension the problem. Below is the memo that Olivia and Charlie write:

Memo To: Broyles Phillips

From: Olivia Completed-Ham
Charlie Multiple-Franks

RE: Issues in our Customer Service Department

Date: November 15, 2012

===

During our routine monitoring of customer calls, we noticed some complaints from our customers regarding our telephone service.

Some of the more alarming complaints from our customers were:

- our phone representatives are sometimes rude to our customers
- our phone representatives often lack the knowledge to solve our customer's problems
- our customers often wait a long time on hold before talking to a customer service representative
- when our customers do get through to a phone representative, they are often placed on hold for long intervals

In addition the number of complaints we have noticed has increased this month over last month.

In both months we monitored 80 calls. The table that follows summarizes our findings:

Complaint	Last Month	This Month
Rude	3	11
Lack of Knowledge	4	3
Long Wait Time	10	14
On Hold Too Long	3	5
TOTAL PROBLEMS	20	30

Since we get over 10,000 calls a month, the 80 monitored calls is not a significant number of samples.

<NOTE - Olivia recently took a course in statistics and it included sample size analysis; and took a course in market research that included the correct way to construct, field and analyze a survey; Broyles, her supervisor, does not know this>

Therefore, we believe that the first step is to field a survey to help dimension the problem.

We further recommend that the survey be conducted monthly so that we can track the problems over time. This helps in two ways:

- first, if there is no major problem, to ensure it is staying that way
- second, if there is a major problem, to determine if the solutions implemented are fixing the problem

In either case, the phone monitoring is highlighting specific incidences where problems are occurring. So our second recommendation is that we set up refresher training courses which phone representatives who show a pattern of errors during monitoring, are required to attend.

Our third recommendation is to update our procedure manual. It is out of date regarding some of the problem resolutions so the phone representatives do not use it. If it was updated, the phone representatives could use it if they find themselves in a situation where they lack the knowledge to resolve a customer problem.

As an aside, many phone representatives look at the monitoring in a very negative light. In addition to using it as a tool to spot errors, you could give some thought to rewarding phone representatives who continually perform perfectly on the monitored calls.

We want to thank Peter and Walter Rook for providing us with the numbers that are contained in this memo.

cc: P. Rook
    W. Rook

After reading the memo, Broyles assigns Peter Rook the task of fielding the survey. Peter has experience with monitoring calls, but has no experience generating and fielding surveys. Remembering that Charlie was the original person to approach him about this problem, he assigns Charlie the task of making a proposal regarding rewarding employees who continually perform well on monitored calls.

Charlie discusses some initial ideas with Broyles in regards to a reward program for employees who continually perform well on monitored calls. Broyles is very impressed and believes Charlie may be on to something good. However, one week, two weeks, one month later, Broyles doesn't get a report from Charlie. Two months later, still no report from Charlie, and Broyles gets wrapped up in a new problem and all thoughts of a program rewarding employees who continually perform well on monitored calls is completely off his mind.

Daryl and Merle are brothers who work at the fast food restaurant Hershel's Fresh Farm Burgers. The burgers are so tasty, that the company's slogan, "Our burgers are so good zombies prefer them to all alternatives," rings true.

Hershel's Fresh Farm Burgers has a company policy, clearly stated in the employee handbook, that all leftover food is thrown out at the end of the day; and that no employee can take any of the food leftover at the end of the day home, for any reason.

At the end of the night, their supervisor, Maggie, leaves the restaurant allowing the brothers to close up shop. Immediately upon Maggie's leaving Merle notices his brother Daryl take four leftover Hershel Fresh Farm burgers and place them aside to take home. The only other person in the restaurant at that time, a local customer named Glenn, also notices Daryl putting the leftover burgers aside to take home. Glenn also witnesses Merle observing Daryl putting the burgers in a bag to take home.

Merle knows what Daryl is doing is against company policy, but he thinks the policy is dumb. Why waste food? Besides, it's not like Maggie can call the sheriff, Rick, and have Daryl arrested. In fact, Merle knows that Daryl is doing a good thing for a struggling family. Daryl has always had a crush on Carol; Carol's daughter Sophia loves Hershel's burgers; and Carol is struggling to make ends meet since the untimely death of her husband Ed. Merle thinks it all adds up, it's good for everyone involved; and it hurts no one.

So Darryl leaves with the burgers, and Merle follows him out the door minutes later. There he notices Glenn writing notes on some forms. What was that all about thinks Merle?

Another New Year, another set of New Year resolutions. However, this year will be different thinks Clara, this year I'm going to meet my work resolutions and get that promotion.

The job Clara is interested in is an important stepping stone for getting on the fast track to management. As Clara looks at the company organization chart she sees lots of people who have taken the same path she wants to take. Donna, head of Strategic Planning; the Marketing Director Rose, Head of Security, Martha; the Sales Manager Jack and his top salesperson Amy; and even the company nurse Rory; all held the position that Clara is interest in prior to getting their promotions.

So Clara starts to develop a formal work plan of action for the New Year. What follows are the items Clara put in her plan.

1. I often have to pass along bad information to customers from the big boss, The Doctor. The responses are often harsh so I need to learn not to take the negative reaction personally.

2. I have to stop going to my supervisor, asking questions when I am unsure of something. I'm smart. Instead I need to figure things out on my own.

3. I need to be more open to other people's ideas. I know I figure things out better than my co-workers (it is true that Clara figures things out better and well in advance of others), but that doesn't mean that they can't have good ideas too.

4. I need to be more careful to avoid office gossip. I never start the gossip, however, I did jump into the juicy conversation regarding whether Amy really liked the big boss, The Doctor, more than Rory. I know that much of the gossip got back to Rory, and he was hurt by all the talk and insinuation.

5. I need to be a better team player. When Jenny (a co-worker) was put in charge of the last project, I resented that I wasn't put in charge, and I didn't recognize her as someone who could assign me work, and judge my work, during the project. I thought I hid it well; I even looked her straight in the eye the whole time during our first long conversation, holding my head still.

6. I have a habit of constantly tapping my fingers, and I need to stop doing that because I think it gives people the wrong idea of what I am thinking.

7. I also have a habit of leaning forward slightly when I am interested in something; I think I may be giving the wrong impression there as well, so I need to be conscious to stop doing that as well.

8. I need to become a better team leader. The last time I was put in charge of a team, the following happened:

a. I started off by telling the group about the project. I then wrote my ideas on the board and asked the group which tasks they would like to work on. After getting their feedback, I assigned roles to the team. Then I informed them what I expected of them, which included what each person needed to accomplish and the timeframes for accomplishing those tasks. I then invited them to the final presentation, which I gave myself. I stated the presentation by saying, "I want to thank management for giving me the opportunity to solve this important issue. I gave a lot of thought to this problem, and came up with a plan to fix it that I think you will all be very please with. I am very proud of the work I accomplished." When the presentation was done, and The Doctor asked who did the financials for the project, I responded, "Mickey did the reports."

b. My lesson: I did a very good job, however next time I need to be sure that I get the proper credit. Therefore, I should have answered The Doctor's question, "I came up with the parameters, but Mickey crunched the numbers and typed the report."

9. I need to follow all the rules of the workplace. Eating lunch at one's desk is against the rules, so I need to stop doing that even though I'm not the only one who does it; and even though I do it to save time to get back to work faster.

10. I need to stand up for myself and stop cow-towing to my supervisor, River, when she criticizes me. I am the one doing the work, I know better than her if it is good or not. And I was right to tell her that I would try the new procedure she wanted, and then ignore it. I knew it wouldn't work.

11. I do, however, have to keep my supervisor, River, better informed. I need to let her know everything that is going on in a timely fashion. Maybe if I do that she will stop trying to give me better ways to do my job.

12. Since I have a good understanding of how the workplace operates, I need to let my supervisor know about some changes that I think will improve the entire operation, even in areas where others do the work. So I will tell her, and then I will follow whatever she thinks is best to do.

Mike works for original Victory Corporation and, once again, it's that time of year. Boy time does fly; and now it's time for Mike's annual performance review once again.

However, much to his chagrin Mike discovers that it isn't his immediate boss Martin who will be giving him his performance review this year; it is the commander, herself, Diana who will be conducting this interview.

As Mike walks into her office, Diana stands and says, "I know I have a reputation as a very tough boss, but if you can at least recognize the things you did right and the things you did wrong this past year I won't "eat you alive," so to say.

Grasping his upper arms, Mike sits down.

The first topic Diana brings up is Mike's presentation to Juliet. During the presentation Juliet asked how many cases his department handled last year. Mike did not have the specifics but knew that it was somewhere between 3,500 and 7,500 cases. So Mike answered that his department handled 5,614 cases.

Next Diana brings up the strategic planning meeting between Mike and Ham. Ham is very set in his ways and is constantly arguing. But the meeting between Mike and Ham went well with no arguments. Diana then asks him how he was able to accomplish that. Chin up, Mike starts to answer; "I started with a strategy to concentrate on what I knew we agreed on first, to get us on the same page and eliminate arguments right off the bat."

Diana then asks if Mike's son ever left the cult he joined. She further adds to Mike that it's a shame that you have to be careful not to let him know how bad you believe the cult leader is. Mike responds, how did you know about that? Diana answers; "Are you kidding; who in the company haven't you talked to about this?"

Diana then follows up that rhetorical question by asking Mike, "Do you have any issues with Victory Corporation?" Mike responds, "Why would you ask that?" Diana says, "Do you think I don't know what goes on in my workplace? I wish if you had complaints that you would bring them up with your supervisor Martin, or me; not discuss them with your co-workers." Stroking his nose, and in a tone similar to Sansa Stark when talking about her pending marriage to King Joffrey in *Game of Thrones*, Mike says, "I have never complained to my co-workers about Victory Corporation."

Diana then says, "Let me lighten the mood a bit. Tell me about the situation with Willie that happened a few months back." Mike then responds, "I saw that Willie was placing products in storage bins before labels where placed on them. I knew that if the labels were missing the wrong products could be shipped to the wrong clients and that could cost the company money, result in customer dissatisfaction, and lost accounts. So I spoke to Willie who then started putting the labels on before putting the products into storage bins. Diana followed up by saying, "Willie doesn't work for you. In fact he is in a different department." Mike, said, "That's right, but I used to do that job so I knew the correct procedure. Boy you really do see all." "Yes" said Diana, "My eyes are the eyes of an eagle."

Next up, Diana asked Mike about the time he was put in charge of the Project Resistance. Diana commented that she was at the oral presentation of the findings, and would Mike please explain to her how he decided on the strategy for the presentation format. Mike answered, "I wanted everyone involved in the project to have a role in the presentation, so that management would be aware of their contributions. After all, it was team effort. However, I wanted to start the presentation to talk about our process and challenges; and then I wanted to conclude the presentation presenting the team's solutions since I was the Team Leader."

Knowing that there were a lot of changes that took place during the year; Diana asks Mike, "How did all the changes impact you?" Mike responded, "The changes really helped. The process is running more smoothly, there are fewer work stoppages and errors. In addition, I loved learning the new process."

Diana said, "Last topic. I know you are new to the Science Frontiers account. Their CEO, Nathan, can be tough to deal with. How are you holding up? I know our prior two account managers for Science Frontiers thrived in the role, but I know with the tight deadlines, the high employee productivity needed to meet those deadlines, and no-errors-allowed policy, that account can be highly stressful." Mike answers," I'm very glad you recognize that. That account is keeping me up at night. You know what would help, though; do away with all those Quality Assurance people looking over my shoulder. I feel enough pressure without being told if my productivity is falling behind, or my last batch had an error."

After Mike informs Diana what he did right and what he did wrong regarding these situations, Mike walks back to his desk waiting for his written performance appraisal to see if he identified his good workplace actions and his mistakes correctly.

Help Us Help You, Inc. just completed its first round of in-depth customer research regarding its service delivery. The research included both surveys and focus groups. Many reports were generated highlighting both the good and the bad regarding the company's customer service. You have been invited to a strategic planning meeting to discuss the findings and to help decide steps Help Us Help You Inc. needs to take to improve its service delivery.

Lauren has been put charge of the strategic planning session and starts off by stressing the importance of providing superior customer service. Right away Anne jumps in and says, "Why did we spend over $100,000 on this study? Our products and services are the best in the marketplace and that's what drives our business. As far as I am concerned if we offered no customer service we would still sell a lot." Lauren seems taken by surprise and answers, "I know we have great products and services. This is something management wants so let's just do this the best we can."

Lauren continues, "One of the most interesting findings from the study was that a portion of our customers are complaining about something we fixed three years ago. In fact, our fix is what has propelled our product to the top of *Consumer Report* lists." Mr. K says, "They're fools. Ignore them." Ryan chips in with, "Mr. K, how is that different from how you treat all our customers?" Mr. K just smiles.

Lauren, addressing Mr. K, says "Is that true, do you ignore all our customers?" Mr. K smiles and says, "Not usually."

Owen then says, "Isn't this a meeting about our customers. Let's get back on track. I have things to do after the meeting." Lauren says, "You're right. Let's talk about what our customers want. The research shows that they want a price point 20% below our current prices; thoughts anybody?"

Ryan says, "Just because they want lower prices doesn't mean we have to give them that. Everyone wants lower prices. Our sales have been increasing every month at the current prices."

Danny follows up with, "I thought we wanted to be a customer-focused organization. Doesn't that mean give the customers what they want? Let's cut the prices."

Ryan responds," Being customer focused doesn't mean give them everything they want. That's just silly. What if they want you to go to their house and cook them dinner." Mr. K jumps in with, "I've done that."

Ryan continues, "Do you even know what cutting the prices will do to the profit margin; we could lose money on every sale."

Mr. K jumps in again and says, "Yeah, but even if you're right Ryan, we'll sell more products that way."

Lauren says, "Danny and Ryan, you both make good points. Let's table this topic until later. I now want to discuss another thing our customers indicated they wanted. They indicated that they would like music on hold instead of dead air like we currently have. They indicated that they never know if they are still on hold or if the call has been dropped. This was a very big negative that came out of the study. Our phone system can do this easily and it costs us nothing. What do you think?"

George says, "Seems reasonable. They want it, we can do it, and it costs nothing." Lauren, looking at Anne, asks, "Any objections?" Mr. K raises his hand. Lauren, "Yes, Mr. K?" Mr. K says, "I could sing live to the customers on hold." Ryan says, "Mr. K, we want to attract more customers, not drive them away." Lauren concludes, "Done deal, we'll implement music for customers on hold."

Lauren continues, "Now I have to talk about a sensitive topic. Management wants me to install service measurements. This includes ongoing customer surveys, reports by departments, and individual productivity measurements. I'm going to hand out the list of measurements now."

After handing out the list, and giving the group time to review the list, Lauren asks, "Any questions?"

Anne jumps in with, "Why are you measuring the time it takes me to generate the report I give to Yolanda? Our customers don't read the report."

Ryan says, "Yes, but the report contains information Yolanda needs to better understand how our products are used. This helps her when she gets questions from customers."

Anne says, "Ryan, I'm not talking to you." Yolanda then says, "Anne I use the report to better understand how our products are used. This helps me when I get questions from customers."

Anne just sighs.

Lauren, "Anne, that sigh of yours came up in our study as well."

Anne, "What do you mean? How come I was mentioned at all?"

Lauren, "Remember that survey you took on working with other employees; that was part of the customer service study."

Mr. K raises his hand. Lauren, "Yes, Mr K." Mr. K responds, "Yes, I remember."

Shaking her head from side to side, Lauren continues, "Your co-workers indicated that you are difficult to work with because of your negative attitude. That sigh is an example."

Anne says, "I understand that, but what does that have to do with customer service. I don't do that when I interact with customers."

Lauren responds, "That's true, you are good with our customers. I guess management is concerned that if you act that way with your co-workers that maybe that will carry over to your communications with our customers. I'm not really sure, just watch it."

Lauren continues, "One more topic to discuss, and then we'll call it day." Mr. K, "Can I call it Fred instead?"

Ignoring Mr. K, Lauren says, "As far as our employees are concerned, our Phone Center Staff were the most dissatisfied in their jobs. They believe their supervisor, Steven, and his assistant manager, Carrie, are on a power trip and treat them like kids. They feel this way because they are scheduled for lunch, cannot come in late, even a minute to work, and are watched very closely. You know that a report comes out every day that indicates the percent of time they were plugged into the system, their average talk time; and the number of calls they work on every day. This is a serious issue."

Fausta asks, "Why does Steven and Carrie treat them like that. That's not right."

Anne jumps in and says, "Wait a minute. They are just employing good phone center management techniques. In fact, they are being very customer-focused, which is what this meeting is all about anyway. If you want, Lauren, I can talk to them and explain why Steven and Carrie treat them like that. It could be better coming from someone outside their department. Oh, and I'll watch my "sighs.""

Lauren responds, "That would be great Anne. Thanks. Meeting adjourned."

Mr. K. says, "Can I stay another 15 minutes?" However, everyone was already gone.

Hive Mind Inc. is a very busy company with many employees. Below is how the day has been going for some of those employees.

Peter works in phone center as a customer service representative. Having worked in customer service for ten years, Peter has his own ideas regarding customer service. He believes customers need to chill. He is very good at his job and is able to meet their needs. He also feels that after he understands a problem he can work better without them yammering in his ear. So he puts them on hold to get peace and quiet and leaves them on hold until he finishes his work on their problem. This can take up to six minutes, which is twice as fast as most of his co-workers.. Peter also believes that customers should not get the run around. So he studies hard and learns how to fix all kinds of problems so he can deal with all customer problems without having to transfer the call to anyone else. Customers expect a lot, thinks Peter, but that's okay, they should. After all they should not have had problems in the first place.

Peter's office is located in South Florida where many of the company's customers speak Spanish. Unfortunately, Peter does not speak nor understand Spanish. Peter reports to work at 11:00 AM right before the high-volume lunch hour. Before Peter reports to his workstation he notices that three co-workers are out today. This is going to make for a very busy day since the calls will be backed up. As he sits down Peter notices the sign on the blackboard that says, feel free to take off your jackets and ties, the air conditioner is not working. Boy, talk about making a difficult situation even worse! After answering three calls, Peter's supervisor, sits down next to him and says, "Peter, our customer statements that went out last week had errors in them. All our customers are going to see a $1,000 charge that is not a real charge." Boy, Peter thinks this day is getting tougher and tougher.

Peter's fourth call of the day is from an angry, aggressive caller who won't stop complaining about the $1,000 charge. Peter tries to interrupt but the caller just keeps on complaining about the charge. If only the customer would slow down and listen, Peter could tell him that there was an error and the $1,000 charge is being removed from the account. The caller keeps going on and on and on and on. Finally, Peter tunes him out. Three minutes later Peter hears the customer saying, so what are you going to do about it being broken. Peter has no idea what the customer is talking about.

In another part of the building is Peter's kid brother Andrew. Andrew is talking in person to a customer. Watching him very closely is his supervisor, Hyrum. Hyrum notices that Andrew is listening more than talking. When he does say something Andrew often uses some of the words and phrases that the customer just said. Hyrum then notices Andrew start to talk. In fact he just summarized very succinctly the information the customer just told him. In addition, Andrew looks very interested in what the customer is saying. If he didn't know better, Hyrum thinks, Andrew looks as interested in this conversation as he is playing his video games.

Back in the phone center where Peter works, sits his sister Valentine. When the phone rings Valentine says, "How may I help you?" The customer on the phone says to Valentine, "You're company is the worst I have ever dealt with. But you sound nice. Hey, have you ever read the book *Ender's Game*? It's a great book. You must read it. Let me tell you about it."

The next call Valentine gets is from a customer who is very demanding, who wants immediate action. This customer says, "Your delivery men ripped the couch I just had delivered."

Next up is a very angry customer. This customer says, "I do not understand this charge. Why did I get it?"

That call from the very angry customer is followed by a call from a customer who appears on verge of apologizing for having a problem. The customer seems very reluctant to talk about the problem. However, it is a very serious problem and Valentine needs to know more because this problem could be impacting other customers.

In the backroom observing the ongoing customer service is Bean, the new management trainee. As he is witnessing the various acts of service, Hyrum is sitting next to him quizzing him all the time.

The first call Bean observes is Petra calling one of her clients and asking him if there was anything he needed.

Next Bean observes Tom taking a call from an upset customer. However, by the end of the call, the customer was thanking Tom and he no longer seemed upset.

After that call concluded, Bean listens in on the Production Manager, Dink, congratulating Han and his team for their latest run because it had no defects.

For his last monitoring session Bean listens in on Bonzo and his team talking about enhancements needed to the latest product. Bean also notices that Andrew, part of Bonzo's team, is not in the room.

Later Bean finds out that Bonzo sent Andrew to get coffee for the group. It seems that Bonzo is always excluding Andrew. Boy, thinks Bean, one day that situation is going to come to a head.

From this point up to
About the Author not in
the CLASSROOM BOOK

NOTE FROM THE AUTHOR

I am a consultant who has been paid significant money to develop and implement work readiness/customer service certification training programs for workforce development boards. I retained the rights to my materials and this is my own program, which utilizes the best of my past programs as well as a significant amount of new material. In particular, the lecture content now focuses on the why, not just the how, and uses a lot of examples outside the workplace to help underscore key work readiness and customer service c oncepts.

Use the materials in this book to customize your own program, or contact me at **book@dtrconsulting.biz** or go to **www.dtrconsulting.biz** for telephone contact information, and hire me to help you customize this program.

My best recommendation is to make all assessment tests in your program, open book assessments (including the final certification tests). Since the program is demonstrated competency driven, not assessment test driven, this makes the assessment tests learning tools as much as tests. In addition, this helps train the participants on how to use this book to look-up information. To make this learning strategy ideal, the participants should keep their classroom copies of the book so they have a reference tool when they enter the workplace. To optimize the reference tool, if the book is owned by the participants, they can enter their answers to the personal worksheets in the book, and write down the correct answers to all the exercises during the instructor's review of the exercises.

Areas where decisions need to be made regarding your program are:
- Which exercises are for classroom use, which are competencies (all can be for competencies)
- For each section, will the competency exercises be graded as a group of individually
- What constitutes a passing score for each competency (however, must pass all competencies, cannot give impression that is okay in the workplace do to most of these things, must do all of them)
- How will you run the key concept Q&A review (which should become program competencies)
- How will you monitor (audit) the participants' work on the personal worksheets

In addition:
- You will have to generate test questions for the certification scenarios (examples are given in the certification scenario section write-up).
- You should have a name for the program and offer both a grade or a pass/fail (completion of program) and a program award level (certification).

Keep in mind every participant needs to genuinely earn the award (certification), otherwise employers will not be able to rely on it. If everyone gets the award, either by just completing the program (no matter how they perform) or because the award (certification) level is too easy, employers will eventually find the award level (certification) meaningless. This is why I recommend two levels; grade and certification; with either, "completed a work readiness/customer service program" or "earned a certification in work readiness/customer service" on the participant's resume.

ORIENTATION INSTRUCTIONS

Orientation Instructions

It is highly recommended that you run this program like a workplace training program rather than as a typical education course. That means that day one needs to be a new employee orientation and the program itself is the probationary period for those new employees.

Have the participants read the Participant/Employee Rulebook chapter day one and have them initial each rule indicating that they understand and will follow those rules. In fact performing this properly is the first competency for the participants. Think of it as a following simple instructions exercise.

There are competencies relating to every rule in the rulebook (see the competency statement section). Some are their own competencies, some are combined competencies. Most of the competencies are straight forward, however, for some; you need to define your program's parameters.

For the dress code competency, you need to decide if you will have a dress code for the full program or only on specific days. You also need to define what that dress code should be (it will be different for different venues). For generic venues the dress code could be:

- ✓ Dress shoes (no sneakers or work boots)
- ✓ Dress pants (no jeans) or skirt or dress
- ✓ Dress shirt (no t-shirt) or dress

In addition, depending upon your venue, there may be times when program or personal requirements (an athlete on a school team; someone who goes to work directly after class, etc.) whereby this competency cannot be met. These exceptions need to be flushed out and stated in advance. Worst case, whenever possible, participants need to bring up potential exceptions prior to that participant showing up unannounced asking for an exception at that time.

Also, there are some very basic grooming requirements listed in the rulebook, but you can expand it. For example:

- ✓ Must be clean shaven (men)
- ✓ Must use appropriate makeup (women)
- ✓ No visible tattoos

Finally, the competencies call for no unexcused absences or tardiness. So if there are conflicts in advance, the instructor can make an absence or lateness an <u>excused</u> absence or tardiness. In addition, unforeseen emergencies may also arise. This is especially true in situations where the participants are kids who rely on their parents to get them to class on time. In these cases, a conference with the parents to express what is at risk if their child cannot get to class on time (not their grade, they can do fine; but they would lose out on getting a certification because that is based on demonstrated competencies).

In the end, the instructor is the final word on deciding whether or not to grant an exception in emergency situations. Keep in mind that these exceptions should be rare. The instructor needs to think like a boss not a teacher.

In all cases work missed will need to be made up in order for the participant to receive full certification (or honors).

KEY CONCEPTS REVIEWED

Workplace Basics

The list below contains conclusions from the topics taught in Workplace Basics. Ask the class what lessons they learned from each sub-chapter of Workplace Basics. Below are some of the key points that should result from that discussion, although there could certainly be more. You can do this formally by calling on each participant for a response or as an informal discussion where you inform the group that all are expected to participate. You can then use this wrap-up discussion as a competency based on how you ran the exercise. See the optional competency statements section for more information.

"The Profit Motive of Business"

1. It is very important that the business you work for is highly profitable. Your job security, compensation and benefits are directly tied to the profitability of your employer.

2. If a co-worker is doing anything that impacts your employer's bottom line negatively, he or she is not just hurting the business, he or she is messing with your livelihood.

3. When a business pays employees salaries and benefits, it comes out of the pockets of the business owners. As business owners, they take risks; it is their home or other asset on the line if the business fails, so owners are clearly entitled to make profits in their businesses.

"Time is Money"

1. Absenteeism causes problems for a business. When employees are absent from work, the amount of work needed to be completed that day does not change. Therefore, unexpected absences often results in very difficult work days for the absent employee's co-workers.

2. Being late for work, even 10 minutes, can throw off work schedules and cause problems that last for days. These problems can result in customer dissatisfaction which could lead to losing customers and the company earning less money.

3. Sick days are an insurance policy, not an earned day off. They often accumulate so that if an employee gets seriously ill, he or she has the time available to take off from work while still getting paid. Keep in mind, that long absences for illnesses are usually known in advance, so a business can plan around those absences.

4. Just like car insurance, if you never get into a car accident (never get sick), you don't get your insurance payments back (you don't get paid for unused sick days).

"Safety in the Workplace"

1. In addition to a business setting their own safety rules, the U.S. Government, through OSHA, also sets safety standards for businesses.

2. If a business fails an OSHA safety audit it can result in fines and/or shut downs until the safety issue is addressed. In both cases this costs the business money which reduces profits. So follow all safety rules.

3. Bad accidents can also result in negative word of mouth which can result in the loss of current and future customers. Once again this has a negative impact on the business' profitability.

4. Individuals who fake injuries to go on disability and get workman's comp (or who get into accidents by not following the safety rules), are stealing money not only from the company and the government, but from you as well. The more accidents at work, the higher the premiums for the company. That means more expenses, which result in lower profits.

"Be a Positive Force in the Workplace"

1. You must be dependable (get to work on time, etc.) and responsible (finish all work assignments satisfactory) in order for your supervisor to be able to rely on you.

2. Be a glass half-full person, not a half-glass empty person. Do not react poorly to change in the workplace, either vocally or with your personal signals (for example, arms crossed and scowl on your face).

3. Have a positive self-image; know that you have your job because management believes you are beneficial to their bottom line (profits). If not, you would be fired.

4. You have a responsibility to curb your lifestyle outside of work, to ensure you are at your best when you show up for work; and that you do not do anything that will reflect badly on your employer. So watch what you post online at Facebook and other social web sites!

5. Have plans in advance to account for common emergencies that may arise that can cause you to miss work. For example, have backup plans for getting to work (transportation) and daycare.

"Avoiding Problems at Work"

1. Avoid all kinds of harassment (sexual, racial, creed-related, lifestyle-related, age-related, etc.).

2. Do not discriminate against anyone at work; be all inclusive.

3. Do not tell, post, or distribute jokes or anything else (e.g. a controversial article) that could offend any group; no matter how innocent you think the jokes or materials are.

4. Do not come to work high or drunk; and do not use or even threaten violence.

"Social Life at Work"

1. Keep your baggage at the door; do not bring your personal problems to work.

2. Make the people who work near you and whose work you rely on, more like friendly neighbors than good friends.

3. Dating at work is dangerous. Do not even ask out someone who works for you or whose salary you control; that is sexual harassment. If you do ask out someone at work who works in a different department, be sure you are thinking long term relationship, not one night stand.

"Your Employment Relationship"

1. Know the rules of your workplace, whether they are contained in an employee handbook, a series of memos, or are informal, spoken rules passed down from your supervisor.

2. Your job is not just to complete your job functions, but to be a positive force in the workplace.

3. Raises usually come at set times, are often based on a percent increase, and typically contain both a cost of living component, and a performance based component.

4. Promotions are only available when there are open jobs in the company that are at higher levels of responsibility and pay scales than your current job. In addition to being a good employee, **you must possess the specific skills required for that job to be considered**. Therefore, being the top rated employee does not mean you get the promotion. Promotions are not rewards for a job well done; performance raises and bonuses are rewards for doing your job very well.

Workplace Skills

The list below contains conclusions from the topics taught in Workplace Skills. Ask the class what lessons they learned from each sub-chapter of Workplace Skills. Below are some of the key points that should result from that discussion, although there could certainly be more. You can do this formally by calling on each participant for a response or as an informal discussion where you inform the group that all are expected to participate. You can then use this wrap-up discussion as a competency based on how you ran the exercise. See the optional competency statements section for more information.

"Required Workplace Skills"

1. Workplaces are a finely tuned mechanism where work flow is very time sensitive and co-workers often cannot perform their work until other co-workers complete their work. In addition, customers often have expectations in terms of the time it takes to transact business or to get their problems resolved. Therefore, time management is very important for all employees. This includes time on the job, as well as managing breaks and lunches.

2. At home you may get satisfaction starting, but not completing, projects. In the workplace you must complete all work assigned to you. You get no partial credit for bringing a task close to completion.

3. The quality of the work performed in a workplace is very important to a business and has a direct impact on the profitability of that business. So a quality assurance function, where your work gets checked (in full, sampled, or spot checked) is the rule not the exception. Expect it.

4. Procedure manuals, if they exist in your workplace, are excellent tools to use when you are new to a job or a job function; or you encounter a situation new to you.

"Ethics"

1. A behavior is either ethical or unethical.

2. It is the behavior that determines the ethics, not the circumstances, values, beliefs, the people involved, etc.

3. Acting ethically or unethically is a choice, sometimes you may feel acting unethically is the right thing to do for you.

4. Choosing the unethical act doesn't necessarily make you a bad person.

5. However, with an unethical act comes potential consequences, know what they are and be prepared to face them.

"Reading in the Workplace"

1. The way you were taught reading in school is different from reading in the workplace.

2. At work, no "reading between the lines"; when you read something at work it is straight-forward

3. If you read something and it is not clear to you; don't assume, ask questions

4. At work, do not bring any preconceptions to what you read; take what read at face value.

5. When you read an important work document, take notes. Identify the main topic (usually the first sentence in well written business memos) and then list the important details.

"Business Writing"

1. The way you were taught writing in school is different from writing in the workplace.

2. At school, it was using 1000 words or more; in business it is in as few words as possible.

3. At school it was, paint a picture using your words; at work it is be direct and to the point.

4. At school it was allow the reader to reach his or her own conclusion, or build up to a conclusion; at works it is state your conclusion up front (first sentence) and then back it up from most important to least important.

"Understanding Math"

1. While you should use calculators and computer programs to perform math functions at work, you need to understand numbers so you can spot errors, whether your own, or from a co-worker or even a supervisor.

2. Percent change is: the new value minus what you are comparing the new value to (the base); divided by the base. So if you are comparing the cost in 2012 **to** the cost in 2011, it would be: (2012 cost minus 2011 cost) divided by 2011 cost.

3. When there is a double mark down of a product (50% off a product already reduced 50%), the percents are NOT added together; you take the second discount off of the result from the first discount.

4. Math errors that result in situations that favor the customer are rarely caught and cost the business money. Math errors that are in the business' favor are usually caught by the customer (at the time or at a later date), and can cause customer dissatisfaction. So they do not even out.

"Advanced Workplace Skills"

1. Problem-solving skills are very important in the workplace and can help a worker advance his or her career. There are steps in the problem-solving process and many leave out some of them, such as after implementing the solution, monitor it to be sure that the problem is truly resolved. If you are unaware of the steps in the process, reread this chapter in the *Workplace Skills* section.

2. Creative thinking is not a skill that comes easy to everyone. However, it is a skill that can separate you from other workers. While the final work product for a set procedure is usually the same for every worker (quality and time to complete may be different, but the final product is the same), the result from a creative thinking exercise is often very different by worker. So if you demonstrate practical, creative thinking skills on the job, management knows that if they have to replace you, the new worker will, most likely, not come up with the same creative ideas that you would have come up with.

3. You should look at yourself like a stock, and continually do things to increase your stock value. That includes taking continuing education courses. However, to advance in the company, have a plan for the courses you take. It is often advisable to talk to your supervisor or human resources to help develop your continuing education plan.

4. Report generation and analysis uses many of the prior skills contained in the *Workplace Skills* section. You have to write your report using the business writing approach; you need to spell everything out since the readers will not be reading between the lines, your math skills will come in handy during the analysis, new skills obtained through continuing education will help you throughout the process, and following the problem-solving steps and using your creative thinking skills will help you come up with solutions to any problems uncovered in your report.

People Skills

The list below contains conclusions from the topics taught in People Skills. Ask the class what lessons they learned from each sub-chapter of People Skills. Below are some of the key points that should result from that discussion, although there could certainly be more. You can do this formally by calling on each participant for a response or as an informal discussion where you inform the group that all are expected to participate. You can then use this wrap-up discussion as a competency based on how you ran the exercise. See the optional competency statements section for more information.

"Communication Skills"

1. Communicating clearly is very important when interacting with customers, co-workers and supervisors. So speak clearly and choose your words wisely.

2. Do not use lingo when communicating at work. For example, say or write, talk to you later, do not use TTYL.

3. Leave your emotions out of your communications at work. The customers and employees may react in ways you do not appreciate, however, they are reacting to what you said, not to you; it isn't personal.

4. Do not make up facts, guess at answers, assume, or argue. Stay clam; only say what you know is true; and ask questions when you do not fully understand something.

5. Be open to other people's points of view.

6. Watch your personal signals. Verbal communication is only part of communicating with others. Your actions, both voluntary and involuntary are part of the communication package. For a list of how some personal signals are usually interpreted, reread this chapter.

"Getting Along with Co-Workers"

1. Treat your co-workers more like "friendly neighbors", than best friends. You have control over the friends you choose. However, like neighbors, you do not have control over who your co-workers will be.

2. There are behaviors that should be avoided at work. These include gossiping about your co-workers, complaining about the job (or your employer or your supervisor), and being an overbearing know-it-all.

3. Do not get involved in co-workers personal problems, and leave your personal problems at your door when you leave for work.

4. Treat your co-workers like team members, not the competition. And to be a good team member, always perform your job functions to the best of your ability.

5. Be able to get along with all kinds of people.

"Teamwork"

1. When working on projects, an employee is usually assigned to be a team leader. When this is a supervisor, the lines of authority are clear. However, the team leader is often a co-worker assigned a supervisory role just for that project. When this happens, treat that co-worker just like you would a supervisor.

2. If you are assigned a role as a team leader, that is a good thing, management is observing your potential as a supervisor.

3. There are steps you can follow as a team leader to help ensure success, while also demonstrating your ability to lead and manage. These steps can be found in this chapter. It starts by setting goals, and includes obtaining input from all team members, you making the final decisions, sharing the spotlight with your team members, and taking your role very seriously.

"Meeting Supervisor's Expectations"

1. Your supervisor is responsible for his or her work and for your work. Therefore, it is in your supervisor's best interest for you to succeed. Yes, your supervisor is on your side.

2. Often, if you believe your boss is "out to get you," and your work product is excellent, it is because you are a disruption to the workplace. Remember your job is not just to complete your assigned tasks, but to be a positive force in the workplace. This can include the obvious such as you coming in late, to the not so obvious such as you dating and dumping your co-workers.

3. While workers often look at tough assignments as punishment, supervisors look at them as providing their best workers with assignments that can help them get good raises and grow in the company.

4. Supervisor often get recognition for work you do. That is fine, in fact that is the way it should work. Supervisors assigned you the work, allowed you the time to complete the work, and recognized its value. Be confident that senior management knows the supervisor had staff perform that task and also knows your name and contribution. In fact, if your supervisor does not share that information, that will be looked at negatively by most in senior management.

5. There are steps you can follow to help you consistently meet your supervisor's expectations. Reread this chapter for a full list. Some of these steps include accepting the fact that your supervisor controls your work life; ask questions when not sure of something; follow the rules of your workplace; and take criticism well (if your supervisor thought you were a "lost cause" he or she wouldn't waste his/her time criticizing you).

6. Don't avoid your supervisor when you need to communicate something bad.

7. Seek out your supervisor to ask for feedback on your job performance in advance of your performance appraisal so you have time to improve your performance (if needed) prior to the official appraisal.

"Business Basics"

1. A business plan is an in-depth document that needs to be generated before a business starts. It contains strategies the business will follow and has projections for what it will cost the business to operate. While all the strategies in a business plan are not always successful, without set strategies and goals there is no way to know if the business is operating as expected, lagging behind, or performing better than expectations.

2. Strategic planning picks up where business plans end. It includes business objectives, strategies, tactics and goals that allow a business to take advantage of its strengths, overcome/eliminate its weaknesses, find opportunities, and manage threats.

3. Marketing involves generating strategies, processes and tools, for prices, products, promotions, and distribution channels.

4. All businesses that sell products and services have a sales process. Learn it and follow it.

Customer Service

The list below contains conclusions from the topics taught in Customer Service. Ask the class what lessons they learned from each sub-chapter of Customer Service. Below are some of the key points that should result from that discussion, although there could certainly be more. You can do this formally by calling on each participant for a response or as an informal discussion where you inform the group that all are expected to participate. You can then use this wrap-up discussion as a competency based on how you ran the exercise. See the optional competency statements section for more information.

"Focusing on the Customer"

1. Problems will occur in the workplace. However, if they are dealt with head on, and resolved to the customer's satisfaction, the company can avoid losing the majority share of those customers due to those errors.

2. On the flip side, if a problem or error arises in the workplace, and a company does not provide good customer service and solve those problems to their customers' satisfaction, the company can lose customers and have negative word of mouth on the street. This leads to lower profits which could cost some workers their jobs.

3. Customer focus means understanding what customers want.

4. Once a company understands what their customers want in terms of service; it needs to determine the ideal trade-off between the costs of providing that service and satisfying as many customers as it can.

5. A company needs to be aware of potential problems caused by customer perceptions, even when those perceptions are not true. The answer to incorrect customer perceptions is usually educating the customers as to the true facts.

6. Everyone has different natural strengths and weaknesses regarding their customer focus (focusing on product and services, dealing with negatives, building the positives, delivering quality). It is important to know your strengths and weaknesses so you can use your strengths and be aware of your weaknesses.

"Identifying Your Customer"

1. Your customers can be both the company's customers (the consumers that purchase the company's products and/or services) and your co-workers who rely on your work to perform their job functions.

2. To understand the needs of your customer you must put yourself in your customers' (external and internal) shoes. To help do this ask questions such as what products or services do they use; when and where do they need those products or services delivered; why do your customers need those products or services; who is the decision-maker regarding purchasing (or determining the quality of) those products or services and how much of your products or services (combination of quantity and price) are your customers willing to purchase.

"Service Measurements"

1. Since providing quality service to ensure customer satisfaction is important for keeping and growing a company's customer base; the company needs to measure service delivery to ensure that quality service is actually being provided to customers.

2. Service measurements need to be department (or work function) based (e.g. service measurements for the problem resolution department) and individual based (e.g. productivity measurements by individual employee). The department based service measurements let management know what the customers are experiencing while the individual based service measurements provide a way to help fix or improve service delivery.

"Customer Service Phone Center"

1. Efficiently run customer service phone centers use capacity planning and volume forecasting models to determine the staff needed on the phone every hour of the day to ensure that there is adequate staff to meet the service standards set up by the company to meet customer satisfaction goals.

2. Since the number of available staff on the phone is the key to meeting service standards and goals in a customer service phone center; experienced phone center supervisors will manage their phone representatives' time very closely. This means not coming in even 10 seconds late, scheduled lunches and breaks; ensuring that not a lot of staff is on bathroom breaks at the same time; etc. Therefore, when you experience this, it is not a supervisor who is a control freak, is power hungry or is treating you like a child; it is part of that supervisor's job.

3. While many may look at customer service as only a necessary expense, it is really a profit center for any business that provides superior customer service. However, remember, there is a trade off between the level of service being delivered and the cost for that service. Perfect usually costs too much.

"Service Attitudes"

1. There are 10 truisms regarding service delivery. Go to this section and review them; they are important.

2. In summary, a proper service attitude is one where the focus is on the customer, not on you (the worker) or the company. The customer is very important and is the reason you have a job (no customers, no sales, no jobs). You are there to serve them, they are not there to make your job easier or to be forced to remember things you can remind them of. They also do not expect to have any problems in the first place (how successful a marketing message like "most of our customers do not have problems" would be; not very successful) so they have a right to expect quick, easy resolutions even when they created the problems themselves.

"Active Listening"

1. Listening is 50% talking and 50% listening. Active listening is 20% talking and 80% listening.

2. There are three components to active listening: actually and showing that you are paying attention (positive personal signals and invitations to talk); repeating key words and concepts exactly as said by the customer; and being able to summarize correctly and concisely what the customer is talking about. You need to use all three together when interacting with customers.

"Conquering Communication Barriers"

1. Even when possessing excellent customer service skills there can be obstacles to determining what a customer is communicating to you. So be aware of potential barriers so that you can overcome them.

2. Communication barriers include: the customer's inability to communicate the message; the customer service representative's inability to employ active listening skills; the customer's and the rep's primary language may be different; there could be a personality clash between the customer and rep; there could be business policies standing in the way of a productive talk; your work environment could be noisy making concentration difficult.

"Communicating with Customers"

1. When dealing with customers choosing your words is very important. The customer will get an overall impression based on what you say (e.g. "still" at lunch; not back "yet"; Mr. Goldberg is "busy").

2. One specific phrase that should never be used is your problem "should be" resolved. It is always your problem is resolved.

3. Keep personal details (e.g. Mr. Goldberg is at the doctor) out of your communications with customers.

4. A good phrase to keep in mind is: "So and so is unavailable. How may I help you?"

5. Knowing if a customer's communication is a statement, a question (must be answered) or an objection (must be overcome) helps keep customer interactions to a minimum and customers satisfied with their interactions with you.

6. Overcoming objections is a four step process: use your active listening skills to identify the objection; provide an immediate response addressing the objection; talk clearly and concisely; and do not provide unnecessary information or conversation.

7. There is a proper way to answer the telephone at work. Find out the correct way in your workplace. However, all usually include stating your name, being pleasant, using proper hold procedures (ask before placing someone on hold and check back often) and taking notes using the proper business memo format.

8. While most customers will not be a problem, you will have to deal with demanding, laidback, chatty and furious customers as well. When you have one of these customers do not go with the flow. Follow the procedures to handle them set up at your workplace or follow the procedures outlined in this book. You have to satisfy all customers, not just the easy ones. Keep in mind that satisfying the more difficult customers often results in excellent word of mouth, which means more customers for the business and more job security and potentially more money for the company to spend on employee salaries and benefits.

9. Consumer rights is not just a catch phrase. It is law. Consumers have certain rights and businesses need to ensure that they are in compliance. This could have an impact on how your supervisor tells you how you have to perform your job.

EXERCISE ANSWERS

Note – the book contains worksheets and exercises. The goal of the worksheets is to have the participants be as truthful as possible since they are often listing sensitive areas that they need to improve upon. Therefore, the worksheets are not treated as exercises with right or wrong responses. The goal is that the participants take the worksheets seriously and know that they can write anything since they will not be graded or commented upon by the instructor. While filling out the worksheets, I recommend that the instructors walk the room to ensure that the participants are working on the worksheets and to provide a presence in the room so that the participants will be more likely to work on them seriously.

A recommended approach to help ensure that the participants do, indeed, attack the worksheets seriously is:

   a. Make filling out all of the worksheets a competency that needs to be completed satisfactory (fill out the worksheet seriously; not based on content) in order for a participant to get a certification/honors for the course.
   b. Do spot checks by collecting a non-personal, non-embarrassing worksheet or two during the course spur of the moment (stop writing I am going to collect this worksheet and review it to be sure you took filling out the worksheet seriously; this is not a review on the content). This should help keep everyone in check. If the participants are keeping their books (highly recommended), you can have them keep the books with you at random a couple of times and you can check the worksheets and give the books back in the next class.
   c. Call on each student once or twice during the course (same number for each student) at random and have him or her read one item from their worksheet (student picks what they want to share).

Workplace Basics

Exercise WB1

Q1. *How many people will you need to hire?*
At a minimum 10 refs
Could also hire a league secretary, assistant coaches, etc.

Q2. *List all the expenses that might be involved, including staff expenses.*
At a minimum: the staff above, basketballs, uniforms, trophies, liability insurance
Also: telephone expense, web site, printing expense, etc.

Q3. *How much do you think you can charge each team?*
Anything reasonable; see example that follows

Q4. *Total up all your expenses.*
Anything reasonable; see example that follows

Q5. *Calculate your revenue (number of players multiplied by what you are charging each player.*
Anything reasonable; see example that follows

Q6. *Is the league profitable?*
Varies

Q7. *What other factors could impact profits (plus or minus)?*
Plus: getting a sponsor for the league or for the teams could add to revenue
Minus: a lot of bad weather could cause games to be cancelled and result in teams asking for refunds; not being able to get ten teams for the league; etc.

Example is on next page

Example for exercise WB1

Revenue:
Charge per team ($2,400; $200 per player) $24,000

Expenses:
Refs @ $50 per game per ref (2 per game, 135games) $13,500
Insurance $ 2,500
Uniforms ($25 per uniform; 120 players) $ 3,000
Basketballs ($15 per ball, 10 balls per team, 120 total) $ 1,800

Total Expenses $20, 800

PROFIT (Revenue – Expenses) $ 3,200

So if want to make reasonable money in this venture, it would be important to get sponsors for the team uniforms. In that case you can either increase the fees per team, asking them to get sponsors; or you could line up sponsors and get the money directly and keep the charges as is.

Exercise WB2

	Statement	Reason	Explanation
Q1	Your car will not start.	Bad	Make arrangements with a co-worker or neighbor for emergency situations; or take a taxi or bus
Q2	Your child is sick.	Depends	If stay home every time then you could miss too much work; differentiate between common and serious illnesses.
Q3	You stayed out late, are very tired, and wake up with a major headache.	Bad	Save partying for a night when you do not have work the next day. Take aspirin and go to work.
Q4	You have a fever of 102.	Good	As long as it's not as Foreigner would sing, "Hot Blooded," stay home. No one wants you to go into work and get your co-workers sick.
Q5	You have an appointment with the local cable company scheduled that day.	Bad	You need to schedule them to come on a day or during a time when you are not scheduled to work.

	Statement	Reason	Explanation
Q6	There is a death in your family.	Good	Yes, take care of important family matters.
Q7	Your best friend needs to you watch his or her or her kids because they have a doctor's appointment.	Bad	As much as your friend may need you; your priority needs to be your employer. If anything, make suggestions or help your friend find someone other than yourself who can watch his or her kids.
Q8	You had a fight with your spouse and are too upset to work.	Bad	You need to separate your personal life from your work life. Being upset is not a legitimate reason for missing work.
Q9	You have a second, part-time job and they told you, "We need you today three people are out with the flu; if you can't come in today and help out we will need to fire you and hire someone who can fill in when we have emergencies.	Very Bad	If you are allowed to have a second, part time job, it cannot interfere with your full time job. It is easier to get another part time job than it is to get a full time job. Besides, at your full time job your are working towards long term career and life goals, while your part time job is more temporary and is helping out short term.
Q10	Your child's teacher called and needs to talk to you about something very important.	Bad or Depends (explanation is the key)	This is a situation where you need to attend a meeting with the teacher. Your first option is to schedule a time that does not interfere with work. If that is not possible, explain the situation to your supervisor, go to work, and ask for the time (use it as your lunch time that day if you need to) to go meet with your child's teacher. It is also best to explain this situation before going to meet with the teacher so that if the meeting runs late, the supervisor knows in advance why you are away from work longer than expected. If your supervisor will not give you the time off during the day; then use

		a vacation or personal day (known absence; not a sick day) to meet with your child's teacher.

Exercise WB3

INCIDENT NOTIFICATION FORM

READ NOTES / DIRECTIONS PRIOR TO COMPLETION OF THIS FORM – PLEASE PRINT

Type of incident
☒ work injury ☐ serious bodily injury ☐ work caused illness ☐ dangerous event ☐ dangerous electrical event
Notify Department of Industrial Relations ☐ Yes ☒ No   ☐ serious electrical incident
Was injury/illness fatal? ☐ Yes ☒ No   If an electrical incident, has the area been made safe? ☒ Yes ☐ No

Details of injured person

Given names	FIRST NAME	Surname	LAST NAME
Residential Address	ADDRESS	D.O.B.	BIRTH DATE
	Postcode		☐ Male ☐ Female ←

Basis of employment

Full time	☒	Part time	☐
Casual	☐	Volunteer	☐
Member of public	☐	Other	☐
Self-employed	☐		

Type of employment

Occupation: ELECTRICIAN

Administration	☐	Tradesperson	☒	Apprentice/trainee	☐
Technical	☐	Professional	☐	Student	☐
Other	☐				

Nature of work injury or work caused illness, eg. fracture, sprain & strain, electrical shock, burns, etc.   SPRAIN

Bodily location of injury or work caused illness   WRIST

Medical treatment ☐ nil ☒ first aid ☐ doctor only ☐ hospital admitted to: (if overnight)

Mechanism of injury/disease

Falls, trips and slips	☒	Sound and pressure	☐	Biological factors	☐
Hitting objects with part of body	☐	Body stressing	☐	Mental stress	☐
Heat radiation and electricity	☐	Chemicals and other substance	☐	Other and unspecified mechanisms of injury	☐

Agency of injury/disease

Machinery and (mainly) fixed plants	☐	Mobile plant and transport	☐	Animal, human and biological agencies	☐
Powered equipment, tools and appliances	☒	Non-powered handtools, appliances and equipment	☐	Environmental agencies	☐
Chemicals and chemical products	☐	Materials and substances	☐	Other and unspecified agencies	☐

Details of how incident occurred

Day 25 Month 01 Year 2006   Time of incident: |1|1|1|5| am/pm
Description of incident (Attach report)

Fall off a ladder, braced fall with wrist.

Name of employer/self-employed person/principal contractor   ELECTRIC ELECTRICIANS

Address of employer/ self-employed person/ principal contractor	111 MAIN STREET RIDGWAY, PA	Location address of workplace where incident occurred	222 FIRST STREET DuBOIS, PA
Name of W.H.S.O. and phone no. (if any)	BILL JONES	Phone	(555) 111-2222

Employer/Self-Employed Person/Principal Contractor Signature

	Day	Month	Year

OFFICE USE ONLY

District Reference No.	☐☐☐☐☐☐☐	Action
Plant No.	☐☐☐☐☐☐☐	
Date: Day Month Year	☐☐☐☐☐☐	
Workplace/Construction Workplace No.		
Licence No.		

PRIVACY STATEMENT. The Department of Industrial Relations respects your privacy and is committed to protecting personal information. The information provided on this form is for

Exercise WB4

Q1. *If you were Wilma would you have done the same thing?*
No

Q2. *Why or why not?*
If safety equipment (in this case goggles) are required for workers' safety, it is also required for visitors' safety. Wilma should have put on goggles before visting Fred, no matter how brief the visit was going to be.

Exercise WB5

Q1. *How can dependable employee be unreliable?*
This would be an employee who always shows up for work on time, but doesn't complete all of his or her assignments.

Q2. *How can a reliable employee be undependable?*
This would be an employee who always completes his or her assignments, but does not always show up for work on time and/or on days assigned to work.

Q3. *Which is more important, being dependable or being reliable?*
Both are important, all employees need to be dependable and reliable to be highly-valued by their employers.

Q4. *You work as a fact checker and need to be alert on the job so that errors do not occur. You stay up late every night because you have a second job and often come to work very tired. You need the extra money. If your work suffers, will management understand and look the other way? What could be the consequence of working that second job*
No, management will expect you to perform your job well and if you do not, working your part time night job could cost you to lose your full time day job.

Q5. *You show up late for work because you had to bail your best friend out of jail. You call to ask your new supervisor for permission and you get permission. Is that the end of it? Could anything negative come out of this situation for you?*
No, your new supervisor could have a negative impression about you since your best friend needs to be bailed out of jail.

Exercise WB6

If Tony did not know Foad's religious beliefs, what might his reaction be if:
   Q1. *Foad refused to join the group*
   Q2. *Foad joined the group but refused to drink*
   Q3. *Foad joined the group but refused to chip in for appetizers ordered by the group*

In all three cases the group could feel that Foad is rejecting the group and is not part of their team.

Q4. If any of the above situations occurred, what problems could this have caused Foad at work?
Getting along with co-workers is important on the job, this situation could cause friction and lack of cooperation at work (such as a coworker giving helpful tips or switching lunch hours or shifts so Foad can take care of personal business, etc.)

Q5. If Tony knew about Foad's religious beliefs, how might he have reacted to ensure Foad's behavior was not a problem for him with his co-workers?
Everyone could have been made aware of the real reason for Foad not joining in the eating and drinking with the group. No one would feel that Foad was rejecting the group.

Q6. If Tony knew Foad's religious beliefs and still wanted to get his group together, what could he do differently?
Tony could have changed the venue of the monthly Friday after work team building event to one more suitable for the entire team, which included Foad. Maybe a restaurant with a wide variety of food would have been better than a pub.

Exercise WB7

Q1. What problem could this cause for Marie with her coworkers?
Some workers may believe that Marie got her promotion not by merit, but by sleeping with the boss.

Q2. Statement – If a supervisor makes sexual advances to a willing employee; that could still be considered sexual harassment because others in the company might construe that as something the supervisor favors when it comes to giving raises and promotions. Do you agree or disagree with this statement. Please support your answer.
Agree, sexual harassment is about the workplace as much as it is about the individuals involved. This situation can cause workers to believe sleeping with the boss is expected (or helps) to get a promotion and that is obviously sexual harassment.

Q3. If Marie was hired on merit, then Phil and Marie break up, and later the job proves to be too much for he,r and for the betterment of the company Phil needs to replace he; why might Phil be reluctant to do so?
Phil might be reluctant to fire her, which will hurt the company and the performance of his department because if he fired she might contact the Personnel Department and claim it was just because they broke up. Worst case, Phil would be found out about breaking the supervisor/employee no dating rule.

EXERCISE WB8

Q1. What is the difference between a raise and a promotion?
A raise is making more money in your existing job, while a promotion is an advancement in the company into a new job with greater responsibilities.

Q2. What are the reasons for raises?

Cost of living, additional work experience, doing a good job, a re-evaluation of the base compensation for a specific job function, etc. Remember, you are being paid to do a good job. You do not earn a raise just by doing a good job. Some companies do give raises as rewards for exceptional work. However, raises that reflect gained experience and cost-of-living adjustments are usually given to employees once a year. Very often raises are annual and come with a performance appraisal. In these cases, the better your performance appraisal (e.g. the higher your employee performance rating), the higher the raise.

Q3. *What are the reasons for promotions?*
There is a job opening at a higher level than the job you currently have and management determines that you are the best employee to handle that job. Promotions are not rewards for good work. Companies promote employees they believe can handle the new work assignments best.

Q4. *What can you do to put yourself in position for a promotion?*
Learn all you can, both new skills and current job functions; go above and beyond in your work assignments, get along with everyone; get to work on time and display excellent workplace behaviors and skills; follow all directions; get to know the company and company's products; be dependable and responsible; etc.

Q5. *Does getting a better raise than another worker always mean that that worker will receive more money than the other worker?*
No, very often raises are given as percents, not dollar amounts. For example, if Bob, who has two-years on the job was earning $25,000 and received a 6% pay increase, his pay raise would be $1,500. If Carol, who has 10-years on the job, was earning $40,000 and received a 4.5% pay increase, her pay raise would be $1,800. This is often how annual merit pay raises work, as a percent rather than as a specific amount. Therefore, you can be the highest-rated worker, and get the best raise as a percent of salary, but not get the most dollars. Don't let other workers tell you management lied because they got more money than you so you didn't get the best raise. You may have from a percentage viewpoint.

EXERCISE WB9 (role reversal)

After the exercise is completed, please discuss with the group why the correct person was selected and why each individual was not selected.

Q1. *Who would you promote to support person? Explain why you chose that person.*
Person 3 is the individual whom you would choose for the promotion. He/she has a solid work history with you (rating of good) and has some experience with Excel and Access. If needed, you would send Person 3 for additional training. In the meantime, however, you would still get reports and perform your analyses.

Please have a group discussion and review why Person 3 got the promotion and why Person 1 and Person 6 did not:

Person 1 will believe he/she should get the promotion because his/her performance is the best in the unit. However, without any knowledge of the two key skills required of support person (Excel and Access), you may not be able to get the reports you need to write your insightful analyses. Therefore, promoting Person 1 would result in you taking your best phone representative off the phones making your department's phone service worse at a time when staff is being reduced (from 6 to 5), and put Person 1 in an important job that he/she does not currently have the skills to perform. Therefore, no, Person 1 will not get the promotion. The proper way to reward Person 1 is with the best annual raise (percent or amount depending on company policies).

This also highlights the "employee stock" concept. It would have been in Person A's best interest to take computer courses to put himself or herself in the ideal spot to get the promotion. Person A would have helped both himself/herself and the company if that was done.

Persons 2, 4, 5 are behind Person 1 in the pecking order based on computer knowledge and job performance rating.

Person 6 will believe that he/she should get the promotion because he/she has the best Excel and Access skills. However, with a performance rating of poor, promoting Person 6 would cause two problems. First, it would send a terrible message to your other workers if the lowest-rated employee in your unit, a worker who received a poor rating because of tardiness, sloppy work habits, a bad attitude, too many errors, etc., received a promotion. You just cannot do that. Second, you would be putting your faith and trust in someone who could very easily let you down. What good is it if Person 6 can produce reports if he/she doesn't show up? What good is it if Person 6 produced reports but there were errors; and you based your insightful analyses on those errors! No, Person 6 will have to improve performance before ever being considered for a promotion.

Workplace Skills

Exercise WS1

Q1. Stopping bye an attractive single person's desk get to know him or her every time you go to get coffee; even though you have to go out of your way to get to that person's desk. POOR

Q2. Stopping bye an attractive single person's desk to get to know him or her every time you go to get coffee since that person's desk is right next to the coffee maker. POOR

Q3. Going to lunch with your co-worker friends so that you can visit with them during lunch rather than visiting with them during work time. GOOD

Q4. Discussing a work-related topic with a co-worker as a line of customers backs up at your work station. POOR

Q5. Learning new work tasks during your down time on the job. GOOD

Exercise WS2

Q1. What is the completion of the task from Arnold D. Terminator's point of view?

Identifying why the problem regarding the Freeze Machine occurs and developing a plan of action that can be implemented to fix the problem.

Q2. Why is this task needed to be completed?

The Freeze Machine being down is costing the company money, and Mr. Terminator wants the company to make profits. Therefore, a permanent solution to the problem is needed. To do that the problem needs to be identified so that the problem can be fixed.

Q3. Assuming replacing or repairing the Freeze Machine can't happen until tomorrow, what is your last step to take today in your task? Please provide details for that task.

Turn in your status report to Mr. Terminator. The status report needs to identify the scope of the problem (the track record regarding the performance of the machine), the problem with the machine, the steps you have taken to resolve the problem, and the current status of the problem. In this case the status is that problem has been reported to the right department and the machine will be replaced or repaired tomorrow.

Q4. *Since you do not repair machines, and do not have the authority to replace machines, is your task complete after performing the step you wrote in Q3?* NO

Explain you answer: You were assigned to oversee the resolution so you need to inform Mr. Terminator when the machine is repaired or replaced.

Exercise WS3

You should have created a paper hat.

Exercise WS4

Q1. *Jim has worked for a Paper company for 8 years. A customer asks for special shipping procedures that Jim has not used in over 5 years.* YES

Q2. *Pam has worked for a Paper Company for 8 years as well. A customer calls and asks her to send him the same letter she has sent to him many times before.* NO

Q3. *Nellie is a new hire for a Paper Company and is performing a task she just learned two days ago.* YES

Exercise WS5

Q1. *Did the person who took the Teacher Guide do an ethical or unethical act?*
Unethical

Q2. *Explain your answer.*
Any of the following is acceptable:
- ✓ Stealing is illegal.
- ✓ Others in the program would feel it was unfair to them that some participants had all the answers.
- ✓ If it got out that someone passed the program because they stole all the answers to the exercises and quizzes, their chance of getting a job would be worse than if they failed the program.
- ✓ The behavior makes no sense because you will be expected to know all the competencies in the program on the job, so if you cheat, you will only fail on the job and be fired anyway.
- ✓ Stealing the answers is not fair to the other participants.
- ✓ The people running the program will not approve.
- ✓ If someone stole the answers, I, myself would feel cheated.
- ✓ The whole program could be at risk if someone stole the answers and those answers were distributed widely, ruining it for people who passed it legitimately.

Q3.   *What is the ethical thing for you to do?*
Tell someone in authority about the teacher guide being stolen (and obviously not use the answers themselves)

Q4.   *If you decided to say nothing, but did not use the answers, what would happen if your friend was caught and said, "It's no big deal. Even <you> knew about it and didn't think it was a big deal", and you were doing very well in the program?*
Instructors would assume you cheated as well, and you could lose the opportunity to get a certification in the Program.

Q5.   *If your friend was not caught, what negative consequences could happen because of his/her cheating?*
Any of the following is acceptable:
✓ Businesses would lose faith in the program because graduates would not have the competencies advertised.
✓ The answers could get out to a lot of people making the program worthless.
✓ Rumors of answers being in the hands of participants could get out into the business community so that some businesses do not hire graduates from the program.
✓ The cheating could devalue the Work Readiness Credential for participants that earned it.
✓ The person that cheated could take a job from a more deserving participant.

Exercise WS6

The name of the educated rapper is Ed. MC Mahon.

Exercise WS7

Q1.   B. The company is implementing new programs to improve phone service.

Q2.   No correct answer, however answer must support their positive or negative reaction to the memo.

Q3)   FALSE, it was above industry standards.

Q4)   FALSE, they had to log in exactly on time.

Q5)   TRUE, phone equipment, new staff and training.

Q6)   FALSE, they are hiring 10 new employees but training takes place when the phone representatives are not scheduled to be on the phones.

Q7)   FALSE, it is also to determine if the training is working.

Q8)   TRUE, as stated directly in the memo

Exercise WS8

Write a hand written note to your instructor informing him or her of the ranking the top three things you have learned so far in this course that will help you in the workplace. Please use the proper format and proper structure for this assignment.

The hand written note must have the business memo heading (to, from, re/subject, date); there must be a first sentence along the lines of what follows are the three things I have learned in the course that will help me most in the workplace. Then the items should be listed from most important to third most important. Finally, the three items mentioned must be from the course.

Exercise WS9

1.   300 - 290 = 10; 10 ÷ 290 = 3.4% change (improvement)

   40-30 =10; 10 ÷ 30 = 33.3% change (improvement)

   120-100 = 20; 20 ÷ 100 = 20% change (improvement)

2. $225,000 - $130,000 = $95,000 profit expected in 2012

   $95,000 - $80,000 = $15,000; $15,000 ÷ $80,000 = 18.75% change (improvement in profits)

   Revenues = $225,000 - $200,000 = $25,000; $25,000 ÷ $200,000 = 12.5% change in revenues
   Expenses = $130,000 - $120,000 = $10,000; 10,000 ÷ $120,000 = 8.3% change in expenses

   Revenues are growing at a faster rate than expenses.
   (12.5% for revenues vs. 8.3% for expenses)

3. $2.50 x 20% = $0.50; $2.50 - $0.50 = $2.00 (discount price)
   $2.00 x 200 = $400 (cost for 200 books)
   $2.50 x10 = $25 (cost for 10 books)

4.   100 x 10% = $10; new price = $100 -$10 = $90; $90x60 = $540
   Additional 10% discount = $540x10% = $54; $540 -$54 = $486

5.   Discount = $14 x 10% = $1.40
   Sale price = $14 - $1.40 = $12.60

6.   Discount = $1,000 x 30%
        Sale price = $1,000 - $300 = $700

7.   Profit to make per puppy = $100 x 75% = $75
        Selling price = $100 + $75 = $175

8.   The original price for a book is $30. It has been discounted 10% already. Your supervisor asks you to mark it down an additional 10%. Does that make the sale price $24 or $24.30?
        $24.30
        $30 – ($30*10%) = $27
        $27 – ($27*10%) = $24.30

9.   True or false. As long as I have a calculator, computer and point of sale terminal, it is okay if I do not understand numbers; these devices will always give me the correct results.
        FALSE

10.   True or false. Math is very difficult for many people so I know all my supervisors will understand and not hold me accountable if I do not catch simple math errors at work.
        FALSE

Exercise WS10

Use the business memo format and business writing techniques and etiquette to write a report to your supervisor (use the name of your instructor as your supervisor's name). The secretary's name is Pat Jones. Also include a chart summarizing the 10 calls by number of rings.

To: Instructor

From: Participant

RE: Secretary Phone Monitoring Results

Date: Date of exercise

==

Overall, I felt your secretary, Pat Jones, did a very good job. He (or she) is very professional, and courteous on the phone. The people he (or she) talks to respond well to him (or her) and he (or she) answered all questions asked very well.

However there were some concerns.

Of the ten calls answered, 90%, not 100% were answered within 4 rings. The breakdown follows:

# of rings	how many	percent answered
1	1	10%
2	3	30%
3	3	30%
4	2	20%
5	1	10%
TOTAL	10	100%

There were also two incidents where I felt the response could have given the caller a negative impression of the company.

On the fourth call of the day, while you were at lunch, your secretary said you were not back from lunch yet. By adding yet at the end of the sentence, the customer could have gotten the impression that you were late in reporting back from lunch.

On the eighth call of the day, your secretary indicated that you were too busy to take any call now. That could have given the customer the impression that their business is not highly valued by the company.

cc: Pat Jones

Grading: items in memo:
    Correct format
    Summary of findings as first paragraph
    Details to include:
        Report the numbers regarding the time to answer the phone in a chart
        Something about Pat Jones' phone conversations
        All information (numbers and statements) are correct
    Copied Pat Jones on the memo

Exercise WS11

Q1.

Harold's Collectible Knives, Inc.
Task Checklist
Enter first name and last initial upon successful completion of each task

Date: <u>Today's date</u>

FABRICATION Blanking the blades	Name	Time	COMPLETION Knife assembly	Name	Quantity
Machine XYZ cleaned			Model 15 blade proper size	Lisa L.	100
Machine XYZ set			Model 15 blade spinning		
Machine XYZ tested	Mary J.	7:00 AM	Model 15 blade bracketing		
Machine ABC cleaned	Jack S.	8:50 AM	Model 15 final assembly	Cassie D.	100
Machine ABC set	Jack S.	8:55 AM	Model 25 blade proper size	Lisa L.	200
Machine ABC tested	Mary J.	9:30 AM	Model 25 blade spinning		
Machine JAY cleaned	Jack S.	10:15 AM	Model 25 blade bracketing		
Machine JAY set	Jack S.	10:20 AM	Model 25 final assembly		
Machine JAY tested			Quality control models 15 25		15> <u>95</u> 25> ___

Q2. How many model 15 blades did not pass the quality control inspection? 5

People Skills

Exercise PS1

Q1) Good communication; the employee tailored it to specific customers, acknowledged issues, and helped customers solve problems.

Q2) Bad communication; the unemotional, slow, yawn filled talk could communicate boredom and breed disinterest from the listeners.

Q3) Bad communication skills; the examples should have been for the powdered metal industry.

Q4) Bad communication skills; the employee should have explained the recall and projected positive personal signals instead of not answering the customer's question while displaying annoyance and aggression through his/her personal signals.

Exercise PS2

Q1. Jack should not say anything about what he saw. Even if he knew for sure that they were having problems it is not his place to say that at work. However, in this case, what if it wasn't an argument, but a phone call where both Juliet and Sawyer got on the phone to argue with the person on the other end. And then Juliet left to stay with and help a family member who had an emergency.

Q2. Hugo should answer something like, "I know this is a difficult time, but the holiday season will be over soon." He should then continue to work. Even if he needs a break, he should wait until the others return so that everyone does not go on break at the same time.

Q3. Desmond should show Ben how to punch in the numbers. It is the right thing to do and management usually does not look kindly on employees who are not team players. In fact, training a co-worker successfully could help Desmond be looked at as "management material" and be the deciding factor in getting that promotion.

Q4. Locke should not get into a heated argument with Jin about energy at work (employee cafeteria). Therefore, Locke should not mention that he has relatives that work in the petroleum industry since that could lead to an argument, and could also put a strain on their "friendly-neighbor" relationship at work (they are not friends so it is not necessary for Locke to tell Jin details about his personal life). So, Locke should just politely decline to go to the weekend event citing prior commitments.

Q5. Sayid should inform the President that it was Claire who did the analysis. The President will, most likely, find out eventually anyway since Sayid's and Claire's supervisor knows who performed the analysis. So Sayid would be doing the right thing shining the light on Claire, while also gaining points by being honest; instead of doing the wrong thing, and losing points because the President of the company, who will find out the truth anyway, believes he or she cannot trust him.

Exercise PS3

This is a teamwork exercise with no correct answer, as long as a team's answer makes logical and business sense.

Have everyone fill out their forms prior to selecting teams and team leaders. This ensures that everyone comes to the table with an idea of what they want the group to do rather than just agreeing to the first thing that is brought up.

Select team leaders, and then walk the room during the team meetings.

Grades are based on individuals:

- ➢ participate in the team discussion
- ➢ follow the appointed team leader's rules for running the team respectfully
- ➢ participate in the team's oral presentation
- ➢ show interest throughout the team exercise
- ➢ demonstrate with words and personal signals that they are on board with the team leader's final decision
- ➢ team's answer makes business and logical sense

Exercise PS4

This is a teamwork exercise and even though there is a correct answer, as long as a team's has logic for their answer they do not have to get the 8 items correct to get a perfect score.

No team leaders are selected by the instructor; the group decides how they will proceed. Be sure to walk the room during the team meetings.

Grades are based on:

- ➢ participated in the team discussion
- ➢ participated in the team's oral presentation
- ➢ showed interest throughout the team exercise
- ➢ demonstrated with words and personal signals that he/she is on board with the team's final decision

- demonstrated that he or she is a good winner (no taunting) or a good loser (no tantrums – no finger pointing) after the real answers are told to the class (note – light good natured teasing can be okay – rule of thumb – it is a workplace not a ball field)
- team used reasonable logic in picking the eight items
- team used a reasonable method for making group decisions (needs to be a method that takes everyone's opinion in consideration)

NASA Teamwork Competency
ANSWER KEY

Item	NASA Ranking	NASA's Reasoning
Box of matches	15	Virtually worthless -- there's no oxygen on the moon to sustain combustion
Food concentrate	4	Efficient means of supplying energy requirements
50 feet of nylon rope	6	Useful in scaling cliffs and tying injured together
Parachute silk	8	Protection from the sun's rays
Portable heating unit	13	Not needed unless on the dark side
Two .45 caliber pistols	11	Possible means of self-propulsion
One case of dehydrated milk	12	Bulkier duplication of food concentrate
Two 100 lb. tanks of oxygen	1	Most pressing survival need (weight is not a factor since gravity is one-sixth of the Earth's -- each tank would weigh only about 17 lbs. on the moon)
Stellar map	3	Primary means of navigation - star patterns appear essentially identical on the moon as on Earth
Self-inflating life raft	9	CO_2 bottle in military raft may be used for propulsion
Magnetic compass	14	The magnetic field on the moon is not polarized, so it's worthless for navigation
5 gallons of water	2	Needed for replacement of tremendous liquid loss on the light side
Signal flares	10	Use as distress signal when the mother ship is sighted
First aid kit, including injection needle	7	Needles connected to vials of vitamins, medicines, etc. will fit special aperture in NASA space suit
Solar-powered FM receiver-transmitter	5	For communication with mother ship (but FM requires line-of-sight transmission and can only be used over short ranges)

Exercise PS5

Q1. Cause for concern?   Yes   Not really   If yes, why?

Yes, Worker A is having a negative impact on the workplace which has already led to one of the best workers leaving the company and could lead to other top workers either feeling uncomfortable at work or also leaving the company.

Q2. Cause for concern?   Yes   Not really   If yes, why?

Not really

Exercise PS6

Q1. Is this good or poor communication? Why?

Poor communication, Worker A should have left a note (using proper business memo formatting) explaining the situation before leaving for the day.

Q2. Is this good or poor communication? Why?

Good communication, Worker A is asking questions and is not wasting the Supervisor's time by running back and forth each time a contradiction is found; instead finding them all and going to the Supervisor one time.

Exercise PS7

Q1. A business plan is important for all businesses.
TRUE (see business plans)

Q2. If someone asks you about your company and job you should never bring up what your company sells and never give that person contact information for someone in your company.
FALSE (see elevator pitch)

Q3. Businesses need to goals so that they can determine whether or not their business strategies are working. This may mean measuring how much work you complete since the goals could be related to work completed.
TRUE (see strategic planning)

Q4. If you and your fellow co-workers treat customers poorly, that could lead to the business failing.
TRUE (see reasons why businesses fail)

Q5. As long as they are making some money on each product, it doesn't matter what price the company decides to charge on each product; profit is profit there is no strategy to setting prices.
FALSE (see marketing)

Exercise PS8

Note – what follows are my suggestions for answers. These will help as you review the exercise with the class after it is completed. The grading criteria are:

1. At least 1 training item for each of the five employees
2. The training item needs to be logical based on the write-up for each employee
3. A plan of action for each of the five employees
4. The plan of action needs to have at least one item that is logical based on the write-ups
5. The plan of action cannot have any items that clearly do not belong (based on poor work readiness/customer skills or based on the write-ups)
6. There needs to be at least two items in the group meeting that address the change in management and/or items from the write-ups that need are applicable for a group setting
7. The group meeting should not contain any items that are personal and should only have been in the individual meetings.

Suggested Answers

Employee: Mike Dee

Training Plan: Needs to be taught how to analyze the numbers. This can include basic math or a more advanced statistic course, and learning Excel which can help with the analysis through the formulas and graphs.

Plan of Action (what will you cover in your one-on-one meeting with Mike Dee)
- A reminder about appropriate and inappropriate jokes.
- Talk to him about coming in late and why it is important that he comes in on time (sets a good example for the team).
- Since everyone likes him and he has a relationship with Josephine, ask him if he could try to involve her with his group activities.

Employee: Josephina Prof

Training Plan: Give her training in word processing; telling her that with those skills she will be given consideration for his old position should his promotion become permanent. Hopefully, this will give her incentive to stop looking for employment outside the company.

Plan of Action (what will you cover in your one-on-one meeting with Josephina Prof)

- First, I would assume that Mr. Oneyear blamed Josephina for all the activity at her desk. That would explain how she reacted and started not acknowledging people who walked by her desk.
- Given this assumption: Tell her that you recognize that all the visiting at her desk is not her fault and that you will be addressing that issue in a generic way, not bringing

up her name, to help stop it from occurring. Therefore, she does not need to feel that she cannot say a quick hello to her co-workers who pass by her when performing their regular work functions.

- Try to determine if there are any specific problems Josephine is having with the group which could help explain why she does not join in with the group.

Employee: Larry Lip

Training Plan: Allow him to attend trade school (see below for conditions). A backup for Frankie is needed.

Plan of Action (what will you cover in your one-on-one meeting with Larry Lip)

- Talk to him about how his life style is negatively impacting the workplace, and therefore, his potential growth in the company (remember he is taking management courses because he is interested in advancing in the company).
- Therefore, you expect him to show up clean, professionally dressed, and ready to work first thing in the morning. Then, inform him that if he can demonstrate that he can do this; that you will allow him to attend trade school and to be Frankie's back-up.
- This also gives you a potential replacement for your most destructive employee, Frankie. And if that happened, it places Larry in a job where he no longer will be working in close proximity to his co-workers in case he doesn't lock in his life style habit changes long term.

Employee: Jeannine Comeback

Training Plan: Give her training in computer skills.

Plan of Action (what will you cover in your one-on-one meeting with Jeannine Comeback)

- Inform her that changes will be coming to how Mr. Oneyear did things and that you would like her to help you document the changes, by writing a formal procedure manual, to make the transition easier for everyone.
- There are two goals here. First to make good use of Jeannine's documentation skills and second to get her buy in early in the process since she will have a role in the changes from the outset.
- Talk to her about her use of supplies. Do not accuse her of anything. Just that you have noticed that she goes through supplies more quickly than others.

Employee: Frankie Cash

Training Plan: He badly needs sensitivity training. I would also send him to an OSHA course (safety course).

Plan of Action (what will you cover in your one-on-one meeting with Frankie Cash)

- Talk to Frankie about his use of safety equipment. Inform him that it is not up to him when to use it or not; that he must use it all the time. Explain OSHA (topic covered in *Workplace Basics*), and how the company could get fined or shut down if he continues to not wear his safety equipment.
- Inform Frankie that he is entitled to his opinions, but the workplace is not the appropriate place to express them.
- Next inform Frankie that he has no job role dealing with customers so you do not expect him to ever be involved with discussions with them in the workplace.
- Tell Frankie that he needs to respect other workers and allow them to do their jobs. This means stop hanging out at their desks when you have down time. If you want to talk with a co-worker arrange to go to lunch or on break with him or her.

Topics you could cover in your first group meeting with these five employees:

- Discuss the change in management (you) and your plans for the department.

- Discuss your management philosophy.
  - Can bring up that in addition to how individuals perform their specific job functions, their performance rating will also include whether or not they are a positive force or a destructive force in the workplace.
  - Can bring up that you expect people to have lifestyles outside of work that do not interfere with how they perform their job functions.

  These help highlight what you covered with Larry.

- Talking at other employee's desks: there must be a work reason to be at someone else's desk. If you want to visit for non-work related reasons, come to me and I'll try the best I can to schedule your breaks or lunch at the same time.

  This meets the criteria you mentioned to Josephine in your one-on-one meeting.

- Be careful with the use of supplies. The company has noticed an increase in stationary and office supply expense and will be watching those items very closely.

  This underscores your comment to Jeannine in your one-on-one meeting.

- If Josephine did not indicate any obstacles for group get-togethers: tell them that once a month you will be having a team lunch in the conference room on you, and you hope everyone will attend. Then bring in a couple of pizzas (if you discuss this with Mr. Advocate, the company may even pay for the lunch since it is for team building reasons to help integrate Josephine back into the group).

Customer Service

Exercise CS1

Q1. *A customer-focused business gives its customers everything they want.*
FALSE (they understand everything their customers want)

Q2. *Providing "free" customer service that does not cost the company any additional money such as always havening its employees be courteous to customers; is very valuable to businesses.*
TRUE

Q3. *There is a trade off for businesses regarding costs and the level of service provided to customers.*
TRUE

Q4. *Customer-focus is a management only concept and is not something that everyone in the business needs to be aware of.*
FALSE (everyone in the company needs to be aware of what the company's customers want)

Q5. *When trying to improve service delivery, businesses need to deal only with actual problems. If a lot of customers think a problem exists, but it really is not a problem, the company can ignore the perceived problem.*
FALSE (perceived problems need to be addressed)

Q6. *Often, the best way to correct a customer-perceived problem is by educating your customers so that they are better informed to what is actually going on.*
TRUE

Exercise CS2

Please answer the area of customer focus each situation represents (focusing on products and services; delivering quality, building the positives, dealing with the negatives)

Q1. *Harvey is a top notch attorney and always provides the very best defense for his clients.*
delivering quality

Q2. *Donna is very intuitive when it comes to what the law firms clients need. She is always one step ahead of everyone.*
building the positives

Q3. Louis, who is great with numbers, takes it upon himself to review the law firm's accounting reports. And it's a good thing since he often finds and corrects errors.
dealing with the negatives

Q4. Mike, who is a very quick study due to his excellent recall skills, has just added copyright law to the firm's service offerings.
focusing on products and services

Q5. Rachel writes legal briefs and prides herself on never having any errors and always filing her briefs on time.
delivering quality

Exercise CS3

There are many different potential answers. Grade the exercise correct as long as the participant's answers make sense. Below are some examples you can use when reviewing the exercise with the class.

Q1. You are a phone representative for a newspaper. Individuals call you up to place classified ads.

Use this what-if problem: customer complains that he/she was charged the wrong price for their ad.

The billing (accounting) department is an internal customer – the staff there relied on you charging and recording the correct price in order for the company's invoice to be correct. You did not, so the billing department sent out an incorrect invoice.

Use this what-if problem: the content printed in the newspaper was wrong even though the customer said it correctly and it was printed exactly as recorded by the phone representative.

The printing department is an internal customer – the staff there relied on you to record the content of the ad exactly as communicated by the customer. You did not, so the ad was printed incorrectly.

Q2. You work on an assembly line putting together two pieces of a 10 piece product.

Use this problem: customer complains because their product broke. It was your piece that caused the failure (although it was not known, all that was known was that the product broke)

Your co-workers on the assembly line are internal customers. Your mistake will reflect on the whole team, not just you, since the error could not be tracked back to you.

The customer service department is an internal customer for you. That department will receive a complaint call from the customer whose product broke. However, what if this became a bigger problem than one product. That could cause a major increase in calls to customer service.

Marketing department/public relations department is an internal customer. If this is a big problem that will involve a recall, there will have to be people involved in dealing with the negative word of mouth that will result from your errors.

Legal department could be an internal customer. If there were injuries that arose from your mistakes, there could be law suits.

Exercise CS4

Q1. What product and services are used by your customer?
Custom stationary for the law firm

Q2. When do they need the products and services delivered?
Every Wednesday between 9:00 AM and 9:30 AM

Q3. Where do your customers receive their products?
At the law firm (purchasing department)

Q4. How do your customers use your products?
To write letters to and for their clients (implied)

Q5. Why do your customers need this product?
To personalize or brand their law firm during written communications.

Q6. What is the interconnectivity between the how and the why? (bonus question)
It makes the written communications a marketing tool

Q7. Who determines if your product meets your customer's standards?
The manager of the purchasing department

Q8. How much of the product do they use and how much do they spend on the product?
10,000 pieces a week for $1,500.

Exercise CS5

Q1. List three service measurements you would implement to help track the amount, quality and timeliness of the work being done by the company or by individuals.

Here are some examples: # of computer repair customers, # computer repairs fixed for business and by employee; # computer repairs could not fix by business & by employee; average time to repair a computer by business & by employee (note – these are just some, if the participant has others you can ask the participant why he or she chose that measurement and give him or her credit if he or she has decent logic).

Q2. List two service measurements you would implement to help you track who would be the best person to promote to manager down the line.

Two key areas to track based on the exercise are: how satisfied customers are regarding each employee's interpersonal skills and computer repair knowledge and performance (how courteous, how friendly, how timely etc.) using surveys or shops; and repeat customer problems by repairperson. NOTE - these are just a couple of measurements, if the participant has others you can ask the participant why he or she chose that measurement and give him or her credit if he or she has decent logic.

Exercise CS6

Q1. If you are working with a customer and cannot answer his or her question it is okay to pass them off to another customer service representative whether or not that other employee knows the answer the answer since with that employee there is at least a chance that the customer can get his or her question answered.
False; you need to transfer that customer to someone you know can help him or her. Customers hate the run-around where they keep getting transferred from person to person to person.

Q2. If there is a serious customer problem going on at work resulting in a lot of customer calls about that problem, and a customer calls you with a simple question such as how to use a product feature, you have a right to tell that customer to try doing it the best he or she can and if they cannot figure it out to call back tomorrow. After all the other callers on hold have serious problems.
False, every customer believes that their question is important. They know that businesses need customers to survive. Answer the question as quickly and politely and concisely as you can so you can move on to the next call as quickly as you can.

Q3. If a customer does not like the way a conservation with you is going and asks to speak to your supervisor; your response should be that you are the only one who can help the customer so they should relax and be respectful and allow you to fix his or her problem.
False, customers have the right to speak to a supervisor. If you treated the customer courteously and took the right steps; your supervisor will realize that this was just someone who needed to hear a result he or she did not like from someone in authority.

Q4. Customers who expect all their problems will be fixed with one simple phone call are customers the business should cut loose. After all, it will be impossible to always satisfy them.
False, customers can expect to have all their problems fixed immediately; after all they did not expect to have any problems at all. Even if they are dissatisfied for awhile, in the end, statistics show that after their problem is fixed, many return to being satisfied customers in time.

Q5. Customers need to understand that phone representatives have no control over how long they wait on the phone before a call is answered so they have no right to start off your call with them complaining about that long wait.

False, customers do not take into account employee's job responsibilities. Their unhappiness with a long wait on the phone is with the business and you are a representative of that business. So they have every right to complain about the long wait on the phone to you.

Exercises CS7, CS8, CS9, CS10

The instructor needs to walk the room and observe the exercises as they are being performed. The recommended grading for these exercises is:

When speaker; told the story in the manner required in the exercise.
When speaker; provided meaningful feedback after/during the exercise to the listener regarding their performance on the active listening skill being taught.
When the listener; followed the rules required for each active listening skill in the exercise.
For both; takes the exercise seriously (no fooling around).

NOTE – getting the skills perfect is not a recommended component of the grade at this point; however, this can certainly be an added exercise to the final certification test for the Customer Service section and there, getting it correct could be the major component of the grade.

Exercise CS11

There is no grade for this fun exercise. The purpose is to put personal signals on display. Below are the instructions for running this exercise. **You will need to prepare items in advance.**

Assign an outgoing person the role of a guest speaker. Call that person aside (go outside the room) and tell him or her that he or she will be talking about a topic they know nothing about. They should "throw the bull" and be sure to come up with made-up terminology that no one has ever heard of for new discoveries in their topic (e.g. schmaguggel, prodenturing, elongated moons, flying evidentiary sockets, etc.). Then select a topic with them like: a discovery of a new planet with a good chance of life, cloning, a new food processing methodology that eliminates fat, a machine that can find the perfect mate for someone based on breathe analysis, etc.). The speaker will inform the class that the assignment was to talk about a recent article he or she read in a magazine. Then the speaker should make-up a story about their topic using at least one made-up word or phrase (for example – see above, or something like squamish, metronometer, you have to tringe the labotek, etc.). Allow the speaker to be creative if he or she likes or make suggestions for topics and made up words like the ones here.

Tell the speaker to take 5 minutes to gather some thoughts (outside the room) and you'll come and get them.

Next hand out index cards to four people randomly. **Tell them to show the cards to no one**.

One card will say, "The topic the speaker will be talking about interests you greatly. Show your interest and ask questions to understand the topic as best as you can."

One card will say, "Challenge the speaker on what they are saying. Make believe you have read something on that topic and know more about it than the speaker."

One card will say, "The topic the speaker will be talking about bores you. Show your boredom."

One card will say, "The speaker is a close friend of yours and you are proud of him/her. You respect your friend and want everyone to be respectful of him/her."

Then call in the speaker and watch what unfolds.

All participants without a role will then try to figure out the roles of the four in the audience based on their behavior and personal signals.

Exercise CS12

Q1. What's wrong	Re-write
Too much information; do not mention meeting with son's criminal attorney. Take charge of call, eliminate don't know when he'll be back.	Mr. Dean is unavailable. How can I help you?

Q2. What's wrong	Re-write
Do not tell the customer about the internal business of the company. No need to mention that the problem impacted many customers. Get rid of the word should. Either the problem is fixed, or the company is working to fix the problem.	Your problem is now resolved.

Q3. What's wrong	Re-write
Do not mention what Ms. Dean is doing or that Tet Corporation is the company's most important client. No wishy-washy words. Be direct when offering to help	Ms. Dean is unavailable. How can I help you?

Q4. What's wrong	Re-write
Get rid of the word "may."	I'm sorry for the inconvenience this has caused you.

Q5. What's wrong	Re-write
Do not mention the details regarding why Jake left early.	Jake is unavailable. How can I help you?

Q6. What's wrong	Re-write
Get rid of the excuse of the billing department being backlogged. That reflects negatively on the company. Get rid of the word "should."	I apologize for the Billing Department not getting back to you. They will be in touch with you within the next 24 hours.

Q7. What's wrong	Re-write
Yet does not belong in the response. It makes it appear that Mr. Dean is late coming in to work.	Mr. Dean is unavailable. How can I help you?

Exercise CS13

Q1. *I think your service is the best in the business*
Statement

Q2. *Why was I charged a service fee*
Question

Q3. *Your selection of pipes is insufficient*
Objection

Q4. *You delivered the wrong product*
Objection

Q5. *When will you have Boston Terriers in stock*
Question

Q6. *I need the product immediately*
Statement

Q7. *I refuse to pay that bill*
Objection

Exercise CS14

Q1. When dealing with a demanding customer, react only to the customer's words, not the customer's tone.
True

Q2. To overcome a customer objection, change the topic of the discussion to get past the objection.
False, you have to address the objection or the customer will not be satisfied

Q3. When you have to do work on your computer to help solve a customer's problem, leaving them on hold for 10 or 15 minutes straight with no interaction from you is fine, as long as when you come back to them you have resolved the problem.
False, you should check back every minute or two to let the customer know you are still working on the problem

Q4. Consumer rights is something enacted by the U.S. Congress.
True

Q5. When you answer the phone at work, providing your name to the caller is optional, it is not part of standard procedures for properly answering the phone.
False, you always need to provide the caller with your name

Q6. When dealing with a chatty customer who likes to talk to you about things not relating to the company or the reason for the call; it is a good idea to talk continuously so that you do not provide a dead period where the customer can chime in with unnecessary, off-topic talk.
True

Q7. Active listening skills cannot help you when trying to manage difficult customers.
False, active listening is a very important skill that can help you in all of these cases

Q8. When you get an angry caller, the first thing you should do is apologize for the problem or situation without using weak words.
True

COMPETENCY STATEMENTS

Competency Statements for Formal Programs

If you are running a formal work readiness and customer service training program, it is highly recommended that you use the competency statements in this chapter to evaluate whether or not participants have learned the subject matter and demonstrated the likelihood that they will employ what they learned in the training program at work.

The participants need to pass <u>all</u> the competencies, not most, in order to receive certification.

There are four unit tests included in the competency statements below. Use the certification scenarios as the basis for the unit tests. I recommend generating 25 questions per unit test. There should be a test for workplace basics, a test for workplace skills, a test for people skills, and a test for customer service. There are two certification scenarios in the book for each unit. Since the scenarios are in the book, my recommended program has the unit tests, open book tests. That means most questions need to be based on what is happening in the scenarios; with a multiple choice question asking what should have been done; what happened in the scenario or something else, listing other options. You can also contact the author at book@DTRConsulting.BIZ or visit www.DTRConsulting.BIZ; to find out about DTR Inc.'s fee for customizing your program. You can also call 206-350-1859 and leave your contact information.

It is also highly recommended that the required competencies are communicated to the participants prior to the first class so they can be held accountable from the start of the first session. That could involve adding, subtracting, or modifying information in the Participant/Employee Orientation section.

Competency Statements

The participant demonstrates the ability to follow simple directions by reading and initialing all of the rules in the Participant/employee orientation section of this book as evidenced by instructor observation of all initialed rules.

*The participant demonstrates knowledge of the material taught in workplace basics by scoring 80% or higher on the workplace basics unit test as evidenced by the instructor proctoring and grading the exam.

*The participant demonstrates knowledge of the material taught in workplace skills by scoring 80% or higher on the workplace skills unit test as evidenced by the instructor proctoring and grading the exam.

*The participant demonstrates knowledge of the material taught in people skills by scoring 80% or higher on the people skills unit test as evidenced by the instructor proctoring and grading the exam.

*The participant demonstrates knowledge of the material taught in customer service by scoring 80% or higher on the customer service unit test as evidenced by the instructor proctoring and grading the exam.

Note – use the two scenarios provided for each section to generate the unit tests (or use one test as an in-class exercise and the other for the unit test). Your questions can take the form of spotting the correct and incorrect activities. You can also have straight-forward questions that refer to something going on the scenario. Unit tests are not provided since it would be too easy for the questions and answers to the questions to get known by the participants. This way your assessment tests are unique to your venue and you can change them when needed. The tests should be open book tests which helps the participants get used to using their books as reference manuals. Examples of the two types of questions explained her follow.

In the scenario Jay did xxxxxxxxxxxxxx.
> *A. What Jay did was correct.*
> *B. Jay should have done XXXXX.*
> *C. Jay should have done XXXXX.*
> *D. Jay should have done XXXXX.*

This scenario involved solving a problem. Which item below is not part of the problem solving process:
> *A. XXXXX*
> *B. XXXXX*
> *C. XXXXX*
> *D. XXXXX*

The participant demonstrates ethical behavior by completing in full, in a serious manner, all worksheets required throughout the four-module work readiness and customer service training program, as evidenced by the random collection and review of two physical worksheets per participant by the instructor.

The participant demonstrates ethical behavior by completing in full, in a serious manner, all worksheets required throughout the four-module work readiness and customer service training program, as evidenced by the instructor calling on each student in class randomly to share one item of his or her choice on a random worksheet twice during the program.

The participant demonstrates the ability to be a team player by participating in all group exercises, including having a role in all group presentations, as evidenced by instructor observation of group meetings and presentations.

The participant demonstrates the ability to express his or her thoughts effectively by answering at least three questions during classroom discussions in a clear, concise, logical manner, as evidenced by instructor observation.

The participant demonstrates the ability to go to work every day by having no unexcused absences throughout the term of the program as evidenced by instructor observation and attendance records.

The participant demonstrates the ability to not be tardy by never being late for the start of class (not even one second), never extending breaks (in-class, lunch, etc.) and never leaving early as evidenced by instructor observation and tardiness records.

The participant demonstrates that he or she can be attentive when supervisors are talking by always paying attention in class and not talking in class when the instructor is speaking as evidenced by instructor observation.

**The participant demonstrates the ability to get along with supervisors by treating the instructor with respect at all times throughout the program as evidenced by instructor observation.

**The participant demonstrates the ability to get along with co-workers by treating the other classroom participants with respect at all times as evidenced by instructor observation.

> ** Note – there may be times when you want to "turn off" the workplace environment in class (e.g. the Whose Line Is It Anyway exercise). _That is fine, but announce when the environment starts being more classroom than workplace;_ and then announce when the environment is back to workplace. When announcing you are going back to workplace; remind the class what that means in terms of the competencies.

The participant demonstrates the ability to dress appropriately for work by coming to class dressed in the manner established for the Program, as evidenced by instructor observation.

The participant demonstrates good grooming by always coming to class with clean, hair neat, and void of offensive odors as evidenced by instructor observation.

The participant demonstrates the ability to show up prepared to work every day by having all required materials (paper, notebook, pen, assignments, etc.) including the text book, for every class as evidenced by instructor observation (note – a lost book is a fail).

The participant demonstrates personal ethics by (A) always paying attention in class, and (B) not formally performing any of the exercises or worksheets in the book prior to those exercises and worksheets being assigned by the instructor and by not speaking to former participants about the answers to the worksheets, exercises and certification tests prior to completing the worksheets, exercises and certification tests, as evidenced by instructor observation including spot checks of each participant's textbook.

NOTE – for businesses – place the competency statements in employee performance reviews

COMPETENCY TRACKING FORM
customize for day and use one per class session
Use √ in the box that intersects a competency and a participant for a pass, and use X for a fail.

Instructor: _____

Term: _____

Lesson #: _____

Date: _____

Participant →										
Competency										
Following instructions: initialed all rules										
Workplace Basics unit test (80%)										
Workplace Skills unit test (80%)										
People Skills unit test (80%)										
Customer Service unit test (80%)										
Ethics: participate in all worksheets via audit - collect & review										
Ethics: participate in all worksheets via audit - answer questions in class from worksheet										
Team player: participated in group work & presentations										
Communication skills: clear answer for in-class question										
Attendance: no unexcused absences										
No tardiness/leave early start to finish for the day										
Constantly attentive; does not talk over instructor										
Treated instructor with respect										
Treated other participants with respect										
Properly dressed										
Proper grooming										
Prepared for work/class; book/materials every class										
Personal ethics: attention in class and proper approach to worksheets, exercises, and test										

Optional Competency Statements for Formal Programs

What follows are optional competency statements for use in a formal program. These include grading all or some of the exercises throughout the book (individually or as a group), and using the summary of key points as individual question and answer competencies; or as contributed to the group discussion competencies.

For individual exercises:

The participant demonstrates knowledge of <insert the topic for the exercise> by scoring <insert your score for passing the exercise> as evidenced by Q&A.

For exercises as a group:

The participant demonstrates knowledge of <insert Workplace Basics or Workplace Skills or People Skills or Customer Service> by scoring <insert your score for passing the exercise questions combined as one competency> as evidenced by Q&A.

Example – you may use exercises 1,2,4 and 6 which have 20 questions total and the passing grade for competency is 80% or getting any 16 of the 20 questions correct).

For individual questions from the summary of key points:

The participant demonstrates knowledge of <insert Workplace Basics or Workplace Skills or People Skills or Customer Service> by answering <insert a specific number of questions> correctly during the Key Summary review as evidenced by Q&A.

For group discussions from the key points:

The participant demonstrates knowledge of <insert Workplace Basics or Workplace Skills or People Skills or Customer Service> by participating in the wrap-up discussion of up <insert Workplace Basics or Workplace Skills or People Skills or Customer Service> as evidenced by instructor observation.

NOTE – for businesses – place the competency statements in employee performance reviews

OPTIONAL COMPETENCY TRACKING FORM
Workplace Basics
customize for day and use one per class session
Use √ in the box that intersects a competency and a participant for a pass, and use X for a fail.

Instructor: _____

Term: _____

Lesson #: _____

Fill in pass score required for competencies turned on

Date: _____

(for combined exercises turn on the ones includes, use the score in the exercise group competency)

Participant →	On or Off												
Competency													
Exercise WB1 pass =													
Exercise WB2 pass =													
Exercise WB3 pass =													
Exercise WB4 pass =													
Exercise WB5 pass =													
Exercise WB6 pass =													
Exercise WB7 pass =													
Exercise WB8 pass =													
Exercise WB9 pass =													
Exercises as a group pass =													
WB individual Q&A pass =													
WB group Q&A pass =													

OPTIONAL COMPETENCY TRACKING FORM
Workplace Skills
customize for day and use one per class session
Use √ in the box that intersects a competency and a participant for a pass, and use X for a fail.

Instructor: _____   Term: _____

Lesson #: _____

Fill in pass score required for competencies turned on   Date: _____
(for combined exercises turn on the ones includes, use the score in the exercise group competency)

Participant →	On or Off											
Competency												
Exercise WS1 pass =												
Exercise WS2 pass =												
Exercise WS3 pass =												
Exercise WS4 pass =												
Exercise WS5 pass =												
Exercise WS6 pass =												
Exercise WS7 pass =												
Exercise WS8 pass =												
Exercise WS9 pass =												
Exercise WS10 pass =												
Exercise WS11 pass =												
Exercises as a group pass =												
WS individual Q&A pass =												
WS group Q&A pass =												

OPTIONAL COMPETENCY TRACKING FORM
People Skills
customize for day and use one per class session
Use √ in the box that intersects a competency and a participant for a pass, and use X for a fail.

Instructor: _____

Term: _____

Lesson #: _____

Fill in pass score required for competencies turned on

Date: _____

(for combined exercises turn on the ones includes, use the score in the exercise group competency)

Participant →	On or Off											
Competency												
Exercise PS1 pass =												
Exercise PS2 pass =												
Exercise PS3 pass =												
Exercise PS4 pass =												
Exercise PS5 pass =												
Exercise PS6 pass =												
Exercise PS7 pass =												
Exercise PS8 pass =												
Exercises as a group pass =												
WS individual Q&A pass =												
WS group Q&A pass =												

OPTIONAL COMPETENCY TRACKING FORM
Customer Service
customize for day and use one per class session
Use √ in the box that intersects a competency and a participant for a pass, and use X for a fail.

Instructor: _____ Term: _____

Lesson #: _____

Fill in pass score required for competencies turned on Date: _____

(for combined exercises turn on the ones includes, use the score in the exercise group competency)

Participant →	On or Off													
Competency														
Exercise CS1 pass =														
Exercise CS2 pass =														
Exercise CS3 pass =														
Exercise CS4 pass =														
Exercise CS5 pass =														
Exercise CS6 pass =														
Exercise CS7 pass =														
Exercise CS8 pass =														
Exercise CS9 pass =														
Exercise CS10 pass =														
Exercise CS11 pass =														
Exercise CS12 pass =														
Exercise CS13 pass =														
Exercise CS14 pass =														
Exercises as a group pass =														
CS individual Q&A pass =														
CS group Q&A pass =														

AUTHOR'S PHILOSOPHY

The Author's Training Philosophy

When I was hired to develop a work readiness curriculum in 2002 there were already a number of established work readiness training programs. With employers complaining about the lack of job skills and poor workplace behaviors by their employees in focus groups throughout the United States, I knew I had to develop more than a training curriculum; I needed to create a better way to deliver workplace training.

First, let's look at traditional programs.

Traditional Programs

Practically all workplace training programs follow models used in education. That means that they are assessment based. FCAT, SAT, etc., determine success in education and, similarly, a certification test determines success in many workplace training courses. And once workplace training ends there is no formal process to hold the individuals trained accountable for what they learned during training.

In fact, assessment tests have become so important in education that schools not only teach students knowledge, but teach students how to take tests. They must. After all, funding is often tied to their students' performances on tests such as the FCAT. Certainly many high school juniors and seniors enroll in courses to help them learn how to improve their SAT scores. And this is not just the case with kids. How many construction management schools, real estate schools, and even schools to help with the BAR exam for attorneys are out there? These schools often teach their students how to take and pass tests.

What does this mean? It means that if a student truly knows only 55% of the required knowledge, but can reduce the other questions to a possible 1 in 3 choice, the laws of probability conclude that the student's expected result on the test is 70%.

Even worse, if a student truly knows only 60% of the required knowledge, but can reduce the other questions to a possible 1 in 2 choice, the laws of probability conclude that the student's expected result on the test is 80%. That means a student whose knowledge base is an "F" (60% was failing grade when I went to school), appears to be a "B" student.

While educators cling to the argument that assessment tests are good indicators of success, no one can make that case when dealing with job skills and behaviors. As an example let's use the following multiple choice question:

If you wake up in the morning and your car will not start, you should:

A) Have made prior arrangements with a coworker who lives in your neighborhood to serve as an emergency ride to work.

Whether because of actual knowledge or eliminating answers like, "B) Take as many days off of work as you need to get your car fixed," someone answering this question correctly does not mean that that is the behavior he or she will follow if this situation actually happened to him or her. Workplace training is NOT about answering questions correctly. It's about doing the right thing in the workplace. That is accomplished through training materials that not only teach what is expected in the workplace, but *why* that skill/behavior is important in the workplace; and also uses real life examples that everyone can relate to outside of the workplace to help illustrate key points. In workplace training, it is the journey (curriculum) that is the key, not the final destination (assessment test). This is because success is measured in the attitudes changed and instilled in participants, not on how much work readiness knowledge they possess.

While this may be obvious to you and me, it isn't obvious to the powers that be. For example, instead of investing in a structured program with an effective curriculum that would produce high-quality employees that employers could rely on; many states either independently or in groups decided to spend funds on generating work readiness credentials through assessment testing. They appear to care more about formulating the perfect question, than the perfect learning tool.

Work readiness certification test results from programs that do not have effective curriculum that changes and shapes attitudes, are, at best, an indicator for possible success and, at worst, a false hope for the business community that hires the "credentialed graduates."

Jay Goldberg's Workplace Training Philosophy

I have been developing and fine-tuning my workplace training program and philosophy since 2002. What follows is a list of the key components for what I know is the correct way to implement a workplace training program.

(1) The client for employee training programs is the **business community** first, and the classroom participants second. Why? Employers observing the participants in the workplace will ultimately determine if the training program is successful; not how well the participants perform in class or on tests. In addition, if employers like the program and believe they can rely on the participants who successfully complete the training to perform well in the workplace; they will value, hire and promote graduates of the program. And that is the main reason the participants are taking the training; to get jobs, keep jobs, and grow in their jobs. In other words, participants want to increase their value to employers.

This realization separates the training programs developed and implemented by the author from most of the other programs in the marketplace. Schools (for sure) and most other venues as well, take on the strategy to improve their students as much as possible, and then market them as vigorously as they can to the marketplace. The result is often graduates, who the school/ training venue expect may fall short of expectations, getting hired and, in fact, falling short of expectations. This result hurts future graduates of the program.

Therefore, my workplace training programs do not allow participants to achieve full certification unless they demonstrate that the main client (the business community) will be able to rely on them at work.

(2) A curriculum that not only teaches what is expected, but why that skill/behavior is important in the workplace, and uses real life examples that everyone can relate to outside of the workplace to illustrate key points, is the foundation to having a successful workplace training program. By clearly defining important workplace skills and behaviors, and informing participants why those skills and behaviors are important to employers; the program sets a baseline of understanding and helps change the participants' attitudes and behaviors.

(3) The training needs to be run like a place of business not a typical educational classroom. The instructor is not just the trainer, but during training is the supervisor, and the participants treat each other as co-workers, not training buddies or friends.

(4) After taking workplace training courses, exams (certification exams or otherwise) are used NOT to indicate competency, but to demonstrate that the participants understood the concepts taught during training so that their employers can start holding them accountable for demonstrating those competencies on the job.

(5) Since performance on the job is what is important to employers, the key program assessments are not the exams, but demonstrated competencies the participants prove every day in class. This also helps the participants understand how they will be evaluated on the job. As an example, during training, a participant demonstrates the ability to not be tardy by never being late to a training session and never extending breaks during a training session.

(6) Since certified program graduates will have shown that they understand the concepts taught during training, and that they can follow some simple, basic rules that are employed during training (through demonstrated competencies); employers should be encouraged to incorporate the competency statements in the training program into their employees' formal performance appraisals.

(7) Within the training program, all competency statements must be very well defined. There should be no leeway given to individual trainers in scoring pass/fail on competencies.

(8) Hold the participants accountable for meeting all their competencies. Recommend to the employers you work with to help place your graduates, that they tie individual compensation (raises, bonuses, etc.) and individual/work unit rewards (employee of the month, monthly pizza party, etc.) to their employees' performances in meeting their competencies.

(9) In addition to training participants, if there are multiple people giving the training sessions, there needs to be a consistent approach between all trainers. That means there may need to be train-the-trainer sessions to ensure all trainers conduct their training in a consistent manner. This is especially true given that the participants will be held accountable for implementing what they learn in the training session every day on the job. Knowing that everyone was trained the same way provides role models who completed the program, were hired, and are now succeeding in the workplace. And since these former program participants received the exact same training as the current participants, there are no excuses for the current participants to fail once they enter the workplace. Program consistency between trainers means no former graduate will be ale to use the excuse, "my instructor never taught me that" to their employer who hired them because of their work readiness credential.

(10) As you can see my program philosophy is very intricate and everything must work in concert to ensure optimal success. Therefore, in addition to instructor training there must be instructor audits to ensure that all teachers/trainers are following and teaching the program correctly.

Jay Goldberg's Background in Work Readiness

As mentioned previously, in 2002 I was hired to develop a work readiness curriculum that I grew into a work readiness philosophy and program. The program I developed was called the best work readiness certification program in the United States by a member of the National Skills Standard Board at a presentation of the Program in Jacksonville, Florida on 01/13/03.

The results from my initial client far exceeded those of other work readiness programs. Employers lined up to hire the graduates and found that over 85% of the graduates remained employed six months later, and over 30% received promotions.

Later I modified and added to the program for a second client.

Since that time I wrote a well-reviewed work readiness book for individuals titled, *How to Get, Keep and Be Well Paid in a Job* (Outskirts Press, ISBN: 9781432725297).

Now I have constructed a four module work readiness and customer service training program that can be used in teaching venues and for on the job training. The four modules each come with recommended competencies and a final online certification test (to use as proof of knowledge so that these individuals can now be held accountable for demonstrating what they leaned every day at work). Participants should have to pass all of the competencies in order to be eligible to sit for the certification test.

ABOUT THE AUTHOR

About the Author

Jay Goldberg, MBA, is a former Service Director for Citibank. At Citibank, Mr. Goldberg specialized in customer service management, measurement, training, capacity planning, profitability, MIS reporting, and strategic planning.

After almost fourteen years with Citibank, Mr. Goldberg left to form his own consulting firm, DTR Inc. DTR Inc. specializes in writing business plans, developing workplace training programs, designing and implementing customer service strategies, performing strategic planning and market research (e.g., surveys, focus groups, etc.), helping businesses build their brands, and training managers and employees.

At DTR Inc., Mr. Goldberg developed the program parameters, program strategy, curriculum, lesson plans, assessments, competency statements, and certification tests for a Work Readiness Training Program called the best Work Readiness Certification Program in the United States by a representative of the National Skills Standard Board at a presentation of the Program in Jacksonville, Florida on 01/13/03.

Mr. Goldberg later updated, modified and added to that Program for a second client and wrote a book, "How to Get, Keep and Be Well Paid in a Job" (ISBN = 9781432725297), specifically tailored to individuals looking to improve their work readiness skills.

In 2007, Mr. Goldberg was instrumental in helping the Palm Beach County Resource Center develop a revolutionary Entrepreneurship Training Program. The program's structure was unlike any other in the marketplace, and would prove to be highly successful.

In 2012, Mr. Goldberg's entrepreneurship book, "Building a Successful Business," (ISBN = 9781470000639) was published. The book is now being used as a textbook for entrepreneurship courses. The book is both a textbook and a workbook with tools entrepreneurs can use to help start, grow and manage their businesses.

While at the Palm Beach County Resource Center, Mr. Goldberg worked with hundreds of small businesses and got a good handle on how to best structure and implement a work readiness training program to ensure that the benefits of training would be demonstrated in the workplace.

This book/program is the culmination of all of Mr. Goldberg's past experiences.

Contact Mr. Goldberg at Book@DTRConsulting.BIZ. Be sure to write "your work readiness book" in the subject line to ensure that your email is not deleted as junk mail. His business's web site is www.DTRConsulting.BIZ.

JAY GOLDBERG's BOOKS

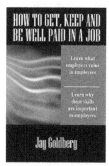

In its first year, about half of all businesses fail. Five years down the line, depending upon which study you look at, only 1 in 10 to 1 in 3 businesses are left standing. The main reasons businesses fail are no business plan and poor management. That is why this book covers both topics.

However, this book goes beyond other books on these topics. The book not only provides a road map for writing a business plan, but also provides a strategy for writing a business plan. A business plan is both a strategic document and a sales document. It also provides the reader with a look into the skills, knowledge and personality of the business owner. Therefore, a good business plan is written to satisfy all of these uses. In addition, this book provides information on how to research and organize the information needed for a business plan, and has worksheets the entrepreneur can use to help make the process easier.

Likewise, management topics such as strategic planning (SWOT analysis plus), advertising, branding, project management, customer service management, cash flow management, sales skills, business writing and more are explained, and a method is provided for each management skill that can be implemented and used in the business. There are worksheets for many of the these topics as well.

In addition to entrepreneurs, this book was written so that venues teaching entrepreneurship can use it as a text book. In fact, I have been teaching entrepreneurship courses since 1997. This book was written to be a stand alone book, to support my business plan mentoring service (I review the worksheets for clients), and to be a text book for my course, How to Start, Grow and Manage a Business.

My intent in writing this book is to provide readers with information vital to helping them get, keep and make good money in their jobs.

However, knowing what to do is not enough. This book covers why workplaces operate as they do, and uses real-life comparisons outside of the workplace that everyone can relate to, in order to help illustrate key points.

Covering topics ranging from customer service to ethics to how to get along with co-workers to how to make yourself valuable to your supervisor to team work to much much more; the worker who reads, understands, and implements the skills and behaviors covered in this book will become as major asset to his or her employer.

To find out more about these books and Mr. Goldberg's consulting and mentoring services; visit

www.DTRConsulting.BIZ

Made in the USA
Middletown, DE
01 May 2021